P9-CDO-407

The Complete Guide to
Investing During Retirement

Turn Your Savings into Earnings

THOMAS MASKELL, M.B.A.

To Rush,
Thanks for the years of insights and entertainment.
Thomas Maskell

BUSINESS

Avon, Massachusetts

DEDICATION

This book is dedicated to Peggy Chapman, a dear friend, who has left this world, but will never leave my heart or thoughts. Thank you for your friendship; it was one of the many gifts God has given me.

Published by
Adams Media, an F+W Media
57 Littlefield Street, Avon, MA 02322. U.S.A.
www.adamsmedia.com

ISBN 10: 1-59869-455-3
ISBN 13: 978-1-59869-455-0

Printed in the United States of America.
J I H G F E D C B A

Library of Congress Cataloging-in-Publication Data
is available from the publisher.

This publication is designed to provide accurate and authoritative information with regard to the subject matter covered. It is sold with the understanding that the publisher is not engaged in rendering legal, accounting, or other professional advice. If legal advice or other expert assistance is required, the services of a competent professional person should be sought.
—From a *Declaration of Principles* jointly adopted by a Committee of the American Bar Association and a Committee of Publishers and Associations

Many of the designations used by manufacturers and sellers to distinguish their product are claimed as trademarks. Where those designations appear in this book and Adams Media was aware of a trademark claim, the designations have been printed with initial capital letters.

This book is available at quantity discounts for bulk purchases.
For information, please call 1-800-289-0963.

Contents

Preface

Why an investment book for retirees? There are hundreds of books on the stock market, investing, and financial planning. They are wonderful excursions into the world of stocks and stock markets. These guided tours are conducted by some of the most accomplished investors Wall Street has ever known, who have forged their credentials in the trenches. They have written on the theory, practice, and manipulations of Wall Street. Their promise, or at least your hope, is that their success can be your success, but it is a hollow promise.

Professor Kenneth Froewiss, a financial professor at New York University Stern School of Business, states, "A good book about personal finance always elaborates on three simple themes: save early, know your risk tolerance and diversify. Any book that suggests it has a new way to riches should probably be a little suspect."[1] That's great advice; but like all good advice, it must be placed in context.

All organic systems follow a life cycle: birth—development—growth—maturity—transition—decline. For humans, each of these stages has unique mental, physical, and financial characteristics. Comparing Professor Froewiss's simple themes in most personal finance books to these life stages yields some interesting results. For instance, look at the possible value of an investment account. You can imagine starting this account at a number of different ages, ranging from one to sixty-one. For purposes of this example, we'll assume that you're risking just $10 per month, or $120 per year. We'll also assume you're getting the average long-term stock market return of 10–12 percent a year, which represents a diversified stock portfolio. Table I illustrates what following the conventional investing wisdom embodied in the professor's themes will get you.

It's clear that if you follow conventional investment advice, the best advice is start early. Unfortunately, not many one-year-olds read the tomes of stock market gurus. The teenagers of stage two and the young adults of stage three are also not high on the mailing lists of the

TABLE I
Conventional Investment Advice
Example: $120 a year invested at a 10% annual return.

State	Life Cycle	Starting Age	Account Value at Age 76
1	Child	1	$1,677,442
2	Teenager	16	$ 400,586
3	Young Adult	31	$ 94,890
4	Mature Adult	46	$ 21,913
5	Retiree	61	$ 4,194

stock market experts. Serious investment decisions are not made until retirement comes into view, a stage four occurrence. By then, it's too late to start early. By age forty-six, following conventional advice won't add much to your retirement fund.

Diversification doesn't help. After age forty-six, the moderate returns of diversification are insufficient to build a meaningful nest egg. The only hope is to increase your contributions. Increasing your yearly investment from $120 to $1,200 or even $12,000 will multiply the account value by ten- or a hundredfold. Can the average forty-six- year-old afford a tenfold increase in contributions? If he can, is he willing to risk it? If he has not made a massive investment plunge by age forty-six, it is unlikely that he will make it after forty-six.

What are aging investors to do when the expert's good advice is not good for them? They have two choices. The first is to find a new expert. There are plenty to choose from. Some are well known, but others are just masters of the fad. They provide sure-fire systems and tales of investment derring-do. They promote their anecdotal expertise in books, newsletters, and mutual funds. Remember Professor Froewiss's warning: "A new way to riches should probably be a little suspect." Many of these fad masters rise and fall like the business cycle.

Even the well-known expert's advice can be contradictory. In Burton Malkiel's book, *A Random Walk Down Walk Street*,[2] he wrote that since small stocks carry greater risk, investors demand greater rewards. Sounds good, but he "proved" his point by showing that small stocks routinely outperformed the major market indexes. He concluded that since the major market indexes are deemed less risky, the higher returns of the small stocks proved his point. Wait a minute! If they are riskier, shouldn't small stocks underperform the major market indexes? If they don't, where's the risk? To use a gambling comparison, if you bet only long shots, over the long term you should win less money, not more. At the very best, you should break even.

The contradiction arises because Mr. Malkiel mixed apples and oranges. When he was explaining risk, he defined it as short-term volatility. When he was comparing returns, he was writing about the tendency of a stock to rise in price over the long term. If the reward is measured in the long term, the risk should also be measured in the long term. I will not make that mistake. My goal is to educate, not confuse.

In this book, I will not be advocating the simple themes, because this book was written especially for retirees. Why especially for retirees? Because retirees are special-needs investors, so the old rules do not always apply to them. Start early, diversify, and know your risk tolerance seem like good rules, but they don't work for all ages. They especially don't work well for the average retiree.

Most books on investing seem to misunderstand who their audience is and what resources they have. They leave out retirees because they focus on the rewards of the stock market rather than the fears of the investors. While retirees are drawn to the market by its rewards, in the end, their fear of it leaves them on the outside looking in. This book seeks to overcome their fears by giving them the knowledge and understanding they need to get into the game.

What knowledge and understanding? First, know yourself. That will be your hardest lesson. Then you will learn about risk, stocks, the markets where they are bought and sold, and finally, the resources you will need to play the game. The greatest enemy of fear is knowledge and understanding. In this book, you'll gain the knowledge you'll need to face your fear.

Acting on the understanding gained from this book, what you will be doing is buying stocks—from a distance. You will be distant from the companies you buy and the people who sell the stocks. You will not be a fly on the wall in their boardrooms or in their back rooms. The information you have will be late in coming, incomplete in content, and devoid of any inside scoop. You will be at the mercy of the market, but you don't need their mercy because you have some formidable weapons in your arsenal.

You Are a Weapon

You are about to explore those weapons, and the first one is you. Remember, as an aging investor you have two choices: Find an expert, or become your own expert. Before you place this book back on the shelf and run screaming from the store, let me explain. I am not talking about becoming a master of spreadsheets, financial statements, and stock market gyrations. I am talking about becoming a master of you. The most important ingredient in stock market success is you. By knowing who you are, what you like, and what you are capable of doing, you can determine how and where you fit in the stock market puzzle. The stock market is a game. In fact, it is three games. The only way to win is to know which of those games you are best at and then play that game.

Of course, you must know something about the stock market, and this book will teach you what you need to know. What it teaches will not be nonsense, or contradictory, or useless; it will be the truth. The truth can be a scary thing, but I won't use it to scare you. I'll use it to open your eyes so that you can see the pitfalls and negotiate your own unique path past those pitfalls to stock market success. If, at the end of this book, you see that path to success, my book will have accomplished its goal. Traveling the path is your goal and your job.

Before you begin, be assured that this book was written with you in mind. I am well aware that you are at the end of your working career. Your little nest egg is precious. To lose it is to be condemned to a life of hard labor for minimum wage at your local McDonalds or Wal-Mart. The opposite is equally true: A nest egg that you hold in a death grip may condemn you to a minimal existence with nothing but a meager savings account and a Social Security check to give you a false sense of safety. There is another way, and this book explores it. It is not necessarily easy. It will take some work, some study, some discipline, and some courage. What it will not take is your nest egg. At age sixty-two, that nest egg is precious, and you should use it sparingly.

Now you know what's in store for you. Are you ready to open up shop and get into the business of buying and selling stocks? Yes? Okay then, let's get started.

Introduction

Americans are notorious nonsavers. The average savings rate in America is less than 5 percent, and the average American worker has only $25,000 in savings when he or she retires. Given the median income in America is now about $37,500 a year, $25,000 is a paltry sum of money. If you are one of those average Americans, $25,000 won't add much luster to your golden years.

If you retire at age sixty-two at the median income, your Social Security check will be $802 a month.[1] Eight hundred and two dollars a month and $25,000 in the bank isn't going to cut it. You'll need much more—a pension or a rich relative. Without those, you will have to delay your retirement. Unfortunately, your present employer may not let you. There are rules. If the rules are against you, you'll have to take a low-strain, low-wage job. It is a very depressing end to a productive career.

Of course, you might be one of the lucky ones with a plump pension from one of the big companies like General Motors, Boeing, General Electric, or the government. Or you might have worked for a small, innovative company that established a 401(k) retirement plan. If you are among those few, you have choices. Combining your 401(k) or pension with your Social Security and savings may provide enough money to pay the bills and cover emergencies. Thus, working beyond age sixty-two becomes a choice. You work to fill the idle hours. You work to fulfill a dream. Or you work to earn the luxuries like gifts for the grandchildren, annual vacations, weekly entertainments, and dinners out. You work because you want to, not because you have to.

Statistics say the lucky ones are, at best, half the population. The other half isn't retired—they continue to work at low-wage jobs. If you have to work during your retirement, why step down? Why not step up? Why not work where the sky is the limit, at a job like the kind you had when you were young and just starting out? There were skills to learn, challenges to meet, promotions to win, and money to make. You weren't winding down; you were building up. This is a book about building up.

Finding the Perfect Job

If you are not in the lucky group, you are going to have to work, or you are going to starve. Even if you don't starve, retirement won't be much fun. More to the point, you really aren't going to be able to retire. You'll have to keep on working. The only real choices you will have are what kind of work you do and how much you will earn. Let's look at the choices available—there are three:

- Work for someone else.
- Work for yourself.
- Get others to work for you.

Your choice will have a big impact on your financial well-being. If you work for someone else, you will always earn less than you're worth. Why? Because you have agreed to give part of your salary to the person who bought the machine, built the factory, or developed the technology that created your job. This is not a bad thing; it is capitalism, part of the free-enterprise system that has made America the greatest economic power on earth.

You can avoid giving away part of your salary by working for yourself. Small shop owners, doctors, lawyers, and some accountants are all examples of the self-employed. While most live well, they are not necessarily wealthy. They spend a lifetime climbing the financial ladder toward wealth, but few of the self-employed reach the top.

Getting others to work for you is your third choice. When you get others to work for you, you are the boss, the owner, the capitalist, "the man." The people who work for you are your employees. You are no longer running a Mom-and-Pop shop; you are running a business with tens, hundreds, even thousands of employees. Each of those employees has agreed to give you part of his or her earnings for the privilege of working for you. For example, if you have just twenty employees who are willing to give you 10 percent of that revenue in the form of profits, and each generates $150,000 in annual revenue, your annual income will be $300,000.

Getting Others to Work for You

When you get others to work for you, you become an entrepreneur. But entrepreneurship is a young person's game. Why? Because, as has been widely reported in business literature, four out of five new businesses will go bankrupt within five years of opening. Many successful entrepreneurs suffer one or more failures before they get it right. If you are thirty-five, it's easier to recover from the psychological and financial trauma of a bankruptcy. Failure is not an option when you are sixty-two. One of the reasons the franchise industry has expanded rapidly over the past ten years is it is a way around this dismal failure rate. Franchising allows entrepreneurs to start already-proven businesses. With a sound business model and a tested market, the chance of failure is greatly reduced. Still, even with the reduced failure rate of a franchise, entrepreneurship is a lot of work for someone ready to retire. The problem with all of the choices described is they are not retirement strategies—they are work strategies.

Earning Without Working

Working doesn't solve the problem because working is the problem: You don't have enough money to retire, so you have to work. What you need is a better way—a real solution. The stock market is your solution.

The stock market is your ticket to entrepreneurship, and entrepreneurship is the road to wealth. Remember, to achieve wealth you have to get other people to work for you. The stock market is a place where you can get other people to work for you. When you buy stock in a company, you are hiring that company—its management, its facilities, and its employees. You become the owner. You collect the profits.

There are many advantages to a stock market venture. First, buying and selling stocks is not work. (At least, not the punch-the-time-clock-and-sit-at-your-desk work you're used to.) You can do it and still retire; you can do it from your home in your spare time. There are no clocks to punch, no bosses to appease, no customers to placate, no employees to suffer, no payrolls to meet. You answer only to yourself, but you benefit from the efforts of hundreds, even thousands, of employees.

Additionally, it doesn't take a lot of money. If you are spending $2 a week on lottery tickets, stop. Place that bet on a stock. The odds of winning are better, it's just as much fun, and a lot of winning stocks can be bought for less than $1. In fact, as you will discover, some of the most promising stock buys are less than $1. For example, a year's worth of lottery tickets would have bought you almost fifty shares of Hansen Beverage in June 2003. Its closing price in June 2006 was $185. Just think, if you had bought $100 worth of Hansen stock in 2003, it would be worth $9,250 by 2006. Looked at another way, if you invested just $5,000 of your $25,000 nest egg in Hansen, you would have $432,243, plus the $20,000 you didn't invest. Not bad for three years of not working.

What Do You Need to Get Started?

If you're looking for a sure-fire stock trading system, you won't find it here. This is not a book about a stock-buying system; it is about a stock-buying business. You will need three things to get into this business: knowledge, understanding, and courage, which are all personal traits. Stock buying and selling is a personal endeavor; no system can do it for you. It isn't the market, the economy, the company, or the stockbroker who controls your success; it's you. It is your knowledge of how the game is played and what kind of player you are. It's true you will need to understand some business basics and some stock market mechanisms, but most of all you'll need to understand yourself.

You'll need courage as well; courage to make the move, take the plunge, buy the stock, accept the risk, and reach for the stars. Courage is the absence of fear, and fear comes from ignorance and misunderstanding. We are creating an upward spiral. With knowledge comes understanding, and understanding leads to courage, and courage gives us the confidence to seek more knowledge that, in turn, brings more understanding and more courage. Before long, you are a risk taker, an investor, a trader, and a player. You are in the business of buying and selling stocks.

Knowledge, understanding, and courage are the pillars on which your stock-buying business will be built. An array of practical insights, rules, techniques, and a computer will be added. If you aren't comfortable with computers yet, you'll need to develop some basic computer skills. Without them, you will be forced to buy stocks through brokers who may be expensive, slow, and self-interested. A computer will allow you to access the Internet and bypass them. You will buy stocks directly and quickly online. Before you get too nervous about not having a computer or knowing how to use it, don't worry. I'll give you some ideas on how to get one or at least access one. You'll be surprised at all the options you have.

Time is another weapon in our arsenal. Finding good stocks to buy is time consuming. It will take time to read this book, even more time to familiarize yourself with the investing websites, and still more time to identify, analyze, select, and monitor your stocks. As a retiree, you may not have the time to compound your interest, but you have plenty of time to search out great investment opportunities. When you see how great some of those opportunities can be, you'll never buy another lottery ticket.

Wisdom is the third weapon in your arsenal. Wisdom is the magical blend of experience and common sense keeping you from buying a bottle of snake oil. You will not be chasing penny stocks here. Nor will you be drilling oil wells or buying corn futures. You will be cautious and will seek exceptional returns through wise choices. It is the purpose of this book to add to your wisdom so you can add to your nest egg.

As a mature adult, you have overcome a lifetime of challenges. This is just one more, and the best way for you to gain the needed courage to face this one is to dispel your fears with knowledge. The more you know about the stock market, the less you will fear it. The more you know, the more you understand, and the braver you become.

It is for this reason we begin our journey with an understanding of ourselves.

CHAPTER 1
Taking Stock of Yourself

Many retirees fear the stock market. They see it as a rich man's playground filled with nefarious characters and suspect institutions. They are right. Unfortunately, it is also the best place to invest their money. If you want to achieve reasonable returns, you must be in the stock market; anywhere else—banks, brokers, government—there will be so many people skimming off the top, your profits will barely cover inflation.

I'll Never Be Able to Understand the Stock Market . . . Will I?

When President Franklin Roosevelt declared, "The only thing we have to fear is fear itself," he wasn't talking about the stock market. He was talking about the economy. The economy was a huge complex of entanglements that began to unwind in 1929, and no one knew how to put it back together. The same is true of the stock market: It is a complex entanglement of seemingly rational and irrational price swings. The torrent of information swirling around this capitalist invention is overwhelming. Yet, if you cut through the nonsense and focus on the fundamental forces driving it, it is simple, understandable, and considerably less scary.

There is no magic in the stock market, but there is something more important and more honest—a predictable set of behavior patterns. Understanding them will allow you to control your fears and discover your own unique road to success. Investing is not really about the stock market, the companies it represents, or the evildoers it attracts; it's about you. Investing is a very personal matter. Once you understand yourself, and it, you will succeed.

Every retiree should play the stock market game, but not everyone will. Some will take their money and go home, hoarding it in coffee cans and under mattresses for fear someone will steal it. While it may be safe from someone, in the end, something will steal it: inflation.

Others will place it in bank accounts and Certificates of Deposit where it is safe from both thieves and inflation. Thus, they have no fear of losing, but no hope of winning. This strategy demands little and yields less.

Players who want more put their money in the stock market. But to make more they must do more. They must learn, then practice what they have learned. Most important, they must know what game they are playing. The stock market is not a single game; it is three different games. Smart players choose the one game they can win, the game they are good at. This reduces their risk, subdues their fear, and raises their confidence level. Risk, fear, and confidence are part of each game. Manage them, and you are on your way to a profitable stock market experience.

The Games People Play

If you want to be a player in the stock market, you better know what game you are playing. While there is only one stock market, there are three games and three kinds of players. They are:

1. Investing
2. Trading
3. Speculating

The most important consideration in choosing a game is you. Who are you? Are you patient, analytical, and logical? Maybe you are impatient, decisive, and self-confident. Perhaps you are none of these. Maybe you're just somebody who wants to win big without the spreadsheets and fancy charts. Well, if one of those fits you, you are in luck. The stock market awaits.

Investing—A Game of Fundamentals

When most people think about the stock market, they think about investors. While it is true many of the players in the market are investors, many are not. It is crucial we understand the difference between an investor and the other market players.

What Is Investing?

When you invest in the stock market, you are actually buying part ownership in a company. As an owner, you share in the prosperity of the company. If the company grows, the value of your stock grows. If the company is profitable, you may receive a share of those profits, which are paid as dividends. Thus, your investment can grow in two ways: stock value and dividends.

Investors are fundamentalists because they look at the business fundamentals supporting a stock's price. These fundamentals include company sales, profits, growth rates, markets, competition, and government regulations. All of these measures have an impact on the health of the company as well as the value of its stock.

To be a fundamentalist (at least a good one), you must be willing to plow through reams of corporate statistics and management propaganda to get to the truth of a company's prospects. The future of the company will determine the future of the stock. If the company is growing in sales and profits, the stock will grow in price and dividends. This is the fundamental assumption underlying all investment decisions. Investors analyze the past in order to project the future.

The Character of an Investor

Not all fundamentalists are good investors because not all fundamentalists are patient. Investing is a slow-moving game; patience is key. Read any book on investing and *patience* will be liberally sprinkled throughout. All stock prices, in time, will reflect the fortunes of their underlying companies. *In time* means you must be willing to wait for the market[1] to catch up to the fundamentals.

Analyzing companies is a rigorous undertaking. One of the fundamentals concerning investors is the price-earnings ratio (P/E). The price-earnings ratio is determined by taking the amount of earnings a company produces in a year and dividing it by the number of its shares of outstanding stock, SO. This result is the earnings per share EPS. The EPS is then divided into the price of the stock to get the P/E (price ÷ EPS = P/E). If this is too much math for you, investing is not your game.

While P/E is an important factor when it comes to investing, there are others. You'll need to understand the other important fundamentals such as debt loads, cash flow, net margins, return on assets, price-to-sales ratio, sales growth, and strategic advantage. An investor needs to analyze all these elements in a logical and systematic manner in order to discover why a stock's price changes. If all these business metrics are a mystery to you and learning them leaves you cold, set your sights on a different game.

Once you have determined a company has a prosperous future, you buy, and you hold. Holding stock is where the patience comes in. You have done all the heavy lifting. Now you must restrain yourself from reacting to the "wiggles and waggles" (as investor and author Peter Lynch[2] called them) of the stock's price. You are looking for long-term gains, not daily or weekly profits. Unless something changes in the fundamentals, there is no reason to sell. Over the past 100 years, the stock market has returned an average of 10–12 percent each year, but it hasn't returned 10–12 percent every year. Along the road to that 10–12 percent average, it has had many short-term fits and starts. You'll need the patience and courage to ignore these wiggles and waggles.

The successful investor's strategy is buy value, not price. Buying value requires a logical approach to the stock market backed by a mathematically rigorous analysis of the targeted company. Add the courage to ignore the stock market's irrational price gyrations and the patience to wait for it to catch up to your analysis, and you have the makings of a successful investor.

Is Investing a Winning Game?

To answer that question, let's look at Hansen Beverage. Hansen produces a line of health-conscious juices, teas, and sodas. Its reported sales at the end of 2003 were $110.4 million, with profits of $5.9 million. The price of the stock at that time was $5 per share. By the end of 2004, its sales increased to $180.3 million (63.3 percent) and its profits increased 245.8 percent to $20.4 million. The price of the stock increased to $18 per share (260 percent). Given the promising product line of health drinks and its history of sales growth, an investor might buy the stock at the end of 2004 ($18).

Would that have been a winning play? Absolutely! At the end of 2005, Hansen's sales continued to increase to $348.9 million (93.5 percent) and profits increased to $62.8 million (207.8 percent). The price of the stock also increased to $80 per share (344.4 percent). A retiree investing just $5,000 of his nest egg in Hansen would have $22,222 within a year.

Trading—A Game of Agility

Investing is all about why a stock does what it does, but stocks don't always do what they should. They often do what the market wants them to do. When that happens, stock prices sometimes go up when they should go down, and down when they should go up. For times like these, we have traders.

What Is Trading?

Traders (or chartists) don't care why a market does what it does or does what it shouldn't; they are only concerned with what it does and when it does it. To discover this what and when, chartists look to the stock chart to spot price movements. Figure 1 is the stock chart for Hansen Beverage.

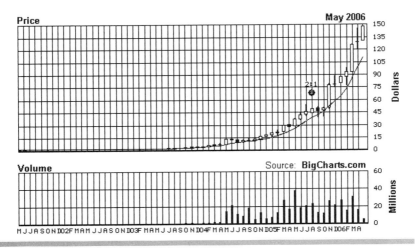

FIGURE 1: Stock Chart for Hansen Beverage (HANS) — Five year Monthly. The stock chart is actually two charts. The top chart measures the periodic changes in price. The bottom chart measures the amount of shares traded in each period. The charts can present different timeframes and periods. This chart is a five year timeframe with monthly periods.

Chartists have their own buy/sell signals. The most powerful is the trend. Once a stock begins a trend, the chartist buys (uptrend), sells (downtrend), or waits (sideways trend). These trends and other buy/sell signals control the entrance and exit of traders into the stock market.

Unfortunately, these trends can be fleeting or fitful, providing chartists with an abundance of false signals.[3] No sooner does our poor chartist buy (or sell), than the stock reverses. Woe is her. She uses agility to protect herself from this market volatility, but agility is not enough; she wants confirmation her signal of choice is valid. Higher volume of shares traded provides confirmation. The increased volume suggests a large number of players have bought the shares. She doesn't know why, she only knows they have, and this makes her confident it is okay to join the crowd.

Confirmation also comes in the form of an elaborate system of technical indicators like the MACD, DMI, RSI, OBV, etc.[4] These are mathematical manipulations of those basic indicators, price and volume. They are designed to clarify the trends and movements of the stock's price. They make it easier for the trader to see what the stock is doing.

The Character of a Trader

Traders are the jackrabbits of the stock market—quick to move and easily spooked. Their agility is their strength; they use their vast array of technical indicators to signal when it is time to buy and sell stocks. Thus, they must be unquestioning, confident, committed, decisive, and focused. Yet, they can be fearful, paranoid, hesitant, undisciplined, and simplistic.

Note the contradictions: confident–fearful, decisive–hesitant, focused–undisciplined. The strength of trading is it is a system designed to overcome these contradictions. For instance, trading allows an undisciplined person to be successful in the stock market because he buys based on a set of disciplined signals. He doesn't have to analyze the company, understand business, or anticipate customer preferences. He only has to watch the chart and react to the signals.

Yet, if the trader is undisciplined and doesn't follow where the technical indicators lead, success will elude him. Therein lies the contradictions: He can be paranoid when it comes to the markets, but he must trust in the indicators. He can be too lazy to do an exhaustive analysis, but he must be ambitious enough to check the stock charts each day, or week, or month. He may never be quite sure of his judgment, but he must be confident in the charts.

For all these contradictions, one thing is certain: Traders must be attentive. To make money as a trader, you must manage the process. Trading is a daily activity. Once you take a position (buy a stock), you cannot walk away from it like investors or speculators. An investment depends on developments within the company. A trade depends on developments within the stock market. Company developments usually take months to mature. Stock market developments are daily events; they change quickly.

Is Trading a Winning Game?

Remember our Hansen example. The stock was increasing as the company's sales and profits increased. That relationship is important to investors because it answers the question "Why?" Traders aren't interested in why, they are only interested in what. To answer the what, they look at the stock chart (Figure 1).

Note what happens to the price of the stock in May 2004: It jumps from $7 to $14. This jump moves it well above its trend line, which is the black line on the price chart. This is a buy signal. Plus, the number of shares sold in May went from 2 million to 17 million shares. This was a strong confirmation a lot of people were buying Hansen. Among those people were some astute traders, who bought the stock at $14 a share.

While the Hansen chart provides a strong buy signal, the sell signal is not as strong. We'll discuss this further in the chapter on trading, but for now there is only one area on the chart indicating a sell signal. In September 2005, the price dips below the trend line. If a nervous trader sold at that point (around $40), she would have gained 185.7 percent on her $14 investment in just 16 months. In other words, investing $5,000 in Hansen would be worth $14,285.

If the trader did not respond to the sell signal in September 2005 and held to the end of the chart, her return would be 971.4 percent. Again, a $5,000 investment in Hansen in May 2004 would be worth $53,571 in just 2 years. Why would she hold past the September 2005 sell signal? The answer lies in the other indicators and rules of trading, which will be discussed in Chapter 10. Until then, whether she sells in September 2005 or holds until May 2006, our trader has won a significant prize with Hansen.

Speculation—A Game of Chance

Speculators are the great gamblers of the market. They take the risks and sometimes reap the rewards. They buy the rumor and sell the news. They buy low and sell high. They are the troublemakers making the market so scary because they buy too soon, sell too soon, and create volatility.

What Is Speculation?

Speculation is the art of buying something with the hope you can sell it for more than you paid for it. What separates the speculator from the investor, trader, or businessman is that he makes his purchase before he has any concrete evidence that he will ever find a buyer. Where the investor has his analysis, the trader his indicators, and the businessman his market surveys, the speculator has only a hunch or a vision or an extrapolation.

The Character of a Speculator

There are actually three kinds of speculators: extrapolators, visionaries, and gamblers. There are many differences between them, but they share some common traits. For instance, they are risk takers. They are also patient. For all its glitz and glamour, speculation can be a waiting game. Many stocks lie dormant, unnoticed, and unmoved for years. Then they explode in a flurry of volume that defies explanation. The entry point for the true speculator is before the move, sometimes years before. Only the speculator sees what isn't seen, knows what isn't known, and reaps the rewards for their clairvoyance. It is here the three types of speculators begin to depart from each other.

The extrapolator is a student of the history of the stock market. She projects this history into the future to predict how the stock market will behave. The extrapolator knows lower interest rates will generate higher stock prices because savers will move their money from low-interest bank accounts to higher dividend stocks, and that raises stock prices. She knows this has happened and why it has happened, and she trusts it will happen again. The extrapolator is not swayed by political hype or personal prejudices; she acts on history, responds to cycles, and heeds cause and effect, not her personal preferences or whims.

The visionary's actions aren't based on history. He goes where no one has gone before, and he goes there first. A visionary has a keen sense of cultural trends and demographic shifts. He may not create the invention, but he realizes its potential soon after its introduction. His insightfulness allows him to cut through the hype and focus on the true worth of an idea.

The gambler plays the odds. He hides his laziness behind a mask of contrarian recklessness. He knows he shouldn't buy the tip, chase the fad, or trust the boiler room, but he does. Greed rules the day and drives his investment strategy. He is an IPO[5] hound who sniffs out winners without the benefit of history. He'll buy Google when it's overpriced, with the confidence there are fools who will price it higher. To the extent he plays this fool's game, he knows the only real fool is the last fool. His goal is to be first, not last.

To many people, speculation looks like an attractive alternative to trading and investing. It seems so much easier to go with rumor, especially when it is published in a fancy newsletter or market report. With speculation, there is no need to understand business or study stock charts. It doesn't require lots of time, money, or smarts. What it does require is trust—in yourself or in the tipster. Add a little intuition to help avoid the losers and vision to help see the winners, and you have the makings of a successful speculator.

Unfortunately, speculation provides fertile ground for the ne'er-do-wells. Since speculative ventures are new, untested, and laden with risk, it is hard to tell the legitimate from the illegitimate. Unless you have honed your speculative skills, you can easily fall victim to brazen manipulators with their pump-and-dump schemes, artificially raising the price of a stock long enough for them to sell it to you.[6] Once you buy, the price drops and your life savings drop with it. Yet it is the occasional winner that draws the honest player to the game, and when speculators win, they often win big.

Is Speculation a Winning Game?

If a speculator purchased a share of Hansen Beverage based on the nature of Hansen's product line and the market trend toward health foods in May 2003, he would have paid $1.12 per share. By May 2006, that share was selling for $150, a 13,290 percent increase. A $5,000 investment in Hansen in May 2003 would be worth $669,643 in just 3 years—a lifetime of savings from just one well-placed speculative stock purchase. To make such a purchase, the speculator must see the value of the product, the potential of the market, and the competence of the company, and he must see it without a historical reference or a rigorous analysis. But, if and when he does see it, the rewards are great.

While this example illustrates the potential of a speculative play, it is important to point out there are over 9,000 stocks listed on the various stock exchanges. In any given year, there are very few speculative opportunities as lucrative as Hansen. You have to be very lucky or a gifted speculator to find one or more of those few. Once you have found one, you have to have the courage to buy it.

Stay in Your Game

If you are going to start buying and selling stock in your golden years, the two things you will need to know are yourself, and the types of players buying a stock. It's a big mistake to play in a game that doesn't match your abilities or personality.

For example, if you are an investor and the market is on a speculative binge, it's time for you to sell. In 2000, the NASDAQ and Dow soared to amazing heights. The Dow is a large-cap portfolio of stocks closely tied to the general economy and the New York Stock Exchange; the various stock exchanges are described in the next chapter. Why did they rise so high so fast? Only the market knows. There was nothing in the technology boom, the Internet revolution, and the expanding economy that would justify the NASDAQ's rise. However, many undisciplined investors abandoned their game and bought into the Internet Bubble.[7] They were late to get in, and many were late to get out. They should have known better, and they probably did, but the lure of the bubble drew them in. If they had stayed in their game, their rewards would have been very different. For example, in July 1996, the Dow was valued at 5,170. The NASDAQ was at 1,009. In the first quarter of 2000, the Dow hit its high of 11,908 (a 130 percent rise) and the NASDAQ peaked at 5,132 (a 408 percent rise). If, in 2000, investors succumbed to the hype of the late nineties and sold their slower-moving Dow investments for the high-flying NASDAQ, they got a rude awakening. Both the Dow and the NASDAQ began a two-year decline in 2000 that ended in late 2003 when the Dow hit 7,177 (a 40 percent decline) and the NASDAQ hit 1,108 (a 78 percent decline).

In later chapters, we will explore why the NASDAQ fell so far. The important point here is if, as an investor, you had sold your Dow stocks and used the money to buy stocks traded on the NAS-DAQ in early 2000, you would have been burned. How badly? In March 2006, the NASDAQ was valued at 2,378. It was still 54 percent below its peak six years after its fall in 2000. Contrast that with the investor-friendly Dow. It was valued at 11,709 in May 2006, less than 2 percent below its peak. If you had stuck with your game, by 2006 you would have recovered from the financial traumas of the 2000–2003 downturn. Not only would you have recovered, your ten-year annual average return (1996–2006) would be about 8.5 percent. If you had shifted to the high-flying NASDAQ, you would still be 54 percent below your peak.

You might conclude from that example the traders and speculators in the NASDAQ were also burned by the downturn. Unlikely! If traders traded and speculators were any good, they probably made a lot of money; they lost only if they stopped playing their game.

Remember, investors hold stocks and are slow to sell. Traders react to the trend and buy and sell quickly. When the NASDAQ turned down, they sold out.

Speculators also sold early in the downturn. Extrapolators may bet on cycles and sectors, but they will always bail when the cycle turns and the sector weakens. Visionaries may bet on a technology or a trend, but they usually place their bets on a specific winning company. Even the gambler, master of the fool's game, would not be so foolish as to stay in once the bubble burst. The speculators were probably out of the market before the traders.

The point of the example is simple: The stock market is a fairly safe place, as long as you don't hop over the fence onto the other guy's playground. As an investor, you need to follow the principles of investing and not try to become a speculator or trader. You need to be true to yourself and your game. To do that, you must know the game and yourself.

Know Thyself

The most important thing you need to know about the stock market is yourself. You can know the economy. You can know the company. You can know the market. You can have all that knowledge, but if you don't know yourself, you can still fail.

Before you read another chapter in this book, you should take stock of yourself. You need to assess your strengths and weaknesses, your likes and dislikes, your prejudices and tolerances, your education and intelligence, your ambition and goals, your courage and fears—and you must do it with brutal honesty. Anything less will cost you money and time. When it comes to investing as a retiree, you don't have the time or the money to waste on delusional self-assessments.

To get you started, turn to Appendix A and look at the personality matrix. Table II is an abbreviated form of the matrix. It illustrates some of the personal traits needed to succeed as a stock market investor, trader, and speculator. The matrix is not based on any exhaustive psychological studies; it is based on common sense. If you are a trader, investor, or speculator and you think the matrix mischaracterizes you, feel free to object, but before you object, are you really being honest with yourself?

Table II assumes you are doing the investing yourself. There are no brokers, money managers, or mutual-fund gurus doing it for you. You are going into the business of buying and selling stocks, and you want to know if you have what it takes to succeed. Creating a matrix like Table II will help you determine who you are and where you fit. So let's use Table II to see how you fit.

Go down the list of personal traits and place an H (high), M (moderate), or L (low) in the check-off column (✓). For instance, if you are highly intelligent, place an H in the column next to Intelligence. If you are a risk taker, place an H next to Risk-Taker. Don't be afraid to admit you lack one of the traits. It is better to be honest now than broke later. If you aren't sure, place an M in the column. Table III illustrates a completed profile.

Now compare your check-off column to the traits most compatible with the various stock market games. In this step, it is okay to highlight lower rankings, but you can't highlight higher rankings. For example, in Table III Business Acumen was marked as H. This allowed you to highlight Very High in the Investing column, but it also allowed you to highlight Low in the Trading and Moderate in the Speculating columns. Having what isn't needed is not a detriment; however, not having what is needed is a problem. In this example, you lack Patience. This precludes you from highlighting Investing or Speculating, because they require something you don't have.

Based on Table III, where is your best chance for stock market success? Before you answer that, notice some of the traits in the various columns were marked as Very High. These traits are considered the most important indicators of success. Thus, to be an investor you should have Business Acumen. Without it, analyzing the income and balance sheets of companies would be difficult. A trader must be decisive, and a speculator needs to be visionary, at least if you want to be a visionary speculator.

Just because you lack a key trait doesn't mean you can't play. It does mean you will have to plan to get or develop that trait. For instance, if

TABLE II
Matching the Player to the Game

Personal Traits Needed to Succeed	✓	Investing	Trading	Speculating
Intelligence		High	Low	Moderate
Knowledge		High	Low	Moderate
Discipline		Very High	Moderate	Low
Math Skills		Moderate	Low	Low
Self-Starter		Low	High	Low
Ambition		High	Low	Low
Patience		Moderate	Low	High
Decisiveness		Moderate	Very High	Low
Visionary		Moderate	Low	Very High
Risk-Taker		Low	High	Very High
Business Acumen		Very High	Low	Moderate

TABLE III
Matching the Player to the Game
(Completed profile)

Personal Traits Needed to Success	✓	Investing	Trading	Speculating
Intelligence	H	**High**	Low	**Moderate**
Knowledge	m	High	**Low**	High
Discipline	L	Very High	Moderate	**Low**
Math Skills	H	**Moderate**	Low	Low
Self-Starter	L	**Low**	High	Low
Ambition	L	High	**Low**	Low
Patience	L	Moderate	**Low**	High
Decisiveness	L	Moderate	Very High	**Low**
Visionary	m	**Moderate**	Low	Very High
Risk-Taker	L	**Low**	High	Very High
Business Acumen	H	**Very High**	Low	**Moderate**

you are not a risk taker but want to trade because you are very impatient, you can control your risk aversion by taking small positions in several stocks. That will dampen your profits, but over time, it will also build your confidence and decrease your aversion to risk.

What game did you decide was best for you? Let's look at the example.

In this example, there is a lack of decisiveness and risk aversion, so trading is not a good choice. Speculating is a possibility, but the lack of vision and risk-taking, which are critical traits, means it isn't the best choice. Given the high intelligence and business acumen, investing would best fit the profile, yet this player could use more knowledge and discipline. When she builds her business plan, she should include the need to develop her knowledge and discipline. Adding these two traits to her profile would bode well for her chances of success in the stock market as an investor.

As you read this book, you will be able to add other traits to the matrix in Appendix A, build your own profile, and compare it to the traits that make for a successful investor, trader, or speculator. Taking stock in yourself before you buy stocks in the market will go a long way toward making your stock buying and selling business profitable.

What You Have Learned

- Through knowledge, we can learn to overcome our fear of the stock market.
- The stock market is made up of three different games: investing, trading, and speculating.
- Investors need to be analytical, patient, and logical.
- Traders are often impatient, but they need to couple their impatience with confidence and decisiveness.
- Speculators need to have vision, good instincts, and a willingness to place a bet and wait for their vision to develop.
- There are three types of speculators: extrapolators, visionaries, and gamblers.
- The best way to succeed in the market is to know who you are and then play your game—the game you know how to win.

CHAPTER 2

Understanding Money, the Stock Market, and the Economy

When you first enter the stock market, you should expect to be misled, lost, and confused. Don't let that deter you. A trek through a well-designed maze can be fun, exhilarating, and in the case of the stock market, rewarding. Sure, you will bump into a few walls, but you always make your way to the exit. In the stock market maze, you will do more than your share of wall bumping, but when you find your way, you will be more than self-satisfied—you will be financially secure.

One of the reasons for all the bumps is the stock market wasn't designed for just one player; the stock market is a maze of mazes. As we discovered in Chapter 1, it is the arena for some very different personalities. These players routinely jump in and out of each other's games. This disrupts the rational flow of play in those games. There isn't much you can do to stop these game crashers; however, you can understand them, recognize their shenanigans, and refuse to play their game.

In later chapters, we will take a closer look at these games, but here we explore the various playgrounds. Before we explore that, let's take a moment to understand money, or at least the uses of it.

The Uses of Money

There are only three things you can do with money: You can spend it; you can hoard it; or you can invest it. Most Americans understand spending money—we do it more than any other nation in the world. America is the world's marketplace. Money not spent is accumulated by hoarding or investing. Hoarding is exactly what it sounds like: You put piles of money in your pocket, your mattress, or your coffee can. It sits idle, waiting for you to spend it or bequeath it.

Money not spent or hoarded is invested. Invested money is out of your possession. You give it to an idea, a company, or an entrepreneur; it is money working for you. Whenever you put your money to work, you expect to be paid. The payment is in the form of interest, profits, dividends, or capital appreciation.

Saving Is Investing

Many retirees think saving is safe and investing is risky. Actually, there is very little difference between saving and investing. Investing can be done through your bank, broker, financial planner, insurance company, family business, neighbor's business, the local casino, etc. Any time you take money out of that coffee can with the expectation you will earn a return on it, you are investing. A decision to buy stocks is not a decision to invest; it is a decision about how and where to invest.

Many people think if their money is in the bank, it is safe. While it is true bank savings are insured, you are paying for that insurance. The average return on a stock investment is 10–12 percent. The average return on a bank savings account is 3–4 percent. The bank is withholding 8 percentage points to cover their losses and provide a profit. They get 73 percent of the return; you get just 27 percent. Yet, they are using 100 percent of your money. So, while your savings may be safe, you are paying a high price for that safety.

How high a price? Consider a $1,000 savings account at 3 percent interest opened at age twenty-one. At age sixty-one, your account is worth $3,262. The same $1,000 invested in the stock market would be worth $92,656. The difference ($89,394) is what you paid the bank to keep your $1,000 safe.

There Is No "Market"

Listen to the stock market gurus, and you'll hear them say, "The market hates uncertainty." "The market consolidated its gains." "The market reacted to higher oil prices." The experts have made "the market" into some mystical being. Only they can talk to it; they are its translators. If you want to talk to the market, you must first talk to them. How convenient and profitable for them—the experts.

There is no market. There is only a collection of individual stocks traded by individual stockholders or institutions. For instance, in 2001 when the Dow was declining from a high of 11,908 to a low of 7,177 (a 40 percent drop), more than 400 individual stocks doubled in price. If you owned one of those stocks and sold because the market was selling, you lost a significant opportunity to make some money. The market, through its indexes, said sell; your stock, through its performance, said hold. Whom should you have listened to?

Don't get caught up in this nonsense of an all-knowing market. At the end of the day, the total of those individual decisions determines what the market did. The market is an after-the-fact invention. Prior to the opening bell (the opening bell starts the day's trading in stocks), there is no market waiting to rush in and buy stocks. There are only individuals, making individual decisions based on their judgments and situations. Each stock has its own following; investors buy it, hold it, or sell it for personal reasons.

I'm not saying there isn't a herd mentality surrounding the market. The big players in the stock market, like market managers and institutional players, account for more than 70 percent of the stock market's daily activity. These players are big enough to move or manipulate the market. They are easily led and easily spooked. If Warren Buffet decided to buy an oil company, 100 institutional sycophants would follow. This flood of buyers could raise prices in the oil sector, but a herd of wild sycophants is not the same as a community of single-minded, rational investors.

This highlights another stock market myth. The experts would have you believe the market is rational. In reality, the market is more maddening than measured. If the stock market were rational, stocks would rise with earnings. Stocks paying dividends would be more valuable than growth stocks, since the market supposedly hates uncertainty. In a rational market, what is known would be rewarded more than what is unknown. The rationality of the market is suspect.

The Stock Market Is Not an Auction

Equally misleading is the notion the stock market is an auction where stock prices are set by supply and demand. When there are more buyers than sellers, demand is up and prices rise. When there are more sellers than buyers, supply is up and prices fall. So runs the conventional wisdom. Sounds good, but is it true?

How an Auction Works

In an auction, the auctioneer holds up an item and elicits bids. If there is just one bidder, the bidder can offer any amount he wants. If there is no minimum price set, the bidder can buy the item for next to nothing. Add another bidder to the process and the situation dramatically changes. Assuming the value of the item to the bidders is greater than the minimum price, the item will sell at the second-highest bidder's highest price. Adding more bidders doesn't change this dynamic. In the end, the two highest bidders control all auctions. Items will always sell at or near the second-highest bidder's highest price.

The auctioneer is neutral—he simply manages the auction. If there are no bidders for an item, he sets it aside and moves on to the next. If there are no items to sell, he tells the bidders to come back another day. Other than informing the bidders a minimum price has not been met, the auctioneer has no role in setting the price.

How the Market Works

The auctioneer at the so-called stock market auction is the market manager (MM) or the market specialist. She is not neutral; she is a participant in the auction. She buys and sells the very items she auctions. Thus, there is always a buyer and seller at the auction because there is always a market manager at the auction.

Since the market manager is a stock seller, she sets the minimum price, which in the stock market is the ask, or offered, price. This is the minimum price at which a stock can be sold on the market exchange.

The market manager (MM) is also a stock buyer. This means he also sets the price at which stocks will be bought—the bid. Thus, when you look at a stock price quotation, it will state something like, "bid 10, ask 11." This means the MM will pay $10 for a stock, but will sell it for $11. The difference between the bid and ask price is the spread, and it is one way the MM makes money.

Another way he makes money is by buying and selling stock. This may seem like the same thing, but it is not. There aren't always an equal number of buyers and sellers. When there are no buyers, the MM must buy the seller's stocks even though he has no one to immediately sell them to. At other times, when there are no sellers, the MM must sell his stocks to the buyers. Therefore, a market manager must maintain an inventory of the stock in order to meet the demands of buyers and sellers. This is part of his responsibility, and depending on market conditions, it can be a very costly or profitable responsibility.

The key point is the buyers or sellers do not set the price in the stock market, the market manager does. He sets the price based on the number of stocks in his inventory, the price he paid for them, the current number of buyers and sellers, and his view of the future demand for the stock. This can lead MMs to set prices that do not reflect the current flow of buyers and sellers to the auction. Thus, in the face of a flood of buyers, prices might go down rather than up. This is counter to what the auction model would suggest. These anomalies have little impact on investors or speculators, but they can have a significant impact on traders. For that reason, I will explore them more fully when we discuss trading. For now, it is important to realize the stock market is not a true auction. In the short run and within the rules and limits of the stock exchanges, stock prices are more about the market manager than they are about buyers and sellers or company performance.

Surveying the Playground

There are 8,000–10,000 individual stocks listed on the major stock exchanges. This is just a sampling of the millions of companies making up the American economy. All companies can be traded (bought and sold), but to be listed on a stock exchange a company must be publicly traded. This means the ownership of the company is offered to many different buyers in the form of stocks.

The companies listed on the various exchanges cover twelve different sectors and more than 100 different industries. A sector is a group of similar industries. For instance, the Health Care sector would include industries such as hospitals, major pharmaceuticals, biotech companies, medical equipment producers, etc. An industry is made up of companies that make similar products or deliver similar services. The pharmaceutical industry contains major drug companies like Merck and Pfizer. Appendix B lists these sectors and examples of the industries and companies they contain.

Polling the Market

To determine the value of all these stocks listed for sale, a poll is taken. The most famous of these polls is the Dow Jones Industrial Average (DJIA or Dow). It consists of just thirty stocks, monitored each day and reported as a single number. The thirty stocks are selected from a cross section of the economy. They include drug companies, oil companies, software developers, computer companies, and banks. Most are very large companies considered bellweathers of the general direction of the economy.

The Standard & Poor 500 (SP500), which includes many moderate-sized companies, is a broader poll. Another, even larger poll is the Russell 2000, which focuses on small companies. The larger sampling is designed to provide a better indication of the overall direction of the market. For your purposes, either the Dow or the SP500 is a good market indicator.

The Stock Exchanges

The stocks of publicly traded companies are bought and sold on stock exchanges. Stocks are just like any other items you buy. They can be sold directly by the company, by individuals that own them, or by retailers. Most stock buyers, especially small investors, go to their local retailer to buy. In the case of stocks, that retailer is a stock exchange. There are four major stock exchanges and many more regional exchanges. We will only deal with the majors here. They are the New York, American, NASDAQ, and Over-the-Counter (OTC) exchanges:

■ **New York:** Like any retail outlet, the major exchanges have their own character. The New York Stock Exchange (NYSE) is the Tiffany's of exchanges. The companies listed there must meet specific financial and reporting requirements. This provides some assurance the stocks purchased there represent viable and transparent companies. Beyond size and quality, each exchange has developed its own persona. For instance, the NYSE is the home of the "old economy" stocks like General Electric, AT&T, and ExxonMobil. They are proven, somewhat staid, and a little less risky.

- **American:** While not as prestigious, the American Exchange (AMEX) demands similar requirements to the NYSE of its listed companies. There are very few really well known or large companies on the AMEX. It appears to be a little market squeezed between the emerging stocks of the NASDAQ and the proven stocks of the NYSE; yet, it offers much of the assurances afforded by the stringent requirements of the NYSE.

- **NASDAQ:** The NASDAQ, while improving, is less restrictive than either the NYSE or the AMEX. The NASDAQ has developed a high-tech persona. Many of the technology companies like Microsoft came of age on the NASDAQ.

- **Over-the-Counter (OTC):** The OTC is the least restrictive. It includes big companies, little companies, emerging companies, failed companies, recovering companies, $100 stocks, and penny stocks. The OTC is a diverse community of companies at various stages of success and failure. Thus, the OTC is freewheeling, wide ranging, and more volatile than the NYSE, AMEX, or NASDAQ.

Of course, these are just general impressions. There are plenty of high-tech stocks on the NYSE, and the NASDAQ has its share of slow growth, tried-and-true turtles. However, for the most part, you will find tech on the NASDAQ and stability on the NYSE and volatility on the OTC.

Although companies and stocks do not have to be bought and sold through exchanges, the exchanges provide an arena in which you can play the investment game with minimal risk. As we will discover, the keys to reducing risk are liquidity and transparency. By providing a marketplace for stocks, exchanges enhance the liquidity of your purchase. By demanding company reporting and stock transaction standards, they promote transparency. In this book, we will rely heavily on the exchanges to subdue some of the dangerous practices of the manipulators.

The Relationship Between the Economy and the Stock Market

There is a strong link between the stock market and the economy. The economy is simply the sum of all the companies comprising it, and the stock market is a sampling of those companies. When the companies making up the stock market decline, it's a signal the economy is declining.

If you understand the cause-and-effect dynamic of the preceding paragraph, you have the makings of a successful stock market player. The stock market is all about cause and effect. When you spot a cause, you invest in the effect. The greater the correlation between the cause and the effect, the greater your profits will be. The cause always leads and predicts the effect. When that happens in economics, it is a leading indicator.

Timing is also an issue. There must be a reasonable time difference between the cause and the effect. In order for a leading indicator to be useful, it must be causal and timely.

Unfortunately, the economy does not lead the stock market. It is at best a concurrent effect, and more often than not, declining stock prices precede economic downturns. Remember, the greatest stock market crash was in 1929, but the Great Depression wasn't until the 1930s. For all its linkage, the economy will not help us play the market. By the time the economy tells us where the market is going, the stock market has already gone there. However, as we will see, the cycles of the economy can provide investment opportunities for those who trust in history.

Stocks Are Not the Only Game in Town

When you invest in the stock market, you're investing in more than just a stock; you are investing in the company behind the stock, and the economy the company operates within. You are also investing in a financial instrument. A financial instrument is any vehicle designed to offer a financial reward. Examples of financial instruments include savings accounts, money markets, certificates of deposit, municipal bonds, corporate bonds, commodities, and stocks. Each of these has a risk and reward associated with it.

How Financial Instruments Interact

These instruments compete with one another for the investor's money. Two of the biggest competitors are bonds and stocks. Because they are so close in their perceived risk and their actual rewards, money often flows between them depending on the interest rate. The interest rate is controlled by the Federal Reserve and can easily rise or fall 4–6 percentage points depending on the condition of the economy and the inflation rate. Without getting technical, when the interest rates rise, the lower-risk bonds become more attractive, and speculators and traders will sell their stocks and buy bonds. When that happens, money is said to be flowing from stocks into bonds. When interest rates are falling, money tends to flow from bonds into stocks.

This sort of interplay between stocks and bonds is the most common, but there are other financial instruments investment money flows into. In times of high inflation and global uncertainty, money will move into commodities like gold and silver. If the market is in transition (from a bull to a bear market[1]), money will flow out of stocks into low-interest-bearing, highly liquid money market accounts. These money flows raise and lower the price of the financial instrument. When money flows in, prices rise; when money flows out, prices fall.

How You'll Make Money from Those Interactions

Since the economy and interest rates are usually in flux, these flows provide investors with a never-ending opportunity to make money. There are economic plays where the speculator (or investor) bets on the direction of the economy. There are sector plays where he bets on growth of a particular sector. There are interest-rate plays where he bets on the intentions of the Federal Reserve and there are inflation plays where he bets on the increase in commodity prices. At any given time, money is flowing and prices are changing.

Think of the stock market as an ocean, and think of the many ways people play in that ocean. Also note the ocean is constantly changing, and these changes influence how people interact with it. As the climate warms or cools, the ocean expands or contracts as it is fed by melting ice caps. The stock market has been expanding 10–12 percent per year because our economy has been feeding it with ever-increasing amounts of earnings. This provides a great opportunity for the long-term investor to go into the ocean and play. Also, within that ocean are currents flowing from one part to the other. These are similar to the money flows from sector to sector within the stock market.

Beyond the currents are the tides. The oceans alternately rise and fall in response to the pull of the moon. The stock market rises and falls in response to the pull of economic cycles and interest rate fluctuations.

Finally, there is the water's edge, where surfers wait for a wave and onlookers watch in awe from the shoreline. Traders, like surfers, ride the undulations of a stock's price in search of a profit. Then there is the shore where onlookers, with their money "safely" tucked away in banks and coffee cans, wonder what might have been if they only had the courage to step into the water. Not everyone can surf the waves, sail the currents, and fish the tides, but the ocean and the stock market offer anyone with the courage and willingness a game to play.

Why You, Why Now?

If you are a typical retiree, you have survived the past sixty years ignoring the stock market, or letting someone else manage your money in it for you. Why should you change now? What's in it for you? To answer those questions, let's look at Table IV.

Ignoring inflation and taxes, Table IV represents your investment choices. You must choose one of them. To do nothing is choice A. Keeping your money in the bank is choice B. Investing it in a balanced portfolio of bonds, stocks, money markets, and treasuries is choice C. Or, you can look to the gurus who tout their targeted mutual funds, money management skills and "in-the-know" newsletters. They might

TABLE IV
Value of Various $5,000 Investments after Five Years

Original Amount	(A) 0%	(B) 3%	(C) 10%	(D) 20%	(E) 100%
$5,000	$5,000	$5,796	$8,052	$12,441	$160,000
Nest Egg	Coffee Can	Bank	Mutual Fund	Gurus	Ten-Bagger

get you to a 20 percent annual return, choice D. It's clear any of those last three choices (B, C, or D) will yield greater returns than choice A. By maintaining a death grip on your meager nest egg, you could lose as much as $7,441 compared to choice D.

The market is a risky place, you say, and you are right, in the short term. In the past 100 years, the market has experienced approximately sixteen major declines, with the average downturn being about 30 percent. The average time of recovery is between twelve and twenty-four months.[2] Based on that statistic, the stock market will experience a downturn every six years. This is why the experts proclaim that over a ten-year period, the stock market has never failed to return a profit. It is a statistic conveniently spanning the six-year projection above.

Table IV represented a five-year investment period without a downturn. What happens if you invest your money and then a downturn hits? This is the very situation retirees fear. What happens to your money under those conditions? This scenario is presented in Table V. The invested amount is still $5,000, and the time horizon is still five years, but now it includes a 30 percent downturn lasting twelve months with an additional twelve months to recover.

The first column in Table V identifies the year in which the downturn occurs. Thus, for Downturn Year #1, the investment in column C would decline 30 percent in the first of the five years. It would

TABLE V
Value of Various $5,000 Investments after Five Years
Includes a Twelve-Month Downturn and a Twelve-Month Recovery

Downturn Year	(A) 0%	(B) 3%	(C) 10%	(D) 20%	(E) 100%
1	$5,000	$5,796	$6,655	$8,640	$160,000
2	$5,000	$5,796	$6,655	$8640	$160,000
3	$5,000	$5,796	$6,655	$8,640	$160,000
4	$5,000	$5,796	$6,655	$8,640	$160,000
5	$5,000	$5,796	$5,124	$7,258	$160,000
	Coffee Can	Bank	Mutual Fund	Gurus	Ten-Bagger

recover to its original value ($5,000) by the end of year two. For the next three years, it would grow at 10 percent per year. Note in all your stock investments the result is the same, whether the downturn occurs in year 1, 2, 3, or 4. As long as the timeframe includes a recovery, the stock returns are higher than either choice A or B. The return of Column C falls below the return on a bank investment only when the downturn occurs in year 5. In that case, there is no time for recovery. In Table V, neither the coffee can option (column A) nor the bank option (column B) is affected by a downturn. Even though interest rates may fluctuate in a downturn, the bank option (column B) is assumed to be unaffected by a downturn.

Table V illustrates that the key to stock market success is to invest funds that will not be needed in the next 3–5 years. In the stock market, time is the antidote for risk.

A New Perspective

Up to this point, I have not mentioned column E in Table IV or V. As an investor in your sixties, seventies, and eighties, you really don't have the time to sit and watch your money grow at 3 percent or even 10 percent per year.[3] I know when I think about my meager 401(k) and compare it to my projected expenses over the next ten or twenty years, a small gray cloud begins to form over my head. One catastrophe, one unexpected mistake, or one medical emergency will leave me broke and dependent on Social Security. A minimum-wage job will not protect me from that fate, but column E will.

Peter Lynch, the investment guru who successfully managed Fidelity's Magellan Fund, had a term for stocks that increase in price tenfold. He called them ten-baggers.[4] In a market of 9,000 stocks, there are hundreds of ten-baggers in play every year. I say in play because ten-baggers don't happen overnight; they usually take about three years to develop. This means ten-baggers usually double in price in each of those three years. The Hansen Beverage Company depicted in Figure 1 is an example of a ten-bagger.

Yet, not all doubles are ten-baggers: Some double and then decline; others run out of steam when they triple or quadruple; and some go beyond ten to increase twentyfold and even fiftyfold. As a retiree, you want to find these stocks, and you only need to find five of them over a five-year period to achieve the results depicted in column E. It is a lofty goal, but it is not an impossible goal. It is also not an exact goal. It would be nice to convert $5,000 into $160,000 in five years, but would you be disappointed if it took six, seven, or ten years? I doubt it! Nor would you be disappointed if, at the end of five years, you only had $25,000, $50,000, or $100,000. By aiming high, even our misses can be big winners.

What You Have Learned

There you have it—the playing field, the players, and the nature of the game. It is a scary game, but as an accomplished adult, you have all the skills necessary to win. You have experience, maturity, and common sense. There is absolutely no reason you shouldn't be in this game save one: fear. It is time to defeat the fear standing between you and financial success. This book provides the knowledge and understanding needed to confront your fears. Hopefully, it will also give you the confidence and courage to reach for financial independence.

- Money can only be spent, hoarded, or invested.
- When you save, you are investing.
- When you hire bankers, brokers, or experts to invest your money, you pay a high price, significantly reducing your returns.
- The stock market is made up of four national exchanges and many regional exchanges. The major exchanges are the New York (NYSE), the American (AMEX), the NASDAQ, and the Over-the-Counter (OTC).
- There are 9,000–10,000 companies listed on the various exchanges. They are only a small fraction of the number of businesses in the country.
- The listed companies are divided into eleven sectors, and those sectors are further divided into industries. There are more than 100 different industries represented.
- There is no such thing as "the market." The market consists of individuals and institutions buying individual stocks.

- The stock market is not a traditional auction. When it comes to small-volume players, buyers and sellers do not set the price, the market managers do.
- The difference between the bid and ask price is the spread.
- The spread accrues to the market manager. It is one way he earns his money.
- The market manager must buy stocks when there are no other buyers, and she must sell stocks when there are no other sellers.
- The most important advantage small investors have in the stock market is liquidity—the ability to buy and sell stocks quickly.
- Time is an antidote for risk. You should only invest money you will not need for the next 3–5 years.
- There are opportunities in the stock market to amass large sums of money with a very small initial investment.
- By developing your ability to spot cause-and-effect relationships, you can profitably predict stock price movements.

CHAPTER 3
It's Not as Risky as You Think

The biggest obstacle between most retirees and the stock market is fear. The biggest cause of fear is risk. Retirees are afraid of the market because it is a risky place. What is risk? How do we measure it? How do we overcome it? Why should you even want to overcome it? Let's answer the last question first.

For Every Risk—A Reward

We want to overcome our fear of risk because we need the rewards. Table IV compared several different investment options. Each one had a risk and a reward associated with it. For instance, the coffee can offered the least risk, but no rewards. The bank account offered the low risk of insured returns, but those rewards barely covered the cost of inflation. The indexed mutual fund offered a much higher reward, but also carried the added risk of uninsured returns. Finally, investments made on the advice of gurus promised an even higher return, but studies show almost 70 percent of these managed funds fail to beat the average returns of an indexed fund. Thus, as we move from column A to column D in Table IV, the perceived risk of failure increases, but the rewards also increase. This is why we take the risk—to get the rewards.

Risk is always there. We can reduce it, control it, or ignore it, but we cannot eliminate it. The very process of living is a risk, and since investing is part of life, it carries the inherent risk of human activity. Remember our supposedly risk-free use of money—hoarding. Is it really risk free? What happens if someone breaks into your house and steals your coffee can? It can happen; it is a risk. Even in the most protected neighborhoods, the risk of burglary, while low, is still present. Our job as business professionals, which is what you are about to become, is to achieve what is achievable and not waste time on what is not achievable. Since it is not possible to eliminate risk, our objective is to simply manage or control it.

Systemic Risk

The experts have identified two kinds of risk in the stock market: systemic and nonsystemic. Systemic risk is also volatility, and it is measured using the beta index.[1] Beta is a comparison between the change in price of an individual stock and the change in value of the Standard & Poor 500 (SP500).

If you are familiar with statistics, you will recognize this view of stock market risk as an adaptation of the normal curve. The SP500 can be viewed as the mean or central point of a normal distribution. When an individual stock parallels the movement of that mean, it is assigned a beta of 1.00. A stock deviating from that parallel track is assigned a beta based on the degree of the deviation. For instance, if the SP500 moves 10 percent, a beta 2 stock will move 20 percent, while a beta 0.5 would move only 5 percent. Also, a negative beta stock would move in the opposite direction of the SP500. When the SP500 increased, the negative beta stock would decrease in price. Thus, beta could be loosely equated to standard deviation, or more precisely, the tendency of an individual stock to deviate from the SP500.

When a normal curve is constructed in statistics, it is based on a single measurement (a metric), and that metric is assumed to come from a single homogeneous population of sources. For instance, if you measure the height of a population of Japanese men, you will be able to construct a normal distribution from those measurements. If you measure another population of men noted for their extreme height, you'll get a very different set of measurements. The distribution of those measurements will still be normal, but the calculated mean and standard deviations will be different from the Japanese population. Figure 2A presents the bell-shaped curves (normal curves) based on these two populations.

You can use the normal curves presented in Figure 2A to make some decisions. If you were to measure the height of man A, you could, without any other information, confidently proclaim him to

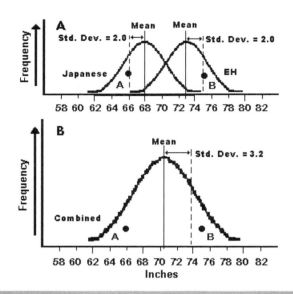

FIGURE 2: Normal Distributions (Curves). A normal curve is constructed by comparing a given attribute (the horizontal axis) to the frequency the attribute is observed in a population (vertical axis). When the population is normal, a bell-shaped curve is produced. One rule of the normal curve is 99.7 percent of all the population is within +/- 3 standard deviations. Thus, 99.7 percent of all Japanese men would be 62"–74". In A, person B is 75", which means you are 99.7 percent confident B is not a Japanese man. Combining the populations (curve B) reduces the confidence person B is not a Japanese man, since it is now within the combined curve.

be of Japanese descent because he falls outside the EH curve. Man B can just as confidently be identified as an EH, because he falls outside the Japanese curve. Making such predictions is one of the purposes of statistics and normal curves. As you will discover, another purpose is to help you understand and overcome your fear of the stock market, since statistics goes to the heart of your stock-buying decision.

However, look what happens when you combine the two populations into one group, Figure 2B. The calculated mean and standard deviation of the combined populations are totally different. Now, you have considerably less confidence in your ability to predict the origins of A and B based solely on their height measurement, since they both fall within the combined normal curve.

The stock market is like Figure 2B. With more than 9,000 stocks from 12 different sectors and 100 different industries, there is no homogeneity. When we combined just two groups of men, the predictive power of the statistic was diminished. If just two different men could diminish its value, imagine how useless beta must be, considering the number of different stocks there are in the stock market. Because of this complexity, beta has very little predictive power.[2]

Yet, to the short-term investor, volatility can be a significant risk factor. Over a long enough timeframe (10–20 years), the market averages a 10–12 percent return on investment.[3] Figure 3 graphically illustrates a hypothetical stock market with a linear growth of 10 percent and an average volatility of 15 percent, with a maximum volatility of 30 percent.[4] Using an average downturn and recovery timeline of twenty-four months, it is clear from Figure 3 the amount of time a stock investment is in the red (meaning you will lose money if you sell in that period) depends on when you enter the market. If you buy a stock just when its price turns down, you may have to wait as long

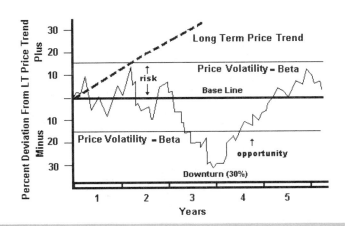

FIGURE 3: Impact of Long-Term Price Growth on Beta Risk. The horizontal solid line represents the price you paid for the stock. The upward sloping line represents the average price of the stock, increasing from your purchase point. The dashed lines represent the upper and lower normal deviation of the current price line around long-term average price. Note that at some point, in this example 3 years, even an abnormal decline in the current price will not penetrate the purchase price line.

as two years before you begin to make any money. However, buying at the low point gives your investment a boost.

In the long term, the fact that stock prices trend upward reduces the impact of beta risk. As Figure 3 illustrates, within two years, the upward trend of the price is greater than the average downward risk of the volatility (beta). Within three years, long-term price growth will even exceed the risk of a 30 percent downturn. In this example, if you can hold a stock for 2–3 years, beta risk is nonexistent, at least with respect to the purchased price of the stock. The real risk for investors, at least as it concerns beta, is you buy at the peak and then have to sell during a downturn. This is a timing decision as opposed to an investment decision; but regardless of when you buy, once you are invested in the market, you are only affected by beta if you have to sell. If you don't have to sell, what do you care if a stock is trading at $1 or $2 or $10 below its average price, if that average price is higher than what you paid for it? What you care about, or should care about, is that the company continues to perform at a level that supports the stock's long-term price rise.

Nonsystemic Risk

Nonsystemic risk is the risk unique to the company. It is caused by new products, management resignations, new competitors, government regulations, or labor difficulties. Anything uniquely affecting the company and impacting its stock price creates nonsystemic or investment risk. This is the risk investors must continually address.

When experts talk about diversifying to reduce risk, they are talking about investment risk. Diversification means buying a group of stocks rather than just one. The goal is to reduce the risk of owning just one stock, which could decline in price, taking your nest egg down with it. The logic of diversification is you cannot be so bad at picking stocks that in a group of thirty stocks you manage to pick thirty losers. Unfortunately, diversification is a misleading and somewhat unproductive antidote to risk.

Diversification is difficult for the small investor because the Capital-Asset Pricing Model[5] suggests in order to significantly reduce investment risk, a retiree would need to purchase twenty or more stocks. If you only have $1,000 or even $10,000 to invest, buying twenty different stocks is difficult. However, by pooling your money with other like-minded investors you can create a diversified fund of stocks benefiting all—a mutual fund. The major problem with diversification through mutual funds is it also reduces your investment returns—it is a ticket to mediocrity. If the risk of picking thirty losers is reduced by diversification, so is the chance of picking thirty winners.

General comparisons of mutual funds to the key market indexes such as the SP500 indicate less than 30 percent of mutual funds outperform these market indexes. While it's true twenty stocks are better than one if that one is going bankrupt, it is also true it is not better than one if that one is going to double, triple, or quadruple in price. Since risk is closely associated with rewards, a real reduction in risk is only accomplished if that reduction does not reduce the expected reward. Given that 70 percent of all mutual funds fail to outperform the SP500, the reward appears to be as reduced as the risk.

The experts are aware of this obvious fact. They have created targeted mutual funds designed to retain the reward while lowering the risk. These funds provide some risk protection compared to individual stocks within their focus. Yet, they allow the investor to reap many of the rewards associated with that sector. Having said that, we are still left with the 70 percent underperformance rate. There are things you can do to reduce risk without sacrificing returns; however, targeted mutual funds doesn't appear to be one of them.[6]

Let's summarize the expert's view. There are two kinds of risk surrounding the stock market—systemic and nonsystemic (investment). Beta compares the price sensitivity of an individual stock to the flow of funds into and out of the stock market. That flow causes stock prices to oscillate over a relatively short timeframe (days, weeks, or years). Investment risk is determined by the company underlying a particular stock. It reflects the good or bad performance of the company with respect to the economy and its competitors.

The experts' solution to beta or short-term risk is to ignore it and focus on the long-term market. As long as you avoid selling stock when it is at a low point, you can reduce beta risk. Experts would have you control investment risk through diversification. Unfortunately, diversification reduces the rewards as well as the risk. It is not a very productive strategy for a retiree with a very small nest egg.

Risk Is Personal

Both systemic and nonsystemic risk are inherent in the stock buying and selling game. There is one other kind of risk, which is personal. The experts address it simply: Don't bet what you can't afford to lose. As a retiree, you can't afford to lose anything, so the experts' definition of personal risk is useless. I don't know anyone who can afford to lose their investment, their nest egg, or their coffee-can stash.

To take this ridiculous concept of personal risk further, reference Table IV. Column E of Table IV was the result of investing $5,000 for five years in a series of ten-baggers (stocks that increase tenfold in value). Assume the initial investment of $5,000 was your risk tolerance. If that is all you are willing to lose, you can't achieve the results depicted in Column E. Column E is not the result of a single $5,000 investment; Column E is the result of a series of investments. In the first year, $5,000 is invested. That $5,000 grows to $10,000, then to $20,000, then $40,000 and finally, at the end of the fourth year, the investment account is worth $80,000. In order to achieve the $160,000 return, you would have to increase your risk tolerance from $5,000 to $80,000 within a four-year period. If you stayed with your original $5,000 by withdrawing the gains at the end of each year, the final total in Column E would only be $30,000.

Of course, the experts have a rebuttal. Their definition of risk tolerance holds because the only money at risk in Column E is the original $5,000. Only $5,000 is your money, the rest is gains, winnings, rewards, interest, paper profits, or as they like to say, "their money." You are no longer playing with your money; you are playing with "their money." I assure you, once your account grows to $10,000, $20,000, or more, it all becomes your money. If your risk tolerance is defined by what you are willing to lose, you will never be a big winner because no one is willing to lose $80,000, especially when they started with just $5,000. Success in the stock market is not based on knowing your risk tolerance; it is based on understanding the real risks and reducing them without also reducing the rewards.

The Real Risks of the Game

Now that we have gotten the experts out of the way, let's talk about real risk, and how you can reduce it without sacrificing the promised rewards. According to *Webster's Ninth New Collegiate Dictionary*, risk is the possibility of loss or injury. That definition is an excellent foundation on which to build our understanding of risk, and it points out two key aspects of it. The first is that risk is inherently negative. No one seeks out risk; we are all risk-averse. We must be induced to risk by some form of incentive, some sort of reward. Without an appropriate reward, no amount of risk, no matter how small, is acceptable.

That risk is only the possibility of a negative outcome is the second aspect of the definition. If it were a certainty—if I knew I was going to fail—I wouldn't do it. This possibility can be, through the magic of statistics, quantified as a probability. Thus, risk can be expressed in mathematical terms such as a percent or odds. For instance, when you flip a coin, you have a 1-in-2 chance it will come up heads. Thus, a flipped coin has a 50 percent chance of being heads or tails.

When the outcome calculated is bad, the probability determines the risk of the outcome happening. For instance, if we bet on tails, the risk a heads will appear is 50 percent. If the outcome is good, the calculated probability is the confidence level. In our example, the confidence level you will win the coin flip is also 50 percent. Risk and confidence are two sides of the same coin; combined, they will always equal 100 percent.

Let's look at another example. With a six-sided die, the probability of rolling a number 2 is 16.7 percent. Since the total of all the possible outcomes will always equal 100 percent, the risk number 2 will not appear is 83.3 percent. The probability you would win the bet is only 16.7 percent; that is your confidence level. It is considerably lower than the coin flip. Thus, the coin flip is less risky than the die roll.

No one seeks risk; they must be lured to it with some form of reward. The reward must be proportional to the risk. Returning to the examples above, if the coin flip were perfectly proportional, a $1 bet on a coin flip will pay $1. You risk $1 to win $1. Since the probability of success is 50 percent, that is a fair payout. However, that same level of payout would be unattractive if you were betting on the die roll. A $1 bet with a $1 payout and only a 16.7 percent confidence level would only give you one win in every six rolls. Since you must bet $1 a roll and you win only once in every six rolls, after six rolls you would be $4 poorer. Since the risk is determined by the possible outcomes, the payout must be raised to attract bettors to the game. What payout is needed? At a minimum, the die game should pay $5 for every $1 bet. This means you can expect to win once in every six rolls, with each win paying $5. This also means in the long run you win nothing and lose nothing—you break even. In a perfectly fair game, you will always eventually break even.

You will have noticed there is a difference between the risk of a bet and the risk of the game if you are at all mathematically inclined. Probability dictates the risk of a coin flip is 50 percent and the risk of a die roll is 83.3 percent. When you place a bet on a coin or a die, you have a 50 percent or 83.3 percent risk of losing the bet, respectively. However, you have no risk you will lose the game if the rewards are proportional and you play long enough. What is long enough? Hard to say, since very few games are perfectly random, but the minimum length of time required to avoid loss is two bets for the coin and six for the die.

Since the stock market is essentially a game, we'll compare our newfound understanding of risk to the advice of the stock market's experts. They recommend diversification and know your risk tolerance. Let's explore diversification first.

Reducing Risk in the Stock Market

Using diversification, we'll reduce the risk of losing the die roll by betting two numbers instead of one. In effect, we'll create a sort of die-roll mutual fund. Your risk will decrease from 83.3 percent to 66.7 percent, because there are now only four possible losing numbers. If you win, your pay out is still just $5, but you had to bet two numbers and $2 to get it. In six rolls of the die, you will win twice. Each of those wins will payout $5, plus you retain half your initial bet. At the end of six rolls, you will have bet $12 ($2 per bet) and you will have won $12 ($6 per win)—breakeven. In the long run, the outcome is the same. You can extend the risk reduction all the way to a six-number bet where you are 100 percent confident you will win. In that case, you bet $6 and win $6—breakeven. Diversification lowered the risk of the bet, but the risk of the game was not changed.

The reason you failed to improve your outcome is, in reducing your risk you also reduced your reward. In the two-bet solution, when you won, you only won $2.50 per $1. You reduced your reward in proportion to your risk, which gained you nothing. This is exactly what happens when you diversify a stock portfolio. The risk is reduced in proportion to the reward, which means in the long term, you gain nothing. Or, more accurately, diversification will not improve your winnings beyond the game average. In the case of the die roll, that was breakeven.

Now, let's look at risk tolerance. If your risk tolerance is less than $1—say a dime or even a penny—how does that affect the outcome of the bet or the game? It doesn't require much to confirm what you intuitively know—it changes neither. If you bet a penny, the risk of losing does not change. The size of the bet has no impact on the probability of the outcome. The same is true with respect to the risk of the game. In the long run, whether you bet $1, a penny, or $100, you will break even as long as the reward is proportionate—a penny bet, five pennies won. Risk tolerance, as defined by the experts, has nothing to do with the risk of a coin flip, a die roll, or a stock purchase.

How to Win the Game

Clearly games are won. How? There are two ways. The first is blind luck. The second is reasoned luck. Blind luck is self-explanatory. Reasoned luck means you reduce risk (or alternately increase your confidence) without proportionately reducing your reward. Applying reasoned luck requires knowledge, understanding, patience, and diligence. Figure 4 illustrates an example of reasoned luck using a perfectly random die roll.

If you roll a perfectly random die six times, the ideal result will be as depicted in Figure 4A. This is a frequency diagram because it measures the frequency of varying outcomes of a measured process. In this case, the process is die rolling, and the varying outcomes are the numbers 1–6. In six rolls of the die, the expected result, based on the calculated probability of outcomes, is each number will appear one time.[7] If the die is rolled more times, the basic balance of outcomes is not changed. The long-term result (120 rolls) is a reflection of the short-term result (6 rolls), and is illustrated in Figure 4B.

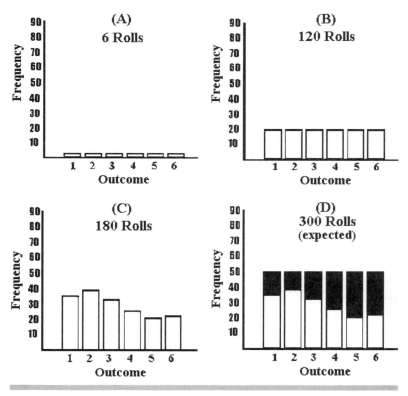

FIGURE 4: Reasoned Luck and the Outcome of a Die Roll. A set of histograms depicting the possible outcomes of a series of die rolls. Like a normal curve, a histogram compares a given outcome to its observed or expected frequency. If the die is fair (not biased), the resulting histogram will not be bell-shaped. It will be box-shaped, like histogram B, with each outcome equally likely.

Blind Luck = Success

However, while Figures 4A and 4B reflect the perfect outcomes, the flow of results does not always exactly match the probability. Abnormal outcomes can develop, like the one depicted in Figure 4C. If you were a player betting the number 2 while that abnormality developed, you would be a winner. How much? You would double your money. Why? Because in sixty rolls the number 2 appeared twenty times, decreasing the risk from 83.3 percent to 66.7 percent. The risk of failure was lowered and the reward of success remained the same, since each bet still paid $5; exactly what we said we wanted to do—lower risk without lowering the reward.

Figure 4C is an example of blind luck. The person betting was unaware the anomaly was developing. She was betting under the old rules of $5 paid for every $1 bet. The pay out was based on the old risk of five losers for every winner, but the anomaly created a new reality of only two losers for every winner. She received a $5 payout in every three bets rather than a $5 payout in every six bets. The problem is she didn't know it was happening. She blindly bet. Call it luck. Call it timing. Either way, she's a winner.

Reasoned Luck = Success, Too!

Figure 4C presents an interesting opportunity. Statistics teach that in the long run, an abnormality cannot be sustained. Continued rolls of the die will ultimately create a distribution like Figure 4B. If you continue to roll the die, you could reasonably expect the next sixty rolls to move the distribution toward normal. Those next sixty rolls are the solid bars of Figure 4D. Now, if you were to bet the number 5, the chance 5 will appear, like the 2 in the previous sixty rolls, has doubled. Again, the payout is still $5, but the risk of failure is reduced. You have a reasonable expectation of winning. It will still require some luck, since there is no guarantee the outcomes will normalize in the next sixty rolls. It may take 70, 100, or 200 rolls to correct the anomaly, but it will correct, and the result is you will be a winner.

Reasoned luck is key to your success in the stock market. In order for you to spot the winning opportunity above, you had to have knowledge, understanding, diligence, and patience. You had to know the anomaly had developed. You had to understand enough probability and statistics to take advantage of that abnormality. You had to have the diligence to count the rolls, record the outcomes, and construct the frequency chart. Finally, you had to have the patience to wait for the opportunity to develop. In a fair game, breakeven is the norm. If you want winning to be your norm, you must wait for the odds to change in your favor.

How Decisions Affect Risk

When you make a decision, you risk making the wrong decision. There are basically two types of wrong decisions. The first is to decide yes when the decision should have been no. This is a Type I error. The second is to decide no when the decision should have been yes. This is a Type II error.

Referring back to Table IV, it is clear that, over a five-year period, deciding not to invest in the stock market is a Type II error, but pointing that out after the fact does not necessarily tell you how to make better (error-free) decisions in the future. For instance, if you bet on the number 2 in our dice game, are you a winner or a loser? Regardless of the outcome of the bet, you don't know. You may lose the bet, but if you continue to play you may win the next bet. Even if you lose the next bet, the third bet might deliver the $5 payout. What you do know is, if you play long enough, you will break even. The decisions you make define your risk, not the bet or the game.

Figure 5 depicts a series of die rolls. On the first roll of the die, you either win $5 or you lose $1. If you decide to stop after your first roll, there is an 83.3 percent risk you will be a loser, but only if you decide to be a loser. You can decide to continue the game. The most likely outcome of that decision is you will eventually break even. In fact, as Figure 5 indicates, 95 percent of the time you will either break even or win a little or lose a little. When you decide to stop betting determines the likely outcome. It's not dependent on the game; it's dependent on your decision.

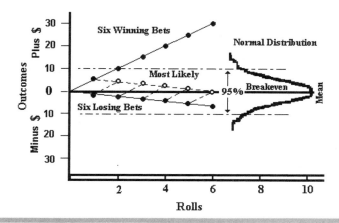

FIGURE 5: Decisional Risk. The graph compares the monetary reward of a fair die roll to a normal curve. The top line denotes the value of six wins in six rolls. The lower line denotes the value of six losses in six rolls. The center line with the hollow circles denotes the most likely outcomes, which is some combination of wins and losses. A normal curve representing all the possibilities is presented. Note the winning line quickly extends beyond the normal curve, while the losing line remains within the curve. The most likely outcome approaches the mean, which is breakeven. Thus, the only way to win the game is to quit while you are ahead. The more you play, the more likely you are to break even—neither win nor lose.

Confidence and Decisions

Decisional risk brings us back to the concept of confidence level. What confidence level do you require to make a decision? This is your real risk tolerance. In the medical field, the decision to introduce a new drug often exceeds a 99.999 percent confidence level. In other words, they must be confident there is only a 1-in-100,000 chance they would make a Type I error and introduce a drug that fails to cure or has debilitating side effects. In many other scientific endeavors, a decision will be made at the 95 percent confidence level. In business, the confidence level most often cited is 85 percent. It has been reported a good business manager is actually correct only about 70 percent of the time, which, by extension, places his confidence level at 70 percent. While the risks inherent in the game are fixed, you control your personal risk tolerance by choosing your own confidence level.

An Example

Let's place three different gamblers at our die roll. The first arrives with a very high risk tolerance; her confidence requirement is less than 10 percent. The minimum confidence level required to bet on a blind-luck roll of a die is 16.7 percent. For our first player, it is more than enough. Our second player requires more confidence before making his bet—say 25 percent. To meet his level of confidence, he watches, waits, and calculates. When he detects an anomaly like the one in Figure 4C that raises the confidence level of a bet decision from 16.7 to 33.3, he makes his bet. The third gambler demands even money or a 50 percent confidence level. The third player recognizes the anomaly, but the confidence level does not rise to her threshold; she refuses to bet. She will require a bigger anomaly with a larger confidence level, or she will require something else. Note the players did not make their decision based on the amount of money they could afford to lose. Nor did they make the decision based on their ability to reduce risk by spreading their bets (diversification). They made their decision based on their understanding of the inherent risks of the game, its opportunities, and their required confidence level.

Yet, there was one player that refused to play. The risk of the game exceeded her confidence level. To play this game, she needs something more, something that will move her to act.

Pay Me More, or Charge Me Less

Up until this point, we have focused on the risk inherent in the game (or process or stock market) and the confidence level required by the players before they will choose to play. By comparing the risk inherent in the game and your required confidence level for action, you can decide to make the bet. What happens when the game is so inherently risky and your confidence requirement is so high the two never meet? That was the case with our third player, and is probably the case with many retirees. There is no rational reason for them to be in the game, yet some are there. This can only mean there is an irrational reason.

How does the stock market entice the risk-averse player to the game? It uses an enticement inducing him to ignore his confidence level. It is the reverse of diversification; it is concentration, or more appropriately, the lottery strategy.

In the lottery strategy, you increase the rewards a million-fold, which increases the risk a million-fold. Now the risk of failure is astronomical, and the confidence level of the bet is infinitesimal. This allows you to lower the cost of the bet. Now, a $1 bet will get you $1 million. The reward is so great it induces a player to abandon all rationality—he joins the game. It is totally irrational, but as millions of lottery players will attest, it is an irrationality they can bet on as long as the bet is only $1 and the reward is $1 million. This is the attraction of penny stocks.

The lottery strategy illustrates an important aspect of blind luck—timing. In a losing or breakeven game, to be a winner you must decide to quit while you are ahead. In the die roll, that is difficult to do because rewards are so low. With the lottery, one win is a life-changing experience. There is no need to play again, and even if you did, you would not break even in your lifetime. Even with timing, it is the decision, not the game, that made you a winner.

In the stock market, the lottery strategy is found among the penny stocks, the backbone of the Over-The-Counter market. Ten dollars can buy a thousand of them, and if they simply increase in price to the market average,[8] your $10 will become $34,686. Like the lottery strategy, this low buy-in brings with it very high risks. This can induce investors to suspend rational analysis and simply buy cheap stocks, but it doesn't have to be as irrational as the lottery. With stocks, you can exercise knowledge, understanding, patience, and diligence to reduce the risk—somewhat.

Dramatically increasing rewards or lowering costs are not designed to reduce risk; they are designed to get you to ignore it. In many cases, they actually increase risk. However, the increased rewards or low cost can induce a player to abandon all reason and ignore his confidence level requirements. Don't let the lure of big payouts or cheap entry fees entice you to the game. Always remember to play the game you can win.

An Insurance Policy

There is another way to lure our recalcitrant third player to the game. However, in order to properly describe it, we will abandon the die roll and lottery examples and take a trip to the racetrack. In this case, a horse race is a much closer analogy to the stock market than either a die roll or a lottery ticket.

If a six-horse race were like a die roll, its outcome would be predicted by a simple application of probabilities. Horses are not sides of a die; they are affected by such variables as track condition and jockey competence; the horse's health, age, and stamina; and myriad other criteria. Unlike the fair die, these variables create a predictable bias in the outcome. One horse will be favored to win, while others are deemed less likely victors. The chance each of the six horses might win is reflected in their odds. (The same is true in the stock market—the odds of an individual company being a winning investment are reflected in their valuations.)

Our race will have six possible outcomes, with odds ranging from even for heavily favored horses, to 100-to-1 for the most unlikely winner. This provides a range of confidence levels ranging from just under 50 percent to 1 percent. These are still below our third player's 50 percent threshold. To get her in the game, she needs more.

A one-mile horse race is run in segments. It begins at the starting gate, progresses along the backstretch, through the turn, down the homestretch, and to the finish. The horses surge and fade as the race progresses. Then, in the final hundred yards, they battle for the lead in an exciting finish, bringing the crowd to its feet. Like the stock market, horseracing isn't just a gamble; it's also entertainment.

While the entertainment is a good enticement for our third player, it is not the offer. The offer is a chance to opt out of the bet as the race progresses. Let's say she bets $100 on a horse with 100-to-1 odds. At the start of the race, her horse takes the lead—a very good start. Her bet is looking very promising. Along the backstretch, her horse begins to falter and drops back to second place. Our player didn't expect this, so she reduces her bet by $50. Going into the turn, her horse revives and retakes the lead. Our player, with renewed confidence, increases her bet by $25. In the homestretch, the horse demonstrates why it was a 100 to 1 shot. It falls back to second, then third, then out of the money. Our player quickly reduces her bet to $25, cutting his losses.

The racetrack scenario just described is a fantasy. At the racetrack, you can only bet on a horse before the start of the race. You can't change your mind or your bet mid-race, but what is fantasy at the racetrack is reality in the stock market. There you can make your bet, increase your bet, decrease your bet, or cancel your bet, and you can do it mid-race. It is liquidity, and it is a wonderful bonus and an excellent incentive.

Liquidity is your biggest risk reducer and confidence builder next to knowledge, understanding, patience, and diligence. It allows you to buy and sell stocks quickly, which in turn allows you to correct mistakes and leverage successes. Thus, you can take profits on the upswing or preserve your original investment on the downturn. It's like having the ability to move your bet from horse to horse as the race is being run. It is a tremendous advantage only offered in the stock market.

Bias and Other Manipulations

Right now, there are mathematicians pulling their hair out. What has caused their dismay? In Figure 4C, an abnormal pattern was observed. This led us to conclude there was an opportunity created by the upcoming correction of that abnormality. To that conclusion, the mathematicians will say hogwash. The die doesn't know where it has been or where it is going. Each roll is its own universe and is unaffected by the previous rolls. Thus, the odds of a 5 appearing is exactly the same on the first roll as it is on the next sixty rolls of Figure 4D.

The only problem with our analysis is that, for the purpose of illustration, we assumed the abnormality of Figure 4C would correct in the next sixty rolls. In reality, it may take 100 rolls or 600 rolls, but in the end, it must correct, otherwise the die would not be fair and the outcomes would not be statistically normal, which is what *fair* means. It is not a question of if; it is a question of when. Thus, the mathematicians are in a box. If they argue against our example, they are arguing the bet is normal but the game isn't. However, if the bet is normal the game must also be normal; otherwise it turns the math on its head.

The real issue poised by Figure 4C is, in the example, we declared that the die is fair, but there is no guarantee the die is fair. Therefore, we must decide what Figure 4C is defining. Is it defining a bias or an abnormality? If the die is biased and the game is rigged, then our strategy is not to bet the number 5, but to bet the number 2 because Figure

4C becomes the expected distribution for the biased die. It is expected because the die is biased toward the number 2. In essence, the game is rigged or, at least, not normal, which defines entirely different risk factors for the possible outcomes.

Unfortunately, the stock market is filled with these rigged games. Some are legal, such as a company introducing a new product. Some are illegal, such as the pump-and-dump schemes that change the price of a stock independent of the company's performance. Whatever the reason, more often than not, we have no way of knowing whether the game is biased. However, there are precautions we can take. The same techniques used to reduce risk also apply to uncovering bias, which itself is a big risk.

Look at Figure 5 again. In a normal, fair die roll, the outcome of a series of bets would normally be between +$10 and -$10. That is a two standard deviation spread and encompasses 95 percent of the expected outcomes.[9] If you were to play the game and win two bets in a row, before making the third bet, you should ask yourself this fundamental question: Is the game fair or biased? If you believe it is fair, you would stop betting because to continue to bet would ultimately place you on the most likely track and lower your rewards. If you assume the game is biased, you will continue to bet in the hopes of continuing your run of winning bets. All bets depend on how you answer the question of fairness and normality.

In the stock market, the question is posed in different terms. You must decide if a price movement is a normal fluctuation responding to the ebb and flow of the market or a price trend responding to the success or failure of the company. It is a fifty-fifty proposition, unless you take the time and make the effort to change the odds. If, by answering the fundamental question, you can increase your confidence, you can beat the market. The answer, as before, is found in your decision-making skills.

What You Have Learned

Up to this point, we have defined *risk* in terms of some very simple games. Through simplicity, we have demonstrated that much of the conventional wisdom surrounding the stock market is wrong. Your real risk is personal and decisional. You cannot influence the game; you can only control your decision-making process. Thus, success in the stock market is mostly about you—your personality and your decision-making skills.

- *Risk* is defined as the probability a negative outcome will result from a decision. Risk is measured as a percent. A 0 percent risk means no negative result will occur. A 100 percent risk indicates the negative result is a certainty.
- The opposite of risk is confidence. Confidence is the probability a positive outcome will result from a decision. Confidence is also measured as a percent. A 0 percent confidence level means no positive result will occur. A 100 percent confidence level indicates the positive result is a certainty.
- There are three kinds of risk: systemic, nonsystemic, and personal.
- Systemic risk, or volatility, is the risk the price of your stock will follow the ups and downs of the market, and is measured by beta. Beta compares the volatility of an individual stock to a defined group of stocks such as the SP500. It can also be viewed as short-term risk.
- Nonsystemic risk is the risk the price of your stock will act independently of the market because of some factor unique to the company it represents, such as a strike, a government assault, a natural disaster, a faulty product, or any other negative impact. It is also called investment or long-term risk.
- Personal risk is the risk you will make a Type I or Type II error. It is decisional. It is controlled by your skills as an investor, trader, or speculator. It is not dependent on the amount of money you are willing to lose.
- Unless the retiree is seeking to trade stocks, systemic risk will have little long-term effect on his investments. However, a buy-and-hold investor must be aware of the downside potential of the nonsystemic risks. He must watch over the companies he has invested in to spot any threats that might depress the stock's price or dividend.

■ Diversification will not eliminate systemic risk, and to the extent it reduces nonsystemic risk, it does so at a very high cost, especially for the retired investor who does not have the time to compound the mediocre average returns it portends.

■ Your risk tolerance is not measured by the amount you are willing to lose. Risk tolerance is the confidence level you require before taking action.

■ Liquidity is the ability to buy and sell stocks quickly, and it is an important tool for reducing risk.

■ Stock buyers must be wary of stock manipulations that can give false signals an opportunity is in the making. They must decide whether a stock is acting normally or abnormally—in essence, is it fair or biased, fluctuating or trending?

■ The key to reducing stock market risk is making well-reasoned, well-researched, high-confidence-level decisions without proportionately reducing the rewards of those decisions.

CHAPTER 4
The Rewards of the Game

In the previous chapter, we defined *risk* as the probability a negative outcome will occur when we make a decision. We also distinguished between two kinds of risk: the risk of the bet and the risk of the game. The risk of the bet is determined by the probability of the outcomes, but the risk of the game is dependent on both the probability of the outcomes and the rewards associated with those outcomes. To determine the risk of the stock market game, we must add reward to the equation.

In a fair game, risk equals reward. This means that, like a coin flip or a die roll, the long-range outcome is breakeven. To win a fair game, you'll need a little luck and a willingness to quit when you are ahead. Or, as we discovered in Figure 4, you need to see the game's abnormalities and the opportunities they portend. The stock market presents similar abnormalities and opportunities.

Insight is an important weapon in the investor's arsenal. You need to understand why a stock's price changes. Price movements in the stock market depend on three elements: reason, recognition, and reaction.

1. A price movement must have a reason. It must be caused by something like growing profits, excessive cash, new management, new products, a looming bankruptcy, the madness of the crowd, etc.
2. The reason must also be recognized. If it is hidden from other investors, there will be no mass movement toward or away from the stock.
3. Finally, investors must react. Simply recognizing is not enough; investors must take action if the price of a stock is going to move.

A failure in any of these three Rs dooms the opportunity. James K. Glassman and Kevin A. Hassett proposed the stock market is, "In the long term, . . . no more risky than the market for Treasury Bonds."[1] (Treasury Bonds are often touted as one of the safest investments.) If that were the case, the Dow should be trading at 36,000. Yet, as of this writing, the Dow is at 12,000. Is this a real opportunity? Glassman and Hassett have presented a good reason, but investors either don't recognize it or they refuse to act on it. Thus, the opportunity is unrealized, at least for now. As we assess opportunities in the stock market, we shall be keenly aware of the three Rs.

Fear has caused most retirees to avoid the stock market. This has been a very costly Type II error (saying no when you should say yes), but errors are a matter of perspective. Many retirees would argue they didn't err at all, since their goal was not to maximize earnings but to preserve principal; they committed no error if their principal is intact. However, if Glassman and Hassett are correct, there is no reason retirees can't both protect principal and earn above-average returns. If the stock market is as safe as a Treasury Bond, retirees can ignore the risks of the market and focus on the rewards.

Rewards of a Stock Market Bet

When you buy a stock, you are buying a share of the company. You are an owner. As an owner, the profits the company earns belong to you. The owner's share of those profits is determined by dividing the total after-tax profits of the company by the number of shares the company has outstanding. This is the earnings per share (EPS). As an individual owner, your share of those earnings is the EPS multiplied by the number of shares you own.

Of course, you don't always get those earnings. The amount you get depends on what the management and the board of directors decides to do with the profits. They have three choices.

1. They can give it to the owners of the company (including you).
2. They can reinvest in the company by buying new equipment or inventories or increasing their marketing budget.
3. They can keep it for themselves in the form of pay and benefits.

In short, they can hoard it, invest it, or spend it.

Dividends

When they give it to the owners, it is dividends. These are usually paid in quarterly or annual payments, but they can be paid in any interval from monthly to never. When a dividend is paid, it is described in terms of its yield and payout. The yield is simply the value of the annual dividend divided by the current price of the stock, expressed as a percent. Since yield is based on the current price, there are actually two yields, because there are two prices involved: the current price and the price the shareholder paid for the stock. The current yield is the current annual dividend divided by the current price. Your personal yield is that dividend divided by the price you paid for the stock. These two yields will always be equal at the exact moment you buy a stock.

Over time, a difference will develop between the current yield and your personal yield. The difference between these two yields illustrates an important aspect of stock investing—growth. If you purchased a stock forty years ago with a 2 percent current/personal yield, which was less than most bank rates on savings accounts, you would appear to have made a poor investment. However, if the growth rate of the company and its dividend were just 5 percent per year, today your personal yield from the current dividend would be approximately 14.1 percent. This is because the price you paid for the stock is constant, but the dividend paid by the company has been growing. Yet, the average savings account is still paying 3 percent, less than a fourth of your personal yield for the stock. That is the power of growth. You will see how important that is in later chapters.

Maintaining a long-term investment perspective requires you to be aware of the other important measure of dividends—payout. Payout refers to the amount of the earnings actually paid to the shareholders. Remember, not all earnings are paid to the shareholders; the company keeps some back. Payout defines how much of the profit is paid to the stockholder. Most companies tend to pay out 0–80 percent of their profits.

In Chapter 9, we will explore the subtleties of dividend yields and payouts. For now, it is sufficient to say dividends are one way companies reward you when you invest in the stock market. The other way you're rewarded is when your stock increases in price. When experts proclaim the long-term annual return of the stock market is 10–12 percent, they're talking about this combination of rewards. Of that percentage, about 40 percent comes from dividends and 60 percent comes from price increases.[2]

Increased Stock Price

While increased stock price is the largest source of stock returns, it is also the most controversial. What makes it so controversial? As you will discover over the course of this book, stock prices are influenced by a variety of forces. Some of those forces are grounded in sound economic and business practices. Others are nefarious and dangerous to your financial health. At this point, we won't discuss all the reasons prices increase, but we will discuss one—the impact of company performance.

When a company reinvests part of its profits in new equipment and new products, it grows the sales and profits of the company. As the company grows, the value and price of its stock also grows. As a shareholder, you reap the rewards of price growth.

Let's assume you bought a stock five years ago for $3 a share. The company performed well, with earnings growth of 10 percent per year. If the valuation of those earnings remains the same, the price of the stock will also increase 10 percent per year. Today, it is worth $5 a share with a current yield of 2 percent. Assuming the dividend yield and payout has been steady over the past five years, your five-year return on this stock would be the increase in price and the total dividends paid. The breakdown would be $2 from price ($5 - $3) and $0.40 from dividends ($0.06 + $0.07 + $0.08 + $0.09 + $0.10). The total return would be $2.40, with approximately 83 percent coming from price increases and 17 percent from accumulated dividends. The total average annual return would be about 12 percent, which is an average market return. Notice your return is actually higher than the growth of the company (12 versus 10 percent). That is leverage, and I will discuss it in later chapters.

Note most of the return came from an increase in the average price of the stock. This increase is based on the performance of the company. Beyond the performance of the company is the performance of the stock market—systemic risk. Systemic risk (volatility) can either enhance the price or depress it. As I discuss performance-based stock price increases (or decreases), I will ignore the wiggles and waggles of the market; however, you should keep them in mind, because if you can, you will want to consider them when buying and selling stocks because they affect your rewards at the buy and sell points.

Rewards of the Stock Market Game

The stock market game is simply the sum of all the stocks you buy. Each stock purchase is a bet, and the sum of those bets defines the game—its risks and rewards. In our fair coin flip, the reward of a winning bet is $1, which is a 100 percent return on a $1 investment. However, that single bet does not define the game, because a single flip of the coin provides a distorted view. To really know the game, we must play it more than once. In the case of the coin, we must play it at least two times, because there are two outcomes—heads or tails.

The risk of a bet only depends on the probability of a negative outcome. In a coin flip, it was 50 percent. In the die roll, it was 83.3 percent. However, the risk of the game also depends on the rewards associated with those outcomes. Thus, on the coin flip, if the payout on the coin was 2 to 1—meaning you were paid $2 for every $1 bet—the risk of the bet would still be 50 percent, but the risk of the game would be zero. To see why, simply make two random bets. You lose the first, and you lose $1. You win the second, and you are paid $2. You started with $2 to make two bets, and now you have $3, your second bet, and your winnings. That is a 50 percent return on your investment. It is the long run and the risk plus the reward that defines the game.

Let's look at another example. Roulette offers a very high return per bet. If you win a bet at roulette, you'll reap a $35 payout for every $1 bet. This is a strong inducement to play. Yet, at the game level, it is lousy odds. Why? Because there are thirty-eight numbers on the game table. In the long run, you will always lose. A quick way to see this is to bet every number on the table. It will cost you $38, but at the end of the spin, you will only have $36—your $1 winning bet and the $35 payout—you lose $2. In the long run, roulette is a losing game.

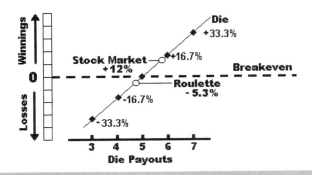

FIGURE 6: Long-Term Rates of Return for Various Games. Various games and their long-term monetary outcomes are presented. Note how the long-term outcome of the die roll changes as the payout is changed. At a $5 payout, the die roll is breakeven. Payouts less than $5 make it a losing game; payouts above $5 make it a winning game. The stock market, which has a long-term history of 12 percent annual growth, is a winning game.

Figure 6 compares the long-term returns of the games described above and the stock market. Included are various forms of the die roll to show the impact of various payouts on game risk. Games delivering returns above the breakeven line are essentially risk free. Play them long enough and you will win. Games falling below the breakeven line are losers. Play them long enough and you will lose. Figure 6 demonstrates that the stock market, over the long term, is, on average, a winning game—it is risk free.

There are some important caveats to that last sentence. First, what is described is the stock market as a whole as measured by the SP500. To guarantee no risk, you cannot bet just any diversified portfolio of stocks. You must bet the SP500 or a mutual fund mirroring that index. In essence, you are betting all the numbers on the roulette table. Second, you are dealing with the long term—five years and beyond. Finally, you are dealing with the average of many investments. Simply making one investment at one time brings short-term beta risk.

This brings us back to Table V, which looked at the returns of various investments. The only risk we had in the stock market was volatility risk—meaning there was a risk we would buy just before a downturn. Again, this is an issue of timing. You can reduce timing risk in three ways.

1. Don't make your investment before a downturn. If you have the patience to wait out the boom, you will be able to bet the bust and benefit from the recovery. You can offset beta risk by choosing when you buy a stock.
2. Invest only in low beta stocks. High beta stocks have high volatility. By choosing less-volatile stocks, you reduce the magnitude of the price swings. The risk of a downturn is still there, but the impact is less.
3. Ignore the risk. As Table V demonstrated, even with a short-term downturn, the stock market protects the investor's original bet as long as he stays in the game. Only if he sells too soon is he subject to market volatility. It is important you only bet with money you can leave in the game long enough to overcome market volatility. As Table V illustrated, the investor only requires a five-year commitment to successfully ignore beta risk.

Thus, we can amend the experts' view of risk tolerance. Risk tolerance isn't how much you can afford to lose; it's how long you can afford to set your money aside.

Given time and on average, the stock market represents the very thing we are looking for: greater rewards without increased risk. In fact, the stock market game, as presently played, is, in the long run, essentially risk free. There is an extremely high confidence level you will earn a 10–12 percent annual return. The only thing you are not confident of is that the return will be linear. Returns in the stock market tend to be sporadic. The thirty-five-year history of the SP500 presented in Figure 7 illustrates the point. The 9 percent linear growth line fits the actual yearly price data,[3] but it does not fit it exactly. There are some significant dips and recoveries in those prices.

Also, note the relative low growth rate of stock prices during the 1970s. In this period of stagnation, the 9 percent growth line pulled away from the actual prices. However, this lack of fit during the 1970s paved the way for the opportunities of the 1980s and 1990s. It is analogous to the abnormality described in Figure 4. It would have been a signal it was time to make a bet.

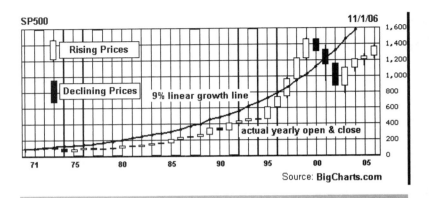

FIGURE 7: 35-Year Price History for the SP500. Price history of the SP500 from 1970 to 2006.

Going Beyond Average

If you invest early and diversify along the lines of the SP500, you can expect average returns of 10–12 percent compounded annually. According to Glassman and Hassett, and our own analysis, you can reap those rewards with very little risk. However, if you are sixty-two with a $25,000 nest egg, you can't afford to deal in averages. Twelve percent of $25,000 is just $3,000 a year, and to get that you have to bet all your money on the game. In the short term, as depicted in Table V, there is beta risk. What you need is a strategy that makes sense for your situation. In Chapter 12, we will look at that strategy.

Of course, this doesn't apply to every retiree. If you have a nest egg of $300,000 or more, a risk-free return of 12 percent is more than enough to supplement your Social Security and pension payments. Why play any other game when you can create an above-average income with an average return $36,000 + $9,624 (Average Returns + Social Security) = $45,624? It's essentially risk-free and work-free. If you don't have $300,000, you have to go beyond average; you have to make individual bets. You have to buy individual stocks. Not only do you have to buy individual stocks, you have to buy them in such a way they do not create a diversified portfolio—to do that would simply bring you back to average. Your buys must be made with an eye toward substantially increasing the rewards without increasing risk.

Remember how you controlled risk in your die game: You observed, analyzed, and picked your opportunities. By understanding the probabilities of success and the current patterns of the game, you selectively made your bets when the risk of failure was diminished and the confidence of success was increased. You will do the same in the stock market. Before you deviate from the average, you will search for opportunities that have historically outperformed the average. This historical pattern of success will give you the confidence to make your bets.

Not only will you seek lower risk and higher confidence, you will seek greater rewards. There is no sense in stepping off the low-risk path of average to buy stock in an average company. Individual bets are inherently riskier than the game. In order to make them, their payouts must provide adequate compensation. In fact, you want more than just adequate compensation; you want extraordinary returns. You want stocks with the potential to be ten-baggers.

Rewards of a Ten-Bagger Strategy

The impact of such a ten-bag strategy is profound. Table V, Column E, illustrated the potential results of a successful ten-bag strategy.

Ten-baggers are not rare. In 2005, when the Dow was bouncing around 10,000, there were 454 potential ten-baggers.[4] Potential ten-baggers made up 5 percent of the total stocks listed. Just blindly picking stocks, the odds were 1 in 20 you could double your investment within a year in 2005. That translates to a 95 percent risk you'd come up empty, assuming a random pick.

But you will not be picking randomly. You are going to improve those odds with thoughtful selection and the use of liquidity (explained later in this book) to correct your mistakes. To do that, you will need a systematic approach, which is the subject of this book.

To fully understand the promise of a ten-bag strategy, we must revisit the risks. What are the risks of failure? We'll determine this using a method called weighted average.

Table VI calculates several degrees of failure using expected rates of return weighted by the confidence of success. The basic assumption in Table VI is a ten-bagger will double in price in a year (a 100-percent gain), and all our erroneous picks will be sold when they decline in price by 50 percent.

TABLE VI
Potential Outcomes of a Ten-Bag Strategy

		Bad Luck	Blind Luck	Reasoned Luck	Good Luck	Breakeven (With the Game)
A	Ten-Bag Return %	100	100	100	100	100
B	Other Loss %	–50	–50	–50	–50	–50
C	Confidence (fractional)	0.0	0.05	0.50	0.80	0.40
D	Risk (fractional)	1.00	0.95	0.50	0.20	0.60
	Average Weighted Return % (AWR) (A × C) + (B × D)	–50	–42.5	+25	+70	+10

Table VI is a useful tool for analyzing various approaches to the stock market. Note that it allows for bad luck and good luck, outcomes presumably out of your control. Blind luck is random guessing, and reasoned luck is a systematic selection. The breakeven is set at the market minimum average or game return of 10 percent. Table VI tells us our worst-case scenario would cause us to lose 50 percent of our investment in a year. With reasoned luck, we could generate an annual return of 25 percent, which would triple our investment in three years.

Try constructing your own Table VI. Change the assumptions; instead of allowing your losers to fall by 50 percent, limit the decline to 30 percent. How would that change the average weighted return? What if your reasoned approach provided a 70 percent confidence level? What would the average weighted return be? Table VI allows you to quantify the most likely outcomes of a stock market strategy. It answers the question: What if? What if you change this or change that? What will the outcome be?

What You Have Learned

The reality of the stock market is average. Its lure is the ten-bagger, but there are many lures beyond the ten-bagger offering greater rewards than average. In your stock buying and selling business, you will leave the comfort of the average and seek out those opportunities. It is a decision you must make in order to achieve financial independence and control. The opportunities are there. You must provide, through reasoned analysis, the confidence level needed to step off the average path. In the next chapter, we explore the nature of those opportunities. In the following chapters, we'll continue to explore the reasoned analysis that will help us capitalize on them.

- Price movements in the stock market involve the three Rs: reason, recognition, and reaction.
- Rewards in the stock market are based on company earnings. They are achieved through dividends and price increases.
- Dividends are payments made to stockholders by the company. They are similar to interest paid to savings account, bond, and certificate of deposit holders. The term used to compare them to other investment returns is *yield*.
- The investor also benefits from an increase in the stock's price.
- Over the long term, the average return on a stock market investment has been 10–12 percent per year. This includes both dividends and stock price increases.
- What makes stock investments more attractive than other forms of investment is their tendency to grow.
- Game risk is different than bet risk. The game risk depends on both the probability of the outcome and the value of the outcome. It is the total of a series of bets. Game risk can be defined by betting all possible outcomes or playing the game long enough to reveal the consequences of all the possible outcomes.
- Bet risk in the stock market is primarily related to beta or volatility. However, when buying individual stocks, it is also related to investment risk.
- Stock-market returns are not linear.
- If average stock market returns are not sufficient to sustain your income needs given the size of your nest egg, you will have to adopt a riskier strategy to improve returns. The weighted average can be used to project the long-term rewards of those adopted strategies.

CHAPTER 5
Stock Market Opportunities

Up to this point, we have focused on the stock market as a whole, and the overall risks and rewards associated with it. It should be clear from that discussion if you are not investing in the stock market right now, you have made a very expensive Type II error (saying no when you should say yes). Because of that, you may need to catch up, which could lead to lapses in judgment and an even more expensive Type I error (saying yes when you should say no). In order to avoid that error, you need to raise your confidence level.

Figure 8 is a simple depiction of the challenge before you. If you take the average path, you will do well. With a sufficiently large nest egg, average is good enough. If you have failed to create a nest egg, you will have to deviate from the average in order to secure your retirement. When you deviate from the average, there is the risk of decreased rather than increased rewards. Your job is to minimize risk, which, in turn, will maximize your confidence level.

Increased confidence comes from a systematic decision-making approach based on knowledge, understanding, and patience; but what

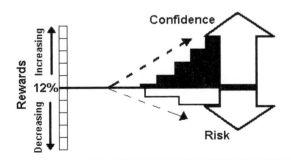

FIGURE 8: Deviating from Average. The average return for a diversified portfolio of stocks is 12 percent. Any deviation from that portfolio should maximize your confidence you will increase your rewards. The ideal would be 100 percent confidence and 0 percent risk.

type of knowledge? What do you need to know? In this chapter, you are going to increase your confidence level by recognizing some of the opportunities presented by the stock market. By knowing the opportunities and understanding the reason behind those opportunities, you can react to them with increased confidence.

The Growth Opportunity

Growth is the fundamental opportunity of the stock market. What makes growth so powerful are the effects of compounding, the impact of leverage, and the relative short forecasting horizon of most investors. Figure 9 illustrates two of the effects: forecast horizon and compounding.

Most investors, amateur or professional, have a difficult time forecasting beyond five years. While their long-term forecasts may be clouded, the impact of various growth rates on the price of a stock is clear. As illustrated in Figure 9, a $10 stock growing at the same rate as the economy (3 percent) would increase to $12 in five years. If the stock were growing at 10 percent per year, it would be worth

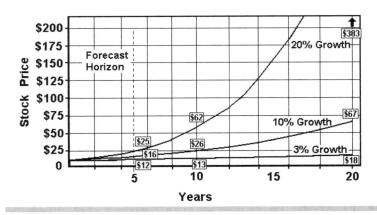

FIGURE 9: Impact of Growth on Price. The comparison among three growth rates for a $10 investment illustrates how the gap between them increases faster than the investments themselves. Thus, small errors in forecasting growth rates can lead to big differences in the ultimate value of the investment, especially when the investment horizon exceeds five years.

$16 dollars. As the two stocks continue their growth patterns beyond the five-year forecast horizon, the price gap between them increases from $4 to $13. With compounding, the gap is growing faster than either of the stocks. Compounding occurs when you reinvest your returns. In essence, you earn interest on the previous year's interest. However, since it is difficult for investors to see past the five-year time horizon, it is difficult for them to build the longer-term growth effect into the current stock price. The market has a potential to provide additional rewards for the patient investor who can see beyond the five-year horizon.

Leverage is another important contributor to the growth effect. In later chapters, we will explore how leverage operates to support the longer-term earnings growth driving the price growth observed in Figure 9.

The Value Opportunity

Two forces drive prices in the stock market: the crowd and the company. The crowd is the so-called market. It consists of various investors with different confidence levels, agendas, and time horizons. The crowd reacts to different environmental, political, and economic events. Its influence over stock prices, while continual, tends to be short term. In the short term, the price of a stock is whatever the market says it is.

There is a difference between the price of a stock and its value. Value is an objective measure dictated by the historical and future performance of the company. Some of the performance metrics used to value a stock are company earnings, sales growth, and debt load. The market provides very little insight into a company's value, but it has a great deal of influence over its price. The metrics used by the market to set prices are interest rates, buyer and seller perspectives, and economic activity. It is the interaction between value and the market's perspectives, as depicted in Figure 10, that determines the ultimate selling price of a company's stock.

Since price must ultimately reflect the underlying value of the company, the interaction between these forces creates a value opportunity. As illustrated in Figure 11, when the market pulls a stock's price below its value, stock investors buy in anticipation this anomaly will correct and the price will return to its value line. Conversely, if the price is pulled above its value, it will subsequently fall back to the value line. Investors avoid buying this stock, since they know its price, in the short term, is going to fall.

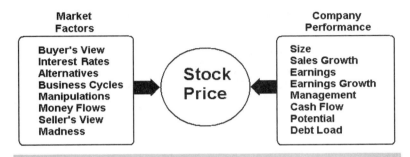

FIGURE 10: Forces Affecting Stock Price. The price of a stock is affected by both market forces and company performance.

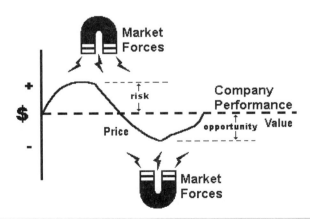

FIGURE 11: Market Forces and Value Opportunities. Company performance can be used to establish the value of a stock, which tends to be more rational and analytical. Market forces tend to pull the price of a stock away from its value line. These forces tend to be emotional and transitory; they reflect the whims of various players in the market.

Emerging Companies Can Be Great Opportunities

Emerging companies are companies moving from their developmental stage to their growth stage. All companies have life cycles like the one depicted in Figure 12. They are born, develop, grow, mature, and decline. Each of these stages offers a different investment opportunity. At the developmental level, there is a speculative opportunity; at maturity, there is usually a low-growth dividend opportunity; and in the growth stage, there is a growth opportunity. There is also an added opportunity when a company is emerging from its developmental stage into its growth stage.

As a company moves from its developmental stage to its growth stage, investors begin to value it differently. Not only do its revenues and earnings begin to grow, its valuation begins to grow because investors will pay a premium for growth, because growth increases the reward of their investment. This places a heavy upward pressure on the stock's current price. This pressure may be short-lived if the company fails to meet expectations, but if the company performs well in this transition and during the subsequent growth stage its stock price will rise dramatically. An investor who spots this trend early will reap immense rewards. This is where you'll find many of the ten-baggers.

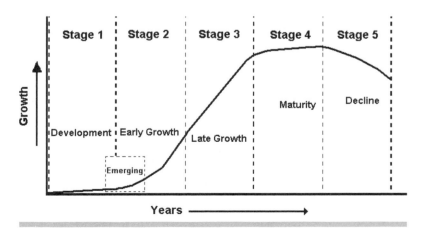

FIGURE 12: Corporate Life Cycle. All corporations experience a lifecycle. Their life cycle can be very short, as was the case with many Internet companies, or very long, as is the case with companies like Ford Motor or Kraft Foods.

Disruptions Can Be Opportunities

At times, the price of a stock will be driven downward by the market's response to a news event or corporate scandal. These price tumbles usually occur over a very short timeframe—a day or a week. These disruptions are usually short-lived; within a few months, or a year at most, the stock's price will fully recover. For example, in September 2001 the SP500 opened the month at 1,133.58. After the September 11 attacks, the SP500 hit a low for September of 944.75, a 16.7 percent decline. However, there was no overall change in the economy, and it rebounded the next month, reaching an October 2001 high of 1,110.61, a 17.6 percent increase. The market overreacted and then corrected. If you did not own the stock when the fall occurred, it was a great time to buy. If you owned it, you should have bought more.

The rewards associated with a disruption can be significant. For instance, a stock declining 50 percent over a two-month period ($10 down to $5) would gain 100 percent upon recovery ($5 back to $10). A series of disruptions can be as profitable as a run of ten-baggers.

But beware; before you jump on board, be sure the price slump is not warranted. If the stock's price has fallen for good reason, there is no opportunity. For instance, the collapse of Internet stocks occurred because investors realized most Internet companies were not making money and never would; their business models were flawed. That realization caused stock prices to decline, and prices have stayed down as one Internet company after another has filed for bankruptcy. True disruptions are not caused by a decline in company performance—they are market-driven. Research the opportunity carefully.

Fads and Bubbles

A disruption is an unreasonable drop in price offering investors a buying opportunity. Fads and bubbles are just the opposite; they are unreasonable increases in price. History is filled with examples of fads and bubbles. You have already read about one in Chapter 1—the Internet Bubble. They are great speculation and trading opportunities, if you know how to take advantage of them.

True investors would not consciously participate in a bubble[1] because they tend to buy and hold stocks, and you don't want to be caught holding stocks when the bubble bursts. Investors can get caught up in one if they own the stock before the rise occurs, but if they are alert, they will recognize the price of their stock has become totally delinked from the performance of the company. When that occurs, investors need to change their focus from long-term gains to short-term profits. There is extra money to be made with a well-timed exit point, but any investor who buys after a bubble begins is playing a trader's game. Unless you are equipped to handle the rigors of stock trading, stay away.

Why are disruptions good for investors, but bubbles aren't? Refer back to Figure 11. When the price of a stock falls below its value (a disruption), it is a buying opportunity for the investor because it reduces her volatility risk. When the price rises above its value (a bubble), the investor needs to wait until the price falls back to the value line before buying. If she doesn't wait, she will increase her volatility risk. Disruptions and bubbles are just extreme examples of the dynamic depicted in Figure 11.

Figure 13 illustrates a recent bubble. In the late 1990s, there was a run-up of Internet stocks. The price of Internet stocks rose above the SP500, increasing in price ten-fold. The rise took only eighteen months, and when the bubble burst, the fall of the Internet stock prices was equally dramatic. If you are a short-term player—a trader—

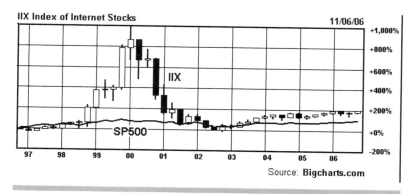

FIGURE 13: Price Comparison Between the SP500 and an Index of Internet Stocks.
The chart above clearly illustrates the Internet Bubble as Internet stocks pulled away from the SP500 and then, just as quickly, dropped back to it.

Figure 13 provided many opportunities to profitably buy and sell on the up-side of the bubble. As an investor, if you were already in, you needed to recognize Internet stock prices were being determined by the actions of traders and speculators. A good investment strategy would have been to look for a profitable exit point, and once out, not look back. Looking back serves no purpose because as an investor, you will never sell at the optimum price, knowing that price is an entirely different game than investing—it's trading.

A fad is like a bubble, except it is isolated to one company. It occurs when a company introduces a new product or service that creates a spike in its sales and profits. This spike can cause investors to buy the stock, which pushes the price up. However, not all products have staying power, and when the public tires of the product or service, the company's sales and profits drop back to previous levels. The stock price also drops. A good example is Mattel, which marketed the Cabbage Patch doll. Its stock price rose during the short-lived craze, and fell after a new toy from a different company caught the public's eye.

Riding the Currents

Money flows are a lot like fads, except they are more reasonable and predictable. The financial market has its currents as funds move from cash accounts, to corporate bonds, to government securities, to stocks, and back again. These flows are driven by economic events like business cycles, interest-rate adjustments, and global events. Since they are routine and reasonable, they provide a continuing series of opportunities for investors, traders, and speculators.

Money can flow into various sectors in the stock market (Appendix B). Since the stock market has some of the qualities of an auction, these money flows will tend to raise prices because more people trying to buy the stock will drive its price higher. This is not necessarily a permanent price increase. Permanent price increases, corresponding to an increase in a company's value, depend on company performance, and flow increases are based primarily on market forces. As a long-term investor, be aware of the temporary nature of a flow opportunity.

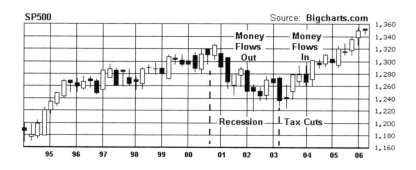

FIGURE 14: Understanding the Impact of Money Flows on the Stock Market. As money flows out of the stock market as it did during the 2001–2003 recession, the price of stocks decline. Once the recession is over and company profits begin to recover, money flows back into the market, which causes prices to increase.

A recent flow example is the performance of the SP500 during the early years of the George W. Bush administration. Figure 14 illustrates the effect of a business downturn on the SP500. When President Bush implemented a series of tax cuts in 2003, savvy investors with an understanding of economic history expected an economic turnaround to ensue.[2] This turnaround would improve company performance, which would provide a flow opportunity as money came back into the stock market. All that was needed to buy stock in 2003, when the SP500 was at its low point, was understanding, courage, objectivity, and some idle cash.

Penny Wise

Stocks priced below $1 are penny stocks. There are no inherent opportunities in penny stocks because the real opportunity in a stock is its value, not its price. A stock priced at a penny may be worth just a penny. There is no reason for the price to increase just because it is cheap. There must be an increase in its value; however, many companies with penny stocks are in the developmental stage of their life cycle. It is in this stage that you can find emerging stock opportunities and overlooked stocks. It is not the fact that a penny stock is low in price that provides the opportunity; it is the fact that it has a large potential for future growth as the company grows.[3] Remember that the three R's (reason, recognition, reaction) still apply. In order for potential to translate into meaningful investment profits, the company must perform, and stock buyers must spot and react to that performance.

Because they are so cheap, there is a significant obstacle to investing in penny stocks: the transaction costs. When you buy a stock, you must pay a brokerage fee. The fee can be $10–$100 for each thousand shares (or less) bought. When you sell the stock, you also pay the brokerage fee. Thus, the cost to buy and sell 1,000 shares of stock can be as much as $200. If you bought 1,000 shares of a $0.10 stock, it would have to triple in price for you to break even on the transaction. Considering that tripling the price only gets you to breakeven, blindly buying penny stocks is a high-risk and, more often than not, losing venture.

However, there are three ways to reduce the negative impact of transaction costs.

1. Buy higher-priced penny stocks, priced closer to $1 than to $0.01.
2. Buy through discount brokers or online, which will lower the transaction costs.
3. Wait for the company to reverse split its stock.

When a company splits its stock, it divides one share into multiple shares without decreasing or increasing the value of the share. For example, a 2-for-1 split would replace one share of stock that cost $100 with two new shares that cost $50 each. The effect of the split is to make the stock easier to buy and sell. When a reverse split occurs, the company combines several stocks into one new stock. For example, a 1-for-20 reverse split would replace twenty stocks that cost $0.10 each with one stock that cost $2. The higher price makes the stock more attractive to active traders because the higher stock price lessens the impact of the brokerage fees.[4] This effect is illustrated in Figure 15, which shows a significant increase in shares traded after a reverse split. Reverse splits will be discussed in greater detail in Chapter 11.

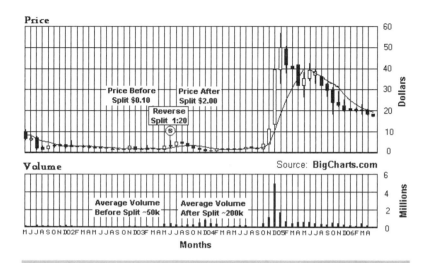

FIGURE 15: Impact of Reverse Split (AMPX). When a stock is split, the stock chart is changed to reflect the split, both before and after the split date. In the chart above, to see what the stock would look like before the split, all the prices would have to be divided by 20. If there were numerous splits on a chart, the chart would reflect the cumulative effect of all the splits.

So where is the penny stock opportunity for retirees? The market for penny stocks is a speculator's playground. If you have a speculator's patience and vision, a penny stock strategy can prove very profitable.

Overlooked Stocks

When a stock is followed by mutual fund and pension plan institutions, analysts will monitor every little change in the company's performance so they can advise their institutions. This leaves very little opportunity for performance pressures to build under these stocks. However, if there are no analysts watching, a company can build a head of steam before anyone notices and begins bidding the price up. These are the overlooked stocks, and they come highly recommended by Peter Lynch in his book on investing, *One Up On Wall Street*.[5]

William J. O'Neil, founder of *Investor's Daily*, focuses his stock analysis on stocks priced at $10 or more, on the basis that most institutions do not buy stocks below that magic number. A recent screen[6] of the companies listed on the various stock exchanges confirms that institutions do have a significantly smaller position in low-priced stocks. The median percent of shares owned by institutions in stocks priced under $10 is just 5.7 percent. For stocks priced more than $10, the median is 55.7 percent. Combining the thoughts of Mr. Lynch and Mr. O'Neil, all things being equal, there is a buying opportunity in a stock with a price above $10 and an institutional ownership below 5.7 percent, especially if its performance and potential is promising. Institutional ownership information for a stock can be found online at investment websites like Reuters.com.

This raises the question of cause and effect. Does the higher price attract more institutions to the company, or does the performance of the company attract more institutions, which then drives the stock price higher? Mr. Lynch and Mr. O'Neil argue the latter. Based on various stock screens run, they may have a good point. All things remaining equal, a well-performing company with very little institutional ownership would appear to offer greater upside potential than a similar company already discovered. When you buy an overlooked company, you can reasonably expect its share price to increase when the institutions discover it, but beware—the stock may have been discovered, analyzed, and rejected. Low institutional ownership of a stock does not guarantee success; it is simply one clue among many that may indicate you have discovered a lower-risk stock buy.

What You Have Learned

The opportunities listed above cover a range of environments and players. Investors will be most comfortable seeking out growth opportunities and using value analysis to reduce their bet risk with well-timed buy-and-sell points. Speculators will be intrigued by the opportunities inherent in emerging companies, penny stocks, and bubbles. Traders would not normally make their moves based on any of the above opportunities, but they certainly can improve their success rate if they are aware of the environment in which their stock is operating. By understanding the opportunities, even the trader can better manage his game.

- If you have failed to create a sufficiently large nest egg, you will have to deviate from the average to ensure a financially comfortable retirement.
- The stock market offers many opportunities for you to outperform the average.
- With knowledge and understanding, retirees can confidently seize these opportunities when they occur. Until they occur, they can reap the relatively risk-free rewards of the average.
- There are opportunities in the market for every type of player.

CHAPTER 6

Your Stock Buying and Selling Business

Up to this point, I've compared the stock market to a game, but now it's time to get down to serious business—the business of buying and selling stocks. The goal of this book is not to coax you into the game, but to put you in the business of buying and selling stocks. As a retiree, it will be a part-time business, with you as its chief executive officer, vice president of research, manager of procurement, and director of sales. You are about to become an entrepreneur. As such, you will put the basic rule of wealth into practice: You don't get wealthy working for others, and you don't get wealthy working for yourself. You get wealthy by getting others to work for you. Buying stocks is getting others to work for you.

Yet, you don't want to hire just any "others." You want to hire the best, and you want to pay them what they are worth—no more and no less. In the manufacturing arena, this is measured by productivity. In the stock-buying business, worth is measured by a series of valuation metrics discussed in Chapter 8. Before we discuss who you should hire, let's explore the basic business model. This will help you run your business and decide which companies to hire.

Why Buy?

All economic activity is based on one simple question: Do you make it, or do you buy it? Figure 16 illustrates the basic underpinnings of that question. Once a customer needs a product or service, she must decide to make it or buy it. If the cost of making is larger than the price to buy, the customer buys. If the price to buy is higher than her cost to make, she makes. To initiate economic activity, there must be a buy decision.

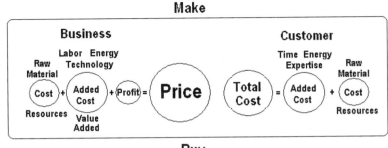

FIGURE 16: Make or Buy Decision. People choose to make or buy a product based on what it costs them to make it versus what someone else is selling it for. When the price is larger than the customer's cost, the customer makes. When the customer's cost is larger than the price, the customer buys. The difference between the price and the customer's cost is the customer's profit. Note, if the customer buys when he should make, his profit is negative; he loses money.

While the cost in Figure 16 was measured in dollars, it can be anything. For example, the cost to make dinner at home is usually cheaper than the price of that same dinner in a restaurant. However, customers will often include their time, convenience, or ability to make a particular meal in the cost. Thus, many economic transactions appear financially suspect, but at some other level, they are perfectly justified.

Understanding the make-or-buy dynamic is fundamental to your stock-buying venture. Your decision to invest in the stock market is a make-or-buy decision. You could choose to make by starting your own business, or you can buy stock in someone else's business. Once you decide, you can choose to pick your own stocks (make) or rely on a broker's recommendation (buy). Finally, if you decide to make, you will need to evaluate the companies behind the stocks you choose. Do they make something people want to buy? Do they make it at a price people will pay? The make-or-buy decision influences almost every step of your business.

Once you choose to buy, you must decide from whom, which is the next step in the business dynamic. There is usually more than one company willing to sell similar products or services—you must choose the best one. If price were the only determinant, this would be a simple question, but, as in the case of the restaurant, price is not just about dollars. It includes quality, performance, style, convenience, psychology, and customer expertise. The same will be true in your stock selections. You will have many to choose from and many selection criteria to use in making your choice. Different stocks compete for your investment dollars. This book will help you decide which stocks are right for you.

The Basic Business Model

The basic business model is simple: Buy, add value, and then sell at a profit. It is the foundation of every successful business. It doesn't matter if it is a manufacturer, wholesaler, retailer, or transporter; their jobs are to take a raw material and convert it into something with more value. The manufacturer might take plastic and convert it to a toy. The wholesaler buys the toys in large quantities efficient for the manufacturer to make, and then sells them in smaller quantities efficient for retailers to sell. The retailer displays those quantities in attractive settings, inducing customers to buy. The transporter moves the product from manufacturer to wholesaler to retailer. Each step between producer and customer adds value in the form of shape, size, movement, or utility. Each bit of valued added provides the opportunity to earn a profit. Figure 16 not only illustrates the foundation of all economic activity, it also illustrates this basic business model.

In your business, you will buy stock. You will add value to the stock by making good selections based on a lifetime of experience, your common sense, the knowledge you gain from this book, your understanding of the company—its products and its markets—your personality, and the discipline to stay in your game. All of this can be done by someone else—a broker, banker, or financial advisor—but in that case you would be buying, not making. If the value you added is recognized by others, you will sell the stock for more than you paid. That difference will be your profit, and you will have done it on your own.

The scary part is, you are on your own. When you open your own business, there is just you and the customer. When you go to work for someone else, there is safety in numbers—you work with a community of people. There are the boss, salesman, engineer, and accountant. You place your trust in them. You hope they have the skills, ambition, and knowledge to keep you employed. This is the norm in a complex society; we travel from the safety of one community to the next. To step outside those communal borders requires courage. Taking that step as a retiree takes immense courage, but safety is costly. In Chapter 2, the safe savings account paid you $3,262, but paid the banker $89,394. When it comes to business, developing the courage (or confidence) to do it on your own pays well.

Keeping Score

Like any venture, the only way to know if you are successful is to keep score. There are three score cards used to monitor a business: the income statement, the balance sheet, and the cash flow analysis.

Income Statement

The first measure of a business is its income statement. The income statement reveals the company's ability to generate sales and profits. It covers a specific period of time—usually a month, quarter, or year. Table VII is a simple, idealized income statement.

The data in Table VII is typical of what you will see on an income statement. Note how Table VII relates to the business model presented in Figure 16. No matter how complex the income statement may appear, it is still built upon the basic elements of the business model. The purpose of the income statement is to record how efficiently the company converts sales into profits. The key metrics on the income statement are sales (or revenue) and net income. Other important metrics are gross profit, operating profit, and interest expense.

The income statement also reveals another attribute of a successful business: Larger companies benefit from the phenomenon of economies-of-scale. This is a form of leverage caused by the nature of the costs.

TABLE VII
Sample Income Statement
Company XYZ

Sales (Revenue)	100		Price
Cost of Goods:	65		
Raw Material	*26*		Cost
Labor	*26*		
Energy	*11*		Value Added
Overhead	*2*		
Gross Profit	35		
Expenses			
Sales and Marketing	5		
Administration	10		**Value Added**
Research and Development	5		
Operating Profit	15		
Interest Expense	2.5		**Value Added**
Other Expense (extraordinary)	1.5		
Income Before Taxes	11		Profit
Taxes	4		Value Added
Net Income	7		Profit

Costs can be divided into two groups: fixed and variable. Fixed costs stay the same no matter how much product a company makes. Variable costs increase in proportion to the volume of products made. The variable costs tend to be in the Cost of Goods. Fixed costs tend to be in the Expenses group. We'll discuss this important effect in more detail in the next section.

Balance Sheet

The second score card is the balance sheet. Unlike the income statement, the balance sheet details the company's assets and liabilities at a particular moment—usually the last day of a month, quarter, or year. Table VIII is the balance sheet for Company XYZ.

The balance sheet describes the assets used by the company to generate the sales and profits listed on the income statement. Assets such as inventories (products the company has made but not yet sold) and receivables (money customers owe the company) are variable. They tend to rise as the volume of business rises. Assets such as plant and equipment tend to be fixed (for example, the company does not build a new factory or buy a new machine every time it makes more product). Having both fixed and variable assets also creates economies-of-scale and leverage similar to those on the income statement.

The liabilities side of the balance sheet details the ownership of the company and will always equal the total assets. In Company XYZ, the shareholders own 50 percent of the company. Their share is the equity portion of the liabilities (30 ÷ 60 = .5 or 50%). Long-term debt holders own 33 percent (20 ÷ 60). Trade partners and other debt holders own approximately 17 percent (10 ÷ 60).

This concept of ownership gets a little more complicated when you relate it to the income statement. It is clear who owns the assets, but who owns the profits? Again, the concept of fixed and variable comes into play. Bond and bank owners are paid a fixed return on their ownership. The equity holders (shareholders) receive a variable portion of the profits. The trade partners generally receive nothing for their investment in the company. Their investment is in the form of credit purchases and delayed payments. This creates an economies-of-scale similar to that observed on the income statement. The exact term for

TABLE VIII
Sample Balance Sheet
Company XYZ

ASSETS			LIABILITIES	
Current			Current	
Cash	2		Payables	8
Receivables	12		Debt	2
Inventories	6		Total Current	10
Total Current	20			
			Long Term	
Plant & Equipment			Bank	10
Plant	30		Bonds	10
Machinery	10		Total Long Term	20
Accumulated Depreciation	2			
Net Plan & Equipment	38		Equity	
			Paid In	10
Miscellaneous	2		Retained	20
			Total Equity	30
Total Assets	60		Total Liabilities	60

this economy-of-scales is *financial leverage*, because it deals with how the company is financed. The more debt a company carries, the more leveraged it is. Again, we will learn more about economies-of-scale and leverage in the next section.

Cash Flow Analysis

The final major score card for the company is the cash flow analysis. Most companies operate on an accrual basis. This is similar to you buying everything on a credit card. When you buy a dress at Kohl's with your credit card, no cash is exchanged. You get a dress, and Kohl's gets a promise to pay, a receivable. When your credit card bill comes due, you pay it, and the credit card company pays Kohl's. Kohl's now removes the receivable from its asset column and places the money in its bank account. The accrual method allows companies to recognize a sale before the item is actually paid for.

Let's apply the above process to Tables VII and VIII. The sales are recorded as 100, but not all those sales resulted in an exchange of cash, some were made with credit. When that happens, the company records the sale and then adds the amount owed to its receivables, which is an asset. Until that receivable is paid, no cash flows to the company. Yet, the company needs cash to pay its bills. It pays its bills, such as wages, interest payments, energy costs, current payables, fees, etc., from its cash account. Where does the company get the cash needed to pay those bills? The cash flow analysis answers that question.

As important as profit is to a company, cash is more important. Profits help the business grow, and growth is important to the investor, but cash keeps the business from going bankrupt, which is even more important. The income statement, which identifies profitability, is a good indicator of a company's growth potential. The cash flow statement monitors their ability to pay their bills. If they can't pay their bills, they could go bankrupt, which is a significant risk for an investor. So keep this rule of thumb in mind when analyzing a company's score card: Profit grows the company; the lack of cash bankrupts it. This explains why many fast-growing and profitable companies go bankrupt. They have the profits to grow the business, but they don't have enough cash to pay their bills.

The cash flow analysis is a very important part of your stock-analysis regimen. Cash flow is one of the most important indicators of a company's financial health and risk exposure. No matter how profitable its income statement, make sure it can pay its bills before you buy its stock. To get more practice reading these business score cards, go online or to your local library and study several examples of companies' income, balance, and cash flow statements.

These are the basic score cards you will use to evaluate a business. If they seem intimidating, they will become less so as you work with them in future sections of this chapter and future chapters. Also, when you set up your stock buying and selling business, you will be using similar statements to track your success. By creating your own business score cards, you will significantly increase your level of understanding of these score cards and how they can help you make profitable stock market decisions.

Back to the Game—Company Stats

The statements for company XYZ provide all the necessary information to determine how effectively and efficiently its owners are operating it. All companies should be scored with those two criteria in mind—effectiveness and efficiency.

One of the first questions you should ask is how effectively the company is using its assets to create a business. The sales-to-asset ratio is a good indicator of this because it measures the amount of sales dollars generated for each dollar invested in the company. Company XYZ has a sales-to-asset ratio of 1.67 (sales ÷ total assets = 100 ÷ 60). The larger the ratio the more effective the company is at generating revenue with its assets. The median sales-to-asset ratio for publicly traded companies is 2.09. Company XYZ would appear to be less effective at generating sales with its assets than most publicly traded companies.

Another important question is how efficiently the company produces the products they sell. Gross profit is a good indicator here because it measures the difference between the price customers are willing to pay for the product and what it costs the company to make it. Large gross profits are good because it is from gross profit the company pays its managers (salaries), creditors (interest), and shareholders (dividends). Company XYZ has a gross profit of 35 percent. The median for publicly traded companies is 34.72. Thus, XYZ is not effectively using its assets, but it is efficiently producing its products. You can make this efficiency calculation at every level of a company's profitability. Each one measures an aspect of the company's operation. Here are some examples:

- The gross profit measures how efficiently the company produces its products.
- Operating profit measures how efficiently the company organizes (administration), develops (R&D), and markets its products.

■ Pretax profits measure how efficiently the company manages its finances and debt loads.

■ Net income measures how efficiently it delivers profits to the shareholders.

You can divide these profit levels by different factors to get a series of ratios such as return-on-sales, return-on-assets, or return on equity. These ratios will also help you, as an educated investor, determine which companies are healthy and which are not.

Table IX presents these and other important ratios that can be calculated to measure a company's effectiveness and efficiency. While they are useful in evaluating manufacturing companies and some service organizations, it is not a universal list. Each industry has its own key ratios to help you monitor their effectiveness and efficiency. If you intend to invest in a bank, be sure to study the ratios used to measure success in the banking industry. They will be different than those used to measure the success of a company making memory chips for personal computers. When it comes to investing, it is always important to compare similar companies.

The ratios presented in Table IX are dynamic and interrelated; one table cannot capture all their nuances. For instance, you might think a company with a low sales-to-asset ratio is not effectively using its assets to generate sales. This view might be especially valid if it is a mature company in a mature market, where its sales growth is flattening (see Figure 12). If it is an emerging company in a growing market, you might conclude that a low sales-to-assets ratio is positive. It could indicate this company has ample room to grow sales without a significant increase in capital spending. This conclusion leads us to a discussion of leverage.

Understanding Leverage

Leverage is the ability of a company to magnify their profits based on a structural or other advantage. There are many forms of leverage in business: operational leverage, technological leverage, marketing leverage, and financial leverage. Most retirees are familiar with financial leverage, especially in the real estate arena.

TABLE IX

Common Performance Ratios
Manufacturing Companies

Performance Measure	Calculation	Data Source	Significance
Sales-to-Assets	Sales ÷ Total Assets	Income Statement Balance Sheet	Measures how effectively the business uses its assets to generate sales. A high number (above 2.0) is good.
Return-on-Sales	Net Income ÷ Sales	Income Statement	Measures how effectively the business generates profits from its sales — the higher the better.
Gross Margin	Gross Profit ÷ Sales	Income Statement	Measures how efficiently the business produces its products or services. Less than 25 percent is worrisome.
Return on Assets	Net Income ÷ Total Assets	Income Statement Balance Sheet	Measures how effectively the business uses its assets to generate profits. The minimum should be 15 percent.
Return on Equity	Net Income ÷ Total Equity	Income Statement Balance Sheet	Measures how effectively the business generates profits for its owners. If the company carries long-term debt, the ROE should be considerably higher than 15 percent.
Debt-to-Equity	Long-term Debt ÷ Total Equity	Balance Sheet	Measures the long-term financial risk and leverage within the company. It should be 1.0 or less.
Days Receivable	(Receivables ÷ Sales) × 365	Income Statement Balance Sheet	Measures the number of days of credit sales in the year's total sales. Forty-five days is normal.
Days Inventories	(Inventories ÷ Cost of Goods) × 365	Income Statement Balance Sheet	Measures the number of days of inventories yet to be sold. Forty-five days would be good; the lower the better.
Current Ratio	Current Asset ÷ Current Liabilities	Balance Sheet	Measures the ability of a company to pay its short-term debts. Two or better is a good number.
Quick Ratio	(Cash + Receivables) ÷ Current Liabilities	Balance Sheet	Measures the ability of a company to pay its short-term debts using cash or assets quickly converted into cash. One or higher is good.
Interest Coverage	(Pretax Profit + Interest) ÷ Interest Expense	Income Statement	Measures the ability of a company to pay the interest on its debt. Very high numbers insulates the company from short-term declines in profits.

Financial Leverage

If you own a $100,000 house and the inflation rate is 10 percent, your return on investment is easy to calculate. It's the 10 percent increase in the price. However, if you borrow $80,000 to buy the house, the return on investment is a little more complex. First, calculate the dollar return, which is 10 percent of the house price, or $10,000. From the $10,000, subtract the interest on the loan, which at a 5 percent rate is $4,000. Divide that difference by your investment, which is only $20,000. The result is your return on investment—30 percent ([$10,000 – $4,000] ÷ $20,000), which is considerably better than the 10 percent return on the cash purchase. Leverage magnified your return because you purchased the house using borrowed money.

In order for financial leverage to work, the return on our total investment must be greater than the cost of borrowing. In the example mentioned above, if your mortgage rate was 10 percent, it would wipe out the advantage. The new return on investment would be $10,000 minus $8,000 in interest divided by your $20,000 investment, which is 10 percent. In this case, you would have taken on the risk of borrowing without the rewards of leverage, which is never a good business practice.

The same problem can occur with companies. They can think they are creating leverage, but in reality they are just taking on debt and increasing their exposure to bankruptcy. Company XYZ provides an example. Let's add 20 in debt to their balance sheet. Based on their sales-to-asset ratio, that will create an additional 33.4 in sales. The calculated profit before interest and taxes will be 4.51. Deducting the added interest (@12%) and the income taxes (@33.3%) leaves an additional net income of 1.342. If they have achieved leverage, they should see improvement in many of the key ratios. Let's calculate some. The first is return on sales (ROS), which was 7 percent, but is now 6.3 percent (8.342 ÷ 133.4). Return on assets (ROA) was 11.7 percent, but is now 10.4 percent (8.342 ÷ 80). Return on equity (ROE) was 23.3 percent, but is now 27.8 percent (8.342 ÷ 30). Debt-to-equity (D/E) ratio was 0.67, but is now 1.33 (40 ÷ 30). Finally, interest coverage was 5.4, but is now 3.7. Taking on debt is a mixed blessing for Company XYZ. They improved their financial leverage as measured by ROE, but they decreased their operating efficiency as measured by ROS and ROA. Also, D/E and interest coverage took a turn for the worse, which indicates risk has increased. XYZ must do more than increase their assets; they need to create additional operating leverage, or economies of scale.

Operating Leverages, or Economies of Scale

Earlier we talked about economies of scale (EOS). This is an important and multifaceted concept you will need to understand. One aspect of it is size—the sheer fact that a company is big implies it has certain advantages over its smaller rivals. It has more resources to weather storms, overcome mistakes, and penetrate markets. Bigger companies also become more efficient the more they do something. They learn to do it better, cheaper, and more profitably with time and volume. Still another aspect is synergy. Big companies bring together a wide array of resources working together to make a more effective and efficient whole. All of these aspects contribute to EOS, but the biggest contributor is the nature of costs.

Costs can be either fixed or variable. A fixed cost is a cost that stays the same over a certain timeframe, usually a year. For this reason, fixed costs are also period costs. Variable costs vary with production. A good example of a fixed cost is insurance. No matter how many items are produced in a factory, the cost to insure the factory against a fire or natural disaster is a constant. On the other hand, the total costs of the raw materials that go into a factory will increase as the production increases—raw materials are variable costs. How do these different types of costs affect profitability? We can figure this out using a breakeven chart.

Figure 17 is the breakeven chart for a simple home-based business. On the vertical axis of the chart are dollars of revenues or costs. The horizontal axis shows the number of units produced. In this case, the units are dresses, and they are being hand-sewn by a seamstress in her basement. The fabrics cost $1 and she pays her daughter $4 per hour to assemble and sew the dresses. The daughter can produce one dress every hour. The customer buys the dresses for $10 each. This leaves our seamstress with a $5 per dress profit. Since all the costs are variable in nature, at zero units produced there are no revenues and no costs. The very first dress produced costs $5 ($1 material + $4 labor) and generates $10 in revenue when sold. This company is profitable from the very first unit of production, which means it has a breakeven of zero units. It doesn't even have to sell one unit to break even, since it does not spend any money until it produces a dress.

Figure 18 illustrates the breakeven chart for the same home-based business, but they have rented a sewing machine to help sew the dresses. The machine costs $700 a year to rent; the daughter can now produce two dresses an hour. The revenue line remains the same, but now we have a fixed cost of $700. This cost must be paid regardless of the number of dresses made. At zero units, the fixed cost is $700. At 100 units, the fixed cost is still $700. A horizontal line drawn through the $700 point of the vertical axis represents the fixed costs. However, the fixed costs have changed our variable cost line. The fabrics still cost $1 per dress, but now the labor cost is just $2 per dress since the daughter can now produce two per hour. The total variable cost is just $3 per dress. This new variable cost line is added to the fixed

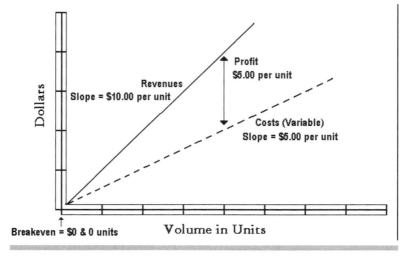

FIGURE 17: Breakeven Chart for a Labor-Intensive Home-Based Business. When there are no fixed costs in a company, the breakeven point is at zero units. Since no costs or revenues are present until a product is produced and sold, both the revenue and total cost line begin at the origin.

cost, and is drawn as a sloping line beginning at the intersection of the fixed cost line and the vertical axis. It now represents the total cost to make the dresses.

The difference between revenues and variable costs is incremental margin, and in Figure 18 it is $7 ($10 - $3). In Figure 17, the incremental margin was $5. This incremental margin is used to offset the fixed costs. Until these fixed costs are paid, the company can't make money. The point at which they are paid is the breakeven point, and can be calculated by dividing the fixed cost by the incremental margin. In our example, the breakeven is 100 units ($700 ÷ $7). In Figure 18, it is the point at which the revenue line crosses the total cost line. Thus, Figure 17 and Figure 18 represent two very different operational results. Table X compares the income statements of these two operations.

The increased leverage is only achieved if there is a significant reduction in the variable costs (which there was—the labor cost decreased). This is the same requirement we had for financial leverage, where the cost of the loan must be offset by significantly greater

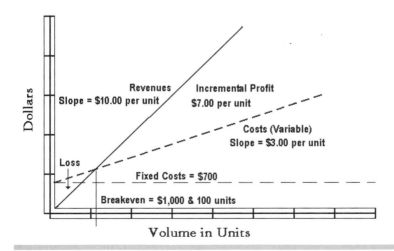

FIGURE 18: Breakeven Chart for a Mechanized Home-Based Business. When fixed costs are added, the total cost line begins where the fixed cost line intersects the vertical axis. The revenue still begins at the origin and has to catch up to the cost line. The point at which revenues equal total costs is the breakeven point. Above that point, the company is profitable. Below that point, it is unprofitable.

TABLE X

Profitability of a Mechanized Versus Labor-Intensive Operation

	Labor-Intensive (Figure 17)	Mechanized (Figure 18)
Revenue 2080 dresses	$20,080	$20,080
Costs to Produce:		
Fixed	$ 0	$ 700
Materials	$ 2,080	$ 2,080
Labor	$ 8,320	$ 4,160
Total Costs	$10,400	$ 6,940
Profit	$10,400	$13,141

returns on the borrowed money. Also like financial leverage, operational leverage brings increased risk. Referring back to Figure 18, the breakeven point has shifted from zero units to 100 units. The company operates at a loss until it manufactures and sells 100 units. Beyond that production and sales level, it is profitable. In Figure 17, there was never a risk it would operate at a loss, but at the 2,080 unit level it was less profitable because it lacked operating leverage.

Using Breakeven Charts

Figure 19 is a breakeven chart for Company XYZ. This required some reasonable assumptions. First, we assumed the price of the product is $1 per unit. If the numbers in Table VII is millions of dollars, the total number of units sold is 100 million. Finally, we will identify all the costs of goods sold to be variable with the exception of $2 million of fixed overhead. These are overhead costs such as depreciation, supervisor's salaries, etc. We will treat all the Expenses, Interest, and Miscellaneous as fixed. Thus, the total fixed costs are $26 million and our variable costs increase at a rate of $0.63 for every unit sold. The breakeven point for XYZ is 70,270,270 units. At 100 million units, the pretax profit equals $11 million, which conforms to Income Statement.

Breakeven charts are very useful in determining the viability of a business model and projecting the potential for future earnings. For instance, let's assume that a competitor of XYZ had $50 million in sales and reported a $7.5 million pretax loss. Let's also assume that it is growing 20 percent per year. We will call this company ABC and plot it on our chart. The first observation we can make is that even though ABC is operating at a loss, it is as efficient as XYZ because we would expect a loss at this low level of sales. Secondly, if its 20 percent growth rate continues, it will be above breakeven in two years and equal to XYZ in less than four years. Thus, the breakeven chart allowed us to better understand the full potential of what would appear, at first glance, to be a failing company.

Calculating Stock Prices with the Breakeven Chart

Now, let's compare the stock prices of these two companies. We'll assume both have 10 million shares outstanding. If XYZ trades at a price-earnings ratio similar to the SP500, which is listed on the Internet as 20, its stock price would be $14 per share. The calculation is

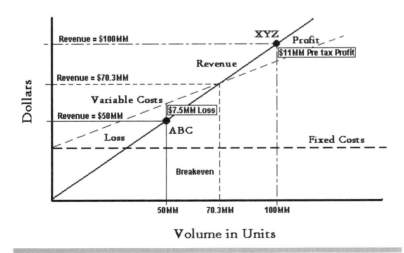

FIGURE 19: Breakeven for the XYZ and ABC Companies. The breakeven chart allows investors to compare similar companies.

the net income ($7 million) divided by the shares outstanding (10 million), to yield an EPS of $0.70, which is multiplied by the SP500's P/E (20) to yield a stock price of $14. Since ABC has no earnings, nor a history of earnings, its price can be based on the equity portion of the balance sheet, which we will assume to be the same as XYZ. That would yield a price of $3 per share ($30 million ÷ 10 million shares). If ABC continues to grow at 20 percent per year, it is reasonable to forecast that ABC's shares will be trading at $14 a share in four years. Investing $5,000 in ABC today, when it's a loser, could yield a $23,333 nest egg in four years. That's a 24 percent annual return over four years, and it illustrates the power of the breakeven chart to identify the growth potential of a company. It also illustrates why speculators and some investors buy stocks with no earnings. They are buying the future, not the present or the past.

Predicting Failures with the Breakeven Chart

Before we leave the breakeven chart, let's look at how it can be used to keep you out of trouble in the stock market. The famous Internet Bubble that burst at the end of the 1990s was said to have occurred because many of the Internet companies had poor business models. What did that mean? How would you know?

Figure 20 compares the breakeven charts of two different business models. The slope of the revenue line is the same in all scenarios. We will also keep the fixed costs the same in order to keep the chart uncluttered. What we will change are the variable costs. Variable Costs A (VCA) represents a typical company with a profitable business model. The slope of the VCA line is lower than the revenue line. This allows the revenues to catch up to it at breakeven and then go on to earn significant profits. Look what happens when the VCA line shifts to Variable Costs B (VCB). The VCB line has a much steeper slope than the VCA line, and the revenue line never crosses it. This occurred in many Internet companies because they were spending almost as much to get and hold a customer (in the form of advertising, promotional discounts, etc.) as the customer was spending to purchase their products or services. This resulted in very small incremental margins, which were insufficient to offset the fixed costs.

Now we need to look at another aspect of our breakeven analysis—capacity. All breakeven charts assume a capacity. This is defined by the size of the factory, the number of production machines, and the organizational structure of the company. These are structural in nature and fixed in cost. In Figure 20, the original assumed capacity was Capacity A. What if the capacity shifted from A to Capacity C? Capacity C defines the maximum new units the company can produce, and it will be reached before the company achieves breakeven, even with the original Variable Costs A. In order for the company to exceed Capacity C, it must restructure the operation, which will add new fixed costs, which will create a new and different breakeven chart.

How can a company's capacity shrink below its breakeven point? Structurally, it could be caused by a failure of design or implementation. More often than not, it is a failure of marketing. Two factors control a company's capacity—its structure and its market. The structural

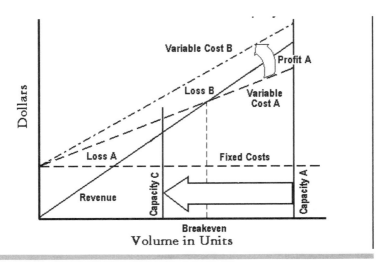

FIGURE 20: Breakeven of an Internet Bubble Company. There are two ways a company can fail to reach breakeven. First, it doesn't achieve capacity. Second, its variable cost increases too fast. Breakeven charts are based on an assumed capacity (capacity A). If the company fails to achieve that capacity (capacity C), it could find itself unable to make a profit. Also, if the variable costs added to the fixed costs are too high (Variable Cost B), the revenue line may not catch up to the total cost line before the capacity of the chart (Capacity A) is reached.

capacity we have just discussed; market capacity is its customer base. Assume that in Figure 20, the company built a plant and organization with a capacity of A. With the fixed cost line as drawn and a Variable Cost A, the company has created a profitable business model. If the market capacity of its product line is C, it will never achieve its profit potential because it cannot produce beyond its market capacity. If it did, there is no one to buy the products—it would simply produce inventory. When working with breakeven charts, be aware of both the structural and market capacity limitations of the chart.

A good example of a marketing capacity dilemma is the Kodak company, which makes photographic film. When film was in demand, Kodak operated its plant at capacity A, which generated healthy profits. The introduction of digital cameras cut into the market demand for film, and Kodak had to reduce their market to capacity C. They could produce more; they just couldn't sell more. Kodak is now struggling to maintain profitability by developing new products, but their film business will remain unprofitable until they restructure that operation to fit the new market realities. In essence, they have to shrink that manufacturing facility until it fits profitably within the limits of their market (capacity C).

Putting It All to Work

The concepts above will be very useful in identifying investment opportunities, but they will be equally useful in helping you understand and operate your stock buying and selling business. When you're feeling comfortable with all these calculations and ratios, you can create an income statement where each individual stock buy is considered the purchase of a raw material. To that cost, you will add any direct expenses incurred in making the selection and the buy. These direct expenses would include analyst's reports, transaction fees, or phone calls to the company. When the stock is sold, that transaction is recorded on the revenue line. Stocks owned but not yet sold are inventory. Money received from a sale not yet reinvested is cash. From the total of these individual trades you will deduct your fixed costs—costs not directly related to any one stock. These could include subscriptions to publications and websites, book purchases, computers, cable hookups, etc. The total of all these individual transactions and fixed costs will allow you to monitor your successes (and failures) as an investor. A score card for one investor might look like the following:

ANNUAL INCOME STATEMENT		BALANCE SHEET	
Revenues:		Assets:	
(3 trades)	$19,500	Current:	
Dividends	$ 300	Cash	$ 7,750
Total Revenues	$19,800	Inventories	$ -0-
		Total Current	$ 7,750
Cost of Goods:			
		Fixed:	
Raw Materials	$15,000	Computer	$ 3,000
Transaction		Depreciation	($ 3,000)
Fees & Reports	$ 450	Total Fixed	$ -0-
Total Variable	$15,450		
		Total Assets	$ 7,750
Gross Profit	$ 4,350		
		Liabilities:	
Fixed Costs:			
		Current	$ -0-
Subscriptions	$ 1,000		
Computer	$ 3,000	Debt	$ -0-
(Depreciation)			
Cable Fees	$ 600	Equity:	
Total Fixed	$ 4,600	Paid In	$ 8,000
		Retained	($ 250)
Net Profit	($ 250)	Total Equity	$ 7,750
Or (Loss)			
		Total Liabilities	$ 7,750

You have learned enough about business in this chapter to analyze the financial statement above. Try answering the following questions:

- Did our investor earn a profit at the end of the year?
- How much equity did he contribute to his business (Paid In)?
- How many stocks does he currently own?
- Was he a successful investor?
- Was he a successful entrepreneur?
- Would it be a good idea for him to add more of his own money to this business; i.e., pay in more equity? Why or why not?
- Name two things he could do to increase his net profit.
- What would his financial statement look like if he borrowed $5,000 in order to double the number of trades he made? (Assume a 10 percent interest rate on the borrowings.)

Answer these questions on a piece of scrap paper and then turn to the footnotes at the end of the book to see how well you did.[1] Exercises like these allow entrepreneurs to test various ideas and scenarios before they commit time, money, and energy to a venture. These what-if scenarios are an important aspect of planning. As you will discover in the next chapter, planning is an important tool in your entrepreneurial arsenal.

What You Have Learned

In this chapter, you have learned a lot about business, but there is more to learn. Over time and with practice, you will be able to understand the subtleties and complexities that swirl around the ratios I have presented. What you have learned so far is an excellent starting point from which you can explore those complexities.

- The basis of all economic activity is a simple make-or-buy decision.
- The basic business model is to buy, add value, and resell at a profit.

- Businesses score their success or failure using financial statements. There are three important ones: income statement, balance sheet, and cash flow analysis.
- The income statement reveals the company's ability to generate sales and profits. It covers a specific period of time, usually a month, quarter, or year.
- The balance sheet describes the assets used by the company to generate the sales and profits listed on the income statement. It also describes who owns those assets—vendors, banks, bondholders, or shareholders.
- The cash flow analysis, or sources and uses of cash, describes how a company has generated and distributed its cash. It draws its information from both the income statement and the balance sheet and covers the same timeframe as the income statement.
- A good rule of thumb to keep in mind when you invest: Profits grow the company; the lack of cash bankrupts it.
- Analysts use a series of financial ratios to measure the performance of the company and compare it to other companies. Some of these ratios are listed in Table IX.
- Companies can improve their profits with financial and operational leverage.
- Financial leverage is achieved by borrowing money at interest rates lower than the return the company can earn with the money.
- Operational leverage, a form of economies of scale, is achieved by using fixed costs to create a proportionate reduction in variable costs. The most common forms of operational leverage are mechanization and automation.
- The breakeven chart is a useful tool to analyze a company's use of leverage and determine its profit potential.
- To create a successful stock buying and selling business, you must be both a successful stock trader and a successful entrepreneur. You must choose stock wisely (effectiveness) and do it at a minimum cost (efficiency).

CHAPTER 7

Tools of the Trade

In any undertaking, some tools are helpful, some even necessary. Tools serve only two purposes: They must add to your effectiveness and increase your efficiency. Effectiveness is how well you reach your objective. Efficiency is how much money, energy, and time it takes to get there. We have already discussed knowledge, patience, and discipline, which are the internal tools you need. We will now discuss some of the external tools that will help you achieve success in your new investing ventures.

Planning for Success

Writing a business plan is the most important and cheapest thing you can do for your business. It is not complicated; it is mostly just common sense. It consists of just six elements: goals, resources, strategies, actions, assumptions, and results. In many ways, it is simply a roadmap that takes you from here to there. The "here" is your current level of finances, expertise, and experience. The "there" is your goal of financial security and independence. Figure 21 illustrates the comparison between a plan and a road map.

Plans usually cover three to five years. This gives the planner plenty of time to acquire resources and implement strategies. As a retiree, you can expect to create four, five, or more five-year plans over the course of your retirement. You should review your current plan annually to determine if the underlying assumptions are still valid and the initial strategies are still productive.

Goals

The first step in planning is to establish your goals. A goal is where you want to go, but we don't want to set just any goals; we want them to be SMART goals. SMART goals are Significant, Measurable, Achievable, Realistic, and Timely.[1] Let's look at each of these attributes.

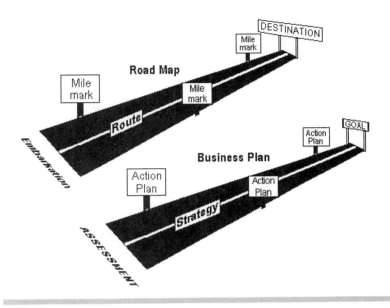

FIGURE 21: Comparison Between a Road Map and a Business Plan. If you can read a road map, you can read and create a plan. Your goal is your destination; your action plans are your mile markers; your strategy is your route.

Significant: Each individual brings different levels of expertise and experience to the business. If you are already invested in the market, continuing your past performance would not be very significant. If you have a fear of the stock market, just moving your nest egg from your bank account to your stock account may be a significant first goal. Your goal must be significant to *you*.

Measurable: Since stocks are quantified in terms of share price and dividends, it is easy to measure how close we have come to achieving our cash flow or capital appreciation goals.

Achievable: There is no incentive greater than success. Set goals that are easy to achieve at your current level of stock expertise. As you achieve, you will learn more and be able to do more.

Realistic: The stock market is filled with examples of investors turning $100 into $10 million in fifteen years. That is achievable, but is it realistic for you? Set goals that reflect your personal understanding, knowledge, and decisiveness.

Timely: A goal needs to be achieved in a reasonable timeframe. Earning $10 on a $100 investment in one year is very different than earning that same $10 over two years. As a retiree, the issue of timeframe is extremely important to you.

Before you can determine if your goal is SMART, you will have to analyze your resources (which you'll do next). An honest self-assessment and resource inventory will allow you to determine how SMART your goal is. If your initial goal appears to be too modest or unrealistic, this is the time to adjust it. Resources will grow, strategies will change, and action plans will be adjusted, but once set, a goal is unwavering. So set them SMART-ly.

Resources

You begin with a self-assessment, an honest look at your internal resources—your strengths and weaknesses. This is where Chapter 1 comes in. If you have completed the self-assessment in Appendix A, you know your strengths and weaknesses. Since strengths tend to define what you can do and weaknesses define what you can't do, any plan that you devise should capitalize on your strengths and eliminate or diminish your weaknesses.

You must also assess your external resources. Examples of external resources are brokers, stock reports, Internet access, library facilities, and online trading capabilities. These are tools of the trade that affect the SMART-ness of your goals. If there are resources you require but don't have, your plan will need to address those requirements.

Strategy

The next question is how do you reach your goal? The answer is your strategy. Your strategy might be to invest, trade, or speculate. There are many different ways to get to the same destination. Once you implement your plan, if one path to your goal becomes blocked, try another. If your safe and staid investments fail to deliver but you seem to have a knack for spotting emerging companies, sell your staid investments and buy your speculations. There is no right strategy. There are only effective and ineffective strategies. In planning, there is a rule: Goals rarely change; strategies always change.

Action

Once you have designed your strategies, you'll need to implement them. A good guide for doing this is an action plan. An action plan is a systematic series of actions designed to help you implement your strategic plan. It consists of an objective, strategy, actions, responsibility, and timing. Note that the action plan has many of the same elements as your business plan. The main differences are the actions, responsibility, and timing. So let's focus on those.

An action is a specific task. Specific people are responsible for the completion of these tasks in fixed time periods. By completing them, you will move toward the action plan objective. Each action plan objective is designed to address an issue that was raised in your business plan. If you successfully complete your tasks, you will meet your action plan objectives. When you meet those objectives, you will achieve your business plan's goals. It is a building process.

The following illustrates a completed action plan. We have decided our best strategy for success is to trade stocks. One of your first action plans will be to open a stock trading account. Since you are a little paranoid, you decide to avoid brokerage houses or online stock trading sites. Instead, you will open the account at your local bank. The action plan to achieve this objective might be as follows:

Objective: To open a stock trading account.

Strategy: Use the services of my local bank.

Step 1: Call the local banks to see which ones offer stock trading.
Responsibility: me
Completion date: 3/1/08

Step 2: Meet with a bank representative to discuss details.
Responsibility: the bank and me

Completion date: 3/7/08

Step 3: Analyze various account details and select a bank.
Responsibility: me
Completion date: 3/14/08

Step 4: Open stock trading account at the bank.
Responsibility: the bank and me
Completion date: 3/21/08

Note that each step in the action plan is a simple task that is within the control of the responsible person or persons. You make the phone calls in Step 1. The bank agrees to meet with you in Step 2. The purpose of the action plan is to implement your strategic goals. To do that, it focuses on the task, person, and timing. In that way, the overall plan is divided into doable chunks. The final step achieves the objective. The sum of the action plan objectives achieves your goal.

By dividing your business plan into a series of simple tasks, implementation becomes less onerous and daunting. It may seem like it is a lot of time and energy, but it is time well spent. In the end, it will save time. It will also prevent you from making some very costly mistakes. Additionally, it will lead to a series of successes that will build your confidence.

Assumptions

As part of your plan, you will want to make some assumptions. For instance, you may assume that over the next five years the economy will be expanding, your health will be good, and your expenses will be modest. Those assumptions will affect your approach to the stock market and the goals and strategies of your business. You will want to make them early in the planning process so you can incorporate them into your thinking.

Results

Finally, your plan should include a projection of results. This will tell you beforehand whether your plan will achieve its goals. In the jargon of the business world, this is a pro forma financial statement. As we discussed in Chapter 6, it consists of an income statement, balance sheet, and cash flow analysis. If the results do not meet your goals, you will have to reformulate strategies or reassess how SMART those goals actually are. It is better to do it now, rather than five years down the road. That is the power of planning; it allows you to correct your faults before they cost you time or money.

It Takes Money to Make Money, or Does It?

You don't need much money to get started in the stock market, but you will need some. Your goal is dependent on three factors: how much money you are willing to invest, how long you are willing to invest it, and your rate of return. Figure 22 illustrates this dynamic relationship as a series of equations.

Figure 22 is not an exact mathematical formula because the rates of return used in the examples presented are compound rates of return (ROR). The actual formulas used to get the answers presented are much more complex. In fact, they are so complex you will never calculate

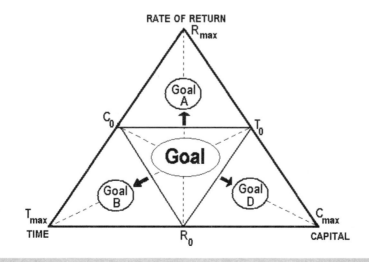

FIGURE 22: Impact of Rate of Return, Time, and Capital on Goals. Strategies are built around your available resources and your ultimate goal. In this case, the resources include your available capital, expected rate of return (based on experience and skills), and your available timeframe.

them yourself. You will use a compound interest table, which can be found in most finance books. (You can also find one on the Internet at *www.us.oup.com/us/pdf/engineeringecon/InterestTables.pdf.*) The compound interest tables do the work for you.

As illustrated in Figure 22, your goal depends on your investment, the time it is invested, and the ROR. Note that the goal doesn't change—how you get there does. With a goal of $100,000, strategies A, B, and C fall short. Even if you have the confidence to invest your entire nest egg ($25,000) in a successful mutual fund (strategy C), you would not achieve your goal. These failures are why you will be investing in individual stocks where RORs of more than 20 percent are possible. All the strategies in Figure 22 assume a small nest egg. However, the formula illustrates by adjusting the amount you have to invest, your confidence in your stock selection skills (ROR), and the time available, you can formulate a winning strategy regardless of your situation. This is the power of planning.

Figure 22 is very instructive with respect to strategy, but what does it tell us about goals? Is $100,000 a SMART goal? It is certainly significant, measurable, and timely, but given the small nest egg, is it achievable or realistic? You have seen that 100 percent stock market returns are possible, but are they realistic given your current level of expertise? Whether your initial goal is SMART depends on you—your resources, your skills, and your timing.

Thus, while money is a necessary resource, the amount you need to start your stock buying and selling business can be very small. As you become a more accomplished stock market professional, the amount you generate could rise to levels beyond your imagination. In order to get to that point, you will have had to execute many successful stock trades. Those successes will give you the confidence you need to make the big bet when the time comes. Until then, bet small, bet often, and learn.

Finding the Money on Your Own

Winning and confidence leads to big money, but where do you get the little money to get started? Obviously, your nest egg is the primary source. If you don't have a nest egg, look around. If you have assets that are not working for you, put them to work. Gather up all those attic and basement treasures and convert them into cash with a garage sale. Instead of using the money for a trip to your local restaurant, open your stock-buying business. If you have few assets but lots of family and friends, ask them to give money in lieu of gifts for birthdays and holidays. Tell them you want to invest in the stock market and their monetary gifts would be a welcome offering. Remember, it doesn't take much to get started.

Borrowing the Money

Another source of funds is borrowing. The only time this is a good option is when you have the confidence that you can successfully earn enough money to pay back the loan. This means you must be an accomplished stock market player with a proven track record, which you're not—yet! But you will be with practice. Set up a pretend business in your mind and operate it for a few years until you have successfully bought and sold stocks at a profit. When you have successfully made money in the pretend business and know why the money was made, then—and only then—should you borrow money to invest.

Where to Get Information

If you are not using stockbrokers for analyses and recommendations, where do you get your ideas? There are several sources, which can be broken down into four categories.

- Print media, such as books, magazines, and newspapers
- Television programs, such as *Wall Street Week* on PBS or *Cashin' In* on Fox
- Newsletters, tipsheets, and services providing stock analysis for a fee
- The Internet

Let's look at a few examples of each.

Print Media

Books

Books are a great instructional source. They provide information on the workings of the stock market, the dynamics of business, and the personalities of the players. The references in the back of this book will get you started. If you are an investor, Peter Lynch's series covers many of the fundamentals of investing. For traders, Clifford Pistolese has a good basic reference on technical analysis, and Toni Turner has provided some additional perspectives in her book on short-term trading. As far as speculators are concerned, Joel Greenblatt's book[2] on "the secret hiding places of stock market profits" provides some recurring speculative opportunities. Another good source of speculative ideas can be found in books on technology or cultural trends, which can be used to predict future business opportunities.

Newspapers

Many localities publish an area business journal that covers local business activities. On a national scale, there are the *Wall Street Journal* and *Investor's Business Daily*. These newspapers specialize in economic, business, and investing news. The *Wall Street Journal* is especially useful since it provides a detailed index of its contents, which allows you to quickly find articles on the stocks you own or the managers who are tending your businesses.

Magazines

Magazines you might find useful include *Smart Money, Forbes*, and *Stocks & Commodities*. These publications cover investing, business, and stock trading, respectively. You can subscribe to these magazines or read them for free at the library.

Many trade journals are also good sources of investment ideas. Trade journals are publications that cater to a specific group of professionals, such as ceramic engineers, metallurgists, physicists, medical doctors, etc. Others are dedicated to hobbyists and educated amateurs like, *Engineering, Psychology Today, AmericanPhoto,* and *Bytes*. These publications are useful to speculators who want to invest in new technologies not yet fully commercialized but showing great promise. Many of these emerging products are the playthings of technophiles long before they become known to the general public.

Television

There are many television shows monitoring the stock market and providing buying and selling recommendations. They include such Fox cable network favorites as *Bulls and Bears, Cashin' In,* and *Cavuto on Business.* Other cable networks have their own in-house gurus, such as Jim Cramer on *Mad Money,* which is an entertaining blend of instruction and stock tips. Consult your local television and radio listings to see what's available in your area.

Newsletters

You can find more precise information from newsletters, tip sheets, and stock selection services. These sources provide in-depth analysis of various companies with varying degrees of bias and accuracy.

Newsletters

Newsletters are offered for subscription fees of $200–$2,000 a year. Using a newsletter to identify stock buys can be very profitable, but be sure they have a confidence level that is conducive to your confidence requirements. To check their confidence level, study their recommendation with the same rigor as you would study your own. Always do your own analysis before buying.

Tipsheets

Tipsheets are usually unsolicited e-mails, print mailings, or phone contacts that provide background information on publicly traded companies in an effort to develop investor interest. They are, at best, a dubious source of information. Beware!

Stock Selection Services

Stock services are more objective, informational sources providing facts about various companies and, in some cases, relating those facts to stock price movements. These services do not usually recommend particular stocks. Their purpose is to identify particular performance traits that correlate to strong stock returns. Two well-known services are Value Line and Zacks. Both can be found in your library or on the Internet.

Internet

The library is one of your best resources for all your informational needs, but as wonderful as it is, the Internet is even more wonderful. The Internet brings the library into your living room. It offers access not just to your local library (with its budget-limited offerings), but to almost unlimited references, advice, and educational opportunities. If you intend to do your own trading, a computer and access to the Internet are invaluable. The Internet will allow you to research companies, search thousands of published documents, track stock movements, access your trading account, and communicate with like-minded investors through chat rooms.

Here are two sites to get you started.

- BigCharts.com provides stock charts for most of the stocks listed on the various national and some regional exchanges.
- Reuters.com is a general informational site with a comprehensive money-and-investing section. The information on various companies and some of the stock market averages in this book can be obtained at Reuters.com.

Both of these are free sites, as are many of the sites on the Internet. Other sites require a subscription fee to access their content. This is especially true of stock trading sites. These fees can range from $50 a year up to $500 per year depending on the depth and timeliness of the information offered. If you choose to subscribe to one of the fee-based sites, be sure the benefits are worth the fees. Remember, you are in business; every investment, even investments in fees, needs to provide a monetary return.

Access to the Trading Floor

You will need access to the various exchanges (such as the New York, American, and NASDAQ exchanges) in order to buy stocks. There are two options available.

Stockbrokers

Before the Internet, investors usually accessed exchanges through a stockbroker. Stockbrokers are compensated with a sales commission, which can range from $50 for small purchases to a percentage of the trade for very large purchases. Their fee, which is paid when you buy and sell a stock, is a fixed cost for each trade.

In the past, individual traders were forced to buy stocks from full-service brokers. These brokers provided access, analysis, and recommendations. Today, recognizing that individual investors have more options (like the Internet), brokers now offer discount services and strictly buy and sell stocks without any analysis or recommendations. These commissions can be one-half to one-third the full-service charges.

Online Trading

One of the new options available to the individual investor is online trading. Online trading allows you to buy and sell stocks on the Internet through a stock trading site. You'll find three types of online trading options:

1. Your local bank
2. A traditional brokerage house (like Charles Schwab)
3. An independent service provider (like eTrade or TDAmeritrade)

These sites charge commission rates as low as $7.99 per 1,000 stocks bought or sold.

Cost

Of the three types of online sites, your bank will charge the highest commission. If the comfort of dealing with your local bank is worth the higher price, you can start there. As you gain comfort and confidence, you may choose to switch to the cheaper and more dedicated trading sites like eTrade and TDAmeritrade.

Tips for Finding a Good Site

When using any of the access options, make sure they are licensed and insured. Investigate them as you would any company, stock, or consultant to ensure they are competent and reputable. A well-chosen access point will protect you from unscrupulous stock-brokers and brokerage houses. Since these houses and sites generally hold your stocks and trading profits for reinvestment, you will want them to be as reliable as your local bank.

Finding a Computer

If you intend to take control of your investment activities, a computer with Internet access is your most important external resource, and it should be the subject of one of your most important action plans. You don't have to buy one; you only need to have access to one, and there are several different strategies you can use to obtain access.

Purchase One

If you have the money, you can buy a new computer for less than $1,000. Even the lowest-priced computers will have more than enough power to satisfy your stock researching and buying needs. If $1,000 is a little steep for your budget, consider buying a used computer. Because of rapid obsolescence, computer geeks will upgrade their computers every two to five years. A two- or three-year-old computer will have all the power and performance you'll need for online stock trading if it has a modem or an Ethernet card. The modem is used to access the Internet using your phone line. The Ethernet card will allow you to access the Internet using a cable or wireless system. The cost of connecting to the Internet by phone is as low as $9.95 per month. Cable connections cost $30–$50 per month.

Borrow One from a Family Member

Not everyone has the resources to implement a buy strategy. Here retirees have an advantage—they can tap into their family, especially a tech-wise grandchild. Let your grandchild show you how to use the computer and access the Internet. Having a computer-savvy child or grandchild will give you an excellent source of instruction and troubleshooting expertise. The beauty of this arrangement is that it isn't a one-way street. As you become a more proficient investor, you can teach your teacher the art of investing—it is a lesson best learned early. You could bestow upon your child or grandchild a gift that every parent seeks to offer—the gift of wealth.

Use One in Your Community

If you don't have the money or access to a family computer, there is the library. Most libraries maintain a bank of computers with Internet access. Many do not even require a library card to use them. If your library hasn't installed computers, request them. The more people requesting a service (or book), the more likely the library will provide it.

If your library has no computers and no plans to install them, there are some other possibilities you can explore. If you have a senior citizens center, check what resources they have. Most local school districts have computer centers. Check to see if they are available to local residents after school hours; also check local vocational schools or community colleges. If all those avenues are blocked, consider creating an investment club. The club could pool their resources and buy a computer. One of the most famous investment clubs was the Beardstown Ladies of Beardstown, Illinois.[3]

Hired Help

If you don't want to pick your own stocks, you have a few resources at your disposal. Each takes you a step away from managing your stocks yourself, but you may want to consider these options when you're still learning the ins and outs of the market.

Stock Gurus

One option is to subscribe to one or more of the numerous newsletters and tipsheets published by stock gurus. Make sure the guru has a good track record before following her advice. They will always tout their winning picks, but you need to know *all* their picks—winners and losers. This will allow you to calculate a confidence level for them. You'll need to know when they recommend you buy the stock and when you should sell it. If they show no losers, be very suspect. If they don't volunteer the information, contact them by phone or e-mail. If you are not confident in them, don't buy what they are selling.

Mutual Funds

Another way to hire people to help you with your investment business is to buy a mutual fund. A mutual fund is a group of stocks bought and sold by a manager. By buying into a family of funds (like Fidelity) or the offerings of your local bank, you get professional management. For a relatively low management fee, you are relieved of the task of finding stocks to buy and sell. If you buy into a family of funds, you are generally allowed to move your money between the various funds they maintain without paying trading penalties, which allows you to alternately focus and diversify your funds.

Exchange Traded Funds (ETF)

Exchange traded funds are similar to mutual funds, except they are not managed and do not carry trading penalties. Yet, they can be bought and sold like individual stocks, which make them more liquid than mutual funds. However, like mutual funds, they are groups of stocks that can be focused or diversified. The major advantages of ETFs over mutual funds are their lower cost (management fees) and their liquidity.

Return on Investment

Whenever you acquire a resource to help you invest in the stock market, be sure to calculate its return on investment. The product or service you buy makes you money and doesn't just cost you money. Any resource you purchase must improve either the effectiveness or the efficiency of your business. Both of these conditions can be quantified, and the return on investment can be calculated.

For instance, if you are traveling to your local library five times a week to use their computers and cable hookup, you are getting a free service. However, if the library is five miles from your home, there is a cost to drive there each week. You need to compare that cost to the cost of a computer, which would allow you to work at home. For instance, if you purchase a $1,000 computer with a five-year life, the cost per year would be $200. If the cost to drive to the library is $260 a year, the cost savings would be $60 ($260 – $200). The return on investment (ROI) is 6 percent ([$60 ÷$1,000] × 100). You have improved the efficiency of your operation by buying a computer.

The above analysis considered efficiency measures. You can also consider effectiveness—how well you do the job. Let's assume over the course of the year you identified five trades that would have earned or saved you $1 a share if you had made them at the opening or closing bell of the stock market. If you owned 100 shares, there is a cost of not being able to make those trades in a timely manner. The cost was $500 dollars (100 shares × $1 × 5 trades). If you had your own computer, you would have reacted faster, and the $1 would not have been lost—you would have been more effective. When you add this level of effectiveness to your analysis, the ROI increases significantly.

What You Have Learned

There are many tools to help you improve the effectiveness and efficiency of your stock buying and selling business. We have only scratched the surface here. As you grow in your experience and skill, you will discover and test the fit of these tools in your business plan. For now, let's review the ones we have discussed in this chapter.

- Like any business, there are tools you can acquire to make you more effective and efficient.
- Any tool you acquire to help you succeed in your stock buying and selling business should provide a return on investment.
- If you have more time than money, spend the time; if you have more money than time, spend the money is a good rule of thumb when it comes to acquiring tools.

- One of the most important tools is a plan—a road map that takes you from where you are to where you want to go—your goal.

- You should build your plan around a set of SMART goals: Goals that are Significant, Measurable, Achievable, Realistic, and Timely.

- A complete plan consists of six elements: goals, resources, strategies, actions, assumptions, and results.

- A strategy answers how you will reach your goal, and it depends on your self-assessment and available resources.

- Action plans are used to help you implement your overall (business) plan.

- Action plans consist of a series of controllable tasks that, when completed, lead to the achievement of the action plan's objective.

- The total of your action-plan objectives equal the achievement of your business-plan goals.

- Other important tools and resources you will need to succeed are capital to invest, information, access to the trading floor, and a computer connected to the Internet.

- When evaluating hired help, make sure their track record meets your confidence requirements—they must deliver more than they cost.

- Your return on investment should consider how the resource improves both your efficiency and effectiveness.

CHAPTER 8

Taking the Measure of the Market

There is a difference between the value of a stock and its price. The value depends on the value of the company it represents. Investors can calculate the company's value using a series of complicated financial formulas adjusted for such intangibles as potential, business attractiveness, and risk. This is the traditional approach used to value a company. The stock value is simply the company value divided by the number of shares of stock issued.

Stock prices are quite different. The price of stock is what people will pay for it. It may or may not be related to the underlying value of the company. Price goes beyond performance; it reflects human behaviors such as greed, bias, fear, and even larceny that are inherent in the market.

Market Value Versus Market Price

Wall Street doesn't always value companies the same as Main Street. Wall Street is a community of investors who buy stocks on the various stock exchanges. Main Street is a community of entrepreneurs who buy businesses in your local community. Wall Street will often value one dollar of profit more than another; Main Street makes no such distinction. There are many reasons for this difference, the most significant being, as you discovered in Chapter 1, the stock market can be divided into three games (investing, trading, and speculating) with three different players (investors, traders, and speculators). That mix of players creates a wide range of attitudes. Before we explore how these attitudes affect stock pricing, let's look at how the market calculates value.

Understanding Capitalization Rate

On Main Street, the value of Company A is the present value of its future earnings. Assuming there is no growth in those earnings, the calculation of present value is simply the current annual earnings divided by the capitalization rate. The capitalization rate is just another way of saying rate of return. The capitalization rate can be anything from the inflation rate to whatever the buyer wishes to earn on her investment (her expected ROR).[1] Let's set it at 10 percent or 0.10. Thus, the overall value of a company with $100,000 in earnings is one million dollars ($100,000 ÷ 0.10). Each share of stock has a proportionate share of that total value. With 1 million shares outstanding, the value of the stock is $1 per share. However, on Main Street, the buyer is buying the entire company (all the shares), so this per-share value will have less meaning to them than Wall Street buyers who are buying just some of the shares.

In the previous calculation, the earnings were known, the growth rate was assumed, the capitalization rate was arbitrarily set at 0.10, and we solved for value. Let's turn the equation around. Let's assume we already know the value of the company—the price of its stock. Since we know earnings and have assumed growth to be zero, we can solve for capitalization rate. With a stock price of $2, the capitalization rate will equal 0.05 or 5 percent ($100,000 ÷ [$2 × 1,000,000 shares]).

Main Street Versus Wall Street

In the above calculations there are only five variables:

1. Earnings
2. Shares outstanding
3. Capitalization rate (or discount rate or expected rate of return)
4. Growth
5. Price

When Main Street calculates the value of a business, it ignores the price of the stock for two reasons. First, most of the companies they buy are not publicly traded on a stock exchange. Second, people on

Main Street don't buy stocks; they buy the entire business. There is one buyer and one business. The buyer is only interested in his return on investment. Thus, he sets the discount or capitalization rate—his personal rate of return.

On Wall Street, there are hundreds of buyers buying small pieces of the company (meaning stocks). One buyer cannot set the discount rate. She knows what it is because she can calculate it based on the price the market has placed on the stock. While she can't set it, it is still important to know because it reflects the financial needs and alternatives of all the buyers and sellers in the market.

Remember, it is the rewards, not the risk, that draws us to the stock market. The capitalization rate tells us what reward the market is demanding in order to invest in a particular company. All performance factors remaining equal, the lower the capitalization rate the lower the reward, and presumably, the lower the risk. This example illustrates the close relationship among capitalization rate, rate of return, and interest rate—they are different ways of expressing the same idea. For instance, when you take your money from a coffee can and place it in a bank savings account, you are promised a 3 percent reward in the form of interest. If that interest rate equals your required rate of return to achieve your goals, a bank account would be a good low-risk strategy.

The capitalization rate is just an inverse use of the interest rate. The interest rate gives you the size of the reward an investment will get you ($100 × 3 percent = $3). The capitalization rate gives you the size of the investment needed to get a given reward ($3 ÷ 3 percent = $100). It is the same number used for different purposes and given a different name. Thus, capitalization rate, interest rate, discount rate, and market attitudes are all derived from similar calculations and can be stated as a single number.

Understanding the Price-to-Earnings Ratio (P/E)

Getting to this revelation required more math than most of us are interested in applying. When it comes to stocks, there must be a simpler measure, and there is. Rather than calculate future earnings adjusted for market attitudes through the capitalization rate, the market simply divides the price of a stock by its earnings per share (EPS).

This shortcut is the price earnings ratio (P/E). It is the heart and soul of stock market valuations.

In the example above, the EPS is simply its net income divided by its shares outstanding (SO) ($100,000 ÷ 1,000,000 = $0.10). The P/E is then calculated by dividing the stock price by the EPS. In the example, where the price is $2, the P/E is 20 ($2 ÷ $0.10 = 20).

What the P/E Means

If all performance factors remain equal, a higher P/E means the market values the company more. Said another way, the market is willing to pay more for the same level of earnings because it believes those earnings are less risky. Everything we need to calculate a P/E is given—the net income of the company, the number of shares it has issued, and the price of its stock. We make no assumptions; there is no guesswork.

The P/E is the inverse of the interest rate (or capitalization rate). Inverting a number means dividing it into the number 1. When we divide 10 into 1, we get 0.10 or 10 percent. Dividing 20 into 1 equals 0.05 or 5 percent. Since you would require a big reward to take a big risk, the reverse is true—a lower reward is associated with lower risk. Since high P/Es equal lower interest rates (rewards), it is clear that higher P/Es also suggest lower risk.

High P/Es indicate that the market considers some earnings more valuable than others, yet a high P/E doesn't tell us why. When you see a stock with a high P/E, try to determine why it carries that premium. Is it the nature of its business, the rate of its growth, the perceived safety of its earnings, or some other factor that has caused buyers to bid up the price of the stock? The same is true for low P/Es. In a future chapter, we will revisit P/E in greater detail.

Pay Me Now

At the common sense level, it seems only reasonable the market would pay more for a certain return than it would for an uncertain return. Yet, the stocks with some of the lowest P/Es (highest risk) pay dividends, which are the most certain form of return. In a pay-me-now or pay-me-later scenario, the market pays a premium for the pay-me-later stocks. Why? You'll discover the answer later. For now, this apparent contradiction is good news for the conservative investor. The market provides a large selection of these low-priced, dividend-paying stocks.

If you are seeking dividends, you'll need to find the value of a dividend-paying stock. You must calculate its yield, payout, earnings stability, and financial exposure. Let's look at each of these measures.

Yield

There are two yields you need to know:

1. The current yield is the annual dividend divided by the current price of the stock.
2. Your personal yield is calculated by dividing the current annual dividend by the price you paid for the stock.

Depending on the success of the company and the length of time you own the stock, personal yields can be drastically higher than the current yield. So if you own a stock with a low current yield, before switching stocks compare the current yield of the new stock to the personal yield of the stock you presently own.

Yields are similar to the interest rate you might get on a savings account, certificate of deposit (CD), or a bond. The difference is, the rates on bonds are fixed and the amount you invested is protected.[2] For instance, the interest rate on a ten-year Treasury Bond is presently 4.78 percent,[3] and the dividend yield on a typical stock is 2.21 percent.[4] However, in ten years, when a $1,000 treasury bond matures, the annual interest payment will still be $47.80, but the stock price and dividend can grow. In ten years, at a typical market growth rate of 12 percent,[5] the new dividend would be $68.64, and the new stock price $3,106. Note that the current yield is still 2.21 percent, but your personal yield is now 6.86 percent. Additionally, there is a $2,106 gain in the price of the stock. Based on lifespan tables, at age 62, the average retiree has fifteen or more years to live, and the practice of automatically shifting money from stocks to CDs or bonds upon retirement could prove very costly. Conversely, shifting your money from CDs to dividend-paying stocks could prove very rewarding in your older years when you need it most.

Payout

Another important measure is payout—the amount of earnings paid to stockholders as dividends. Payouts can range from 0 percent for companies that pay no dividends to 80 percent or higher for companies that pay almost all of their earnings to the shareholders. In general, when it comes to dividend-paying stocks a high dividend yield and a low payout is the ideal situation because it provides a large immediate return on your investment and indicates the company has earnings left over to invest in growth and support future dividends.

Earnings Stability and Growth

Dividends are paid from earnings and cash flow. A stable flow of earnings is necessary if a company is to maintain and grow its dividend payments. Past earnings performance can help you project future performance, but make sure there are no surprises on the horizon by researching the company's upcoming plans.

When buying dividends, you cannot ignore growth. Forecasting earnings growth requires information, common sense, and intuition. For instance, utilities are good dividend stocks, but make sure the utility you buy is serving a vibrant and growing marketplace. If their industrial and commercial customer base is dying and people are moving away, the long-term prospects of the utility may be stagnant or worse. For instance, comparing two electric utilities with similar sales levels but different geographic locations show very different growth and stock price histories. One company located in California with a five-year sales growth of 4.6 percent per year had a five-year stock price increase of 247 percent. A similar company located in Ohio with a five-year sales growth of 2.2 percent per year had a five-year stock price increase of 167 percent. Both companies produced the same product, but one was in a growing market (California) and the other wasn't (Ohio).

Financial Exposure

No matter how high the dividend, you do not want to be holding stock in a bankrupt company. Small investors rarely come out on top in these situations—the first person to feel the pinch of a financial squeeze is the stockholder. Don't be lured to an investment by high dividend yields if the company offering those yields is burdened with high debt. Make sure the company you buy has sufficient cash flow to pay its bills.

Or Pay Me Later

Stock market experts used to contend that the price of a stock is simply the present value of its anticipated dividend stream. Unfortunately, fewer than 30 percent of the companies listed on the various stock exchanges actually pay dividends.[6] Seventy percent of the listed companies either have no earnings or retain all their earnings for internal use. How would these market experts value these dividend-free companies? Do they even have a value?

Of course they have a value, but without a dividend to build on, how do we arrive at that price? Investors have decided it is not the dividends paid that matters, but the dividend that could be paid. In essence, they value the company as if they paid all its earnings to its stockholders, as if it had a 100 percent payout. This brings us back to the price earnings ratio.

Price-to-Earnings Ratio (P/E)

Microsoft, which led the personal computer revolution and has been enormously profitable over the past twenty years, paid no dividends until its recent one-time dividend amounting to less than a 1 percent yield. You may think that such a sorry history of dividend payments would render Microsoft's stock worthless. However, to the market, dividends are not the sole measure of Microsoft's stock price or its value. What's important is what it could pay.

Main Street Versus Wall Street

This leads to the price earnings ratio (P/E), which is a comparison of the price of a stock to the total earnings of the company. You may notice that P/E measures the company's value at the net-income level. Net income is what's left after the government takes its cut in the form of taxes. It is from net income that dividends are paid.

With Main Street valuations, we could choose to use pretax income to value the business and its stock. That's because as a Main Street buyer, you have access to profits at the pretax level. The Main Street owner can take profits in the form of salary, bonuses, pension set asides, and various other perks like insurance, cars, planes, and consulting fees, because she has the power to hire herself into the company. These are all pretax expenditures. Wall Street buyers, especially small investors, have no such power or access. They get their rewards after everyone else gets their cut, including the government. They take their rewards from net income.

Using P/E to Compare Stocks

P/E also allows us to compare the market price of a company to the market value of its peers. Because of the differences in the number of shares outstanding (SO), stock prices are not directly comparable; they need to be adjusted for SO. Because P/E is based on EPS, which is based on SO, the adjustment is built in.

P/E gives us an idea of what the market is thinking, but it doesn't tell us why they are thinking it. To answer that question, we'll have to dig deeper. There are some measures that help us do that.

The Price Earnings-to-Growth Ratio (PE/G)

The stock market is just one way to invest your money, so why choose it? There are two major reasons. The first is liquidity. It is easy to buy and sell stocks. The second reason is growth. It is the promise of growing dividends and earnings that make stocks attractive investments.

Since earnings growth is such an important determinant of a stock's price, it needs to be included in any meaningful stock valuation calculation. Calculations like P/E have the growth component built in, but they also have a multitude of other market attitudes built in. PE/G is an attempt by the analysts to separate the growth component of the P/E from the other components. It does this by dividing the P/E by the forecasted annual earnings growth rate of the company.[7] The resulting ratio is the Price Earnings-to-Growth ratio, or PE/G. PE/G is simply an earnings growth-adjusted P/E.

Comparing Growth Rates

Table XI compares the P/Es and PE/Gs of companies with different growth rates. In Table XI, the company has 1 million in SO. The discount rate used in the present value analysis was 10 percent, and the net incomes were projected thirty years into the future.

In Table XI, the stock price equals the per-share present value. Present value is a method used by finance people to assign a current value to a future payment. Or, as Wimpy in the Popeye comics used to say, "I'll gladly pay you tomorrow for a hamburger today." Present value allows you to determine how big a hamburger you should give him for that promised payment. In this case, you are seeking to set a current price on a stock that promises increasing earnings in the future.

The present value for the 0 percent growth is $943,000. This differs from our previous zero-growth calculation because the earnings are only projected for thirty years. As we add years to the projection, the present value would approach the million dollar valuation calculated

TABLE XI
Impact of Earnings Growth on P/E and PE/G

		1	2	3	4	5	6	7
A	Current Net Income	$100,000	$100,000	$100,000	$100,000	$100,000	$100,000	$100,000
B	Current EPS	$0.10	$0.10	$0.10	$0.10	$0.10	$0.10	$0.10
C	Growth Rate	0%	3%	5%	10%	15%	20%	30%
D	Present Value[8] @ 10%	$0.943 million	$1.267 million	$1.581 million	$3.002 million	$6.431 million	$15.130 million	$96.899 million
E	Share Value (Price) (D ÷ SO)	$0.943	$1.269	$1.581	$3.002	$6.431	$15.130	$96.899
F	P/E (E ÷ B)	9.43	12.67	15.81	30.02	64.31	151.30	968.99
G	PE/G (F ÷ C)	Infinite[9]	4.22	3.16	3.00	4.29	7.56	32.30

earlier. In this example, at 0 percent growth the P/E is 9.43. Any P/Es larger than that would imply the market is assigning other premiums (besides growth) to the price of the stock. The P/E in column 1 becomes our reference point.[10]

From that reference, we can determine the effect of growth. As growth increases, the present value increases, which increases the stock's price. Since both the current earnings and the shares outstanding are fixed, the P/E increases. In this example the variation in the P/E is strictly a function of growth, so we can use the P/Es in Table XI to determine how well the PE/G metric isolates the growth component—the more constant the PE/G, the more accurate the isolation. It works well up to the 20 percent growth rate—the PE/Gs are fairly constant at those lower growth rates.

Comparing Discount and Growth Rates

PE/G is determined by dividing the P/E by the earnings growth rate. The goal is to isolate the impact of growth on P/E from the other factors increasing or decreasing it. We are only partially successful. At the extremes (very low or very high growth rates), PE/G provides very little comparative guidance. However, PE/G does appear to provide some comparative guidance in the midrange (columns 2–5). Even within this midrange, PE/G is not the perfect metric because there is a very big assumption in our calculation.

Let's look at that big assumption in the PE/G—the discount rate. Table XII provides the same information provided in Table XI, except the PV is now calculated with a discount rate of 5 percent instead of 10 percent.

Our attempt to isolate growth and establish an absolute reference point for PE/G is hindered by the impact of the discount rate. When we calculate a PE/G of 7.50, do we conclude the market projects growth to be 20 percent, as in Table XI, with a 10 percent discount rate? Or is it projecting 3 percent growth because it's using the 5 percent discount rate of Table XII? Again, too much is unknown.

While P/E and PE/G allow us to compare various companies and groups of companies, it is clear they are dynamic measures fraught with many complexities and nuances. They are not absolute; they should only

TABLE XII							
Impact of Discount Rate and Earnings Growth on P/E and PE/G							
	1	**2**	**3**	**4**	**5**	**6**	**7**
A Current Net Income	$100,000	$100,000	$100,000	$100,000	$100,000	$100,000	$100,000
B Current EPS	$0.10	$0.10	$0.10	$0.10	$0.10	$0.10	$0.10
C Growth Rate	0%	3%	5%	10%	15%	20%	30%
D Present Value @ 5%	$1.538 million	$2.258 million	$3.001 million	$6.685 million	$16.476 million	$43.162 million	$314.884 million
E Share Value Price (D ÷ SO)	$1.538	$2.258	$3.001	$6.685	$16.476	$43.162	$314.884
F P/E (E ÷ B)	15.38	22.58	30.01	66.85	164.76	431.62	3148.84
G PE/G (F ÷ C)	Infinite	7.53	6.00	6.68	10.99	21.58	104.96

be used as invitations to further investigation. Yet, P/E is probably the single best starting point from which to analyze a company's health and potential, unless—and it is a big "unless"—the company has no earnings. Without earnings, neither the P/E nor the PE/G can be calculated, and in September 2006, after a four-year economic recovery, 42 percent of the companies listed reported zero or negative net incomes. How does the market value a company with no earnings? On Main Street, the focus would shift to assets, but our business is on Wall Street. Without earnings, we will need a new measure, something other than assets.

Price-to-Sales Ratio

While it is true earnings are the true worth of a company, it is also true sales have value. It takes time, money, and labor to generate sales. Thus, the value of an unprofitable business is the sum of the value of its assets and the value of the sales generated by those assets. The stock market recognizes this "business value" by pricing an unprofitable company's stock at something greater than its assets. To determine this price, the market uses sales.

Since sales represent the business value of the assets—that's what the assets have created—they can be isolated and valued. This is done with the price-to-sales ratio (P/S). The price-to-sales ratio answers the question, "How much are investors willing to pay for a dollar of sales?" It is similar to the P/E, which answers the question, "How much are investors willing to pay for a dollar of earnings?" The P/S is calculated by dividing the current stock price by the annual sales per share of stock (Price ÷ [Sales ÷ SO] = P/S). It is basically the same calculation as P/E, using sales instead of earnings.

Why would any investor pay for a dollar of unprofitable sales? They buy with the expectation the sales will generate future profits. Remember our breakeven analysis of the ABC Company in Figure 19 (Chapter 6). This is not far from the illogic of dividends, where dividends in the future are worth more than dividends in hand. In a sales-based valuation, earnings in the future are worth more than earnings in hand.

It was under this valuation scheme that the Internet Bubble inflated and burst. According to the experts, unprofitable Internet companies were good buys because the Internet was the wave of the future, with big profits just around the corner. The experts considered Internet companies such good buys, many were priced higher than old-line companies with a fifty-year history of growth and profitability. Unfortunately, many of these Internet companies not only had sales without profits, but as illustrated in Figure 20 (Chapter 6), the more sales they generated the less profit they made. The experts were wrong: the Internet Bubble burst, and the NASDAQ, the home for most of the Internet stocks, collapsed. One look at Figure 20 and they would have known better.

So why teach P/S if it is a failed valuation method? P/S is not a failed method; it was simply misapplied in the case of the Internet Bubble. The profit potential of sales can be a useful valuation basis. Remember our discussion of breakeven: A low P/S, combined with a good business model as defined by a breakeven chart, could indicate a very lucrative investment opportunity if the company is also growing sales. A measure like P/S is not a stand-alone metric; it is necessary to observe P/S in light of some other measure. Such a measure is earnings growth to sales growth, or EG/SG (earnings growth ÷ sales growth).

EG/SG is a test of a company's business model and its ability to leverage its sales. When sales are leveraged, the earnings grow faster than sales. Thus, the EG/SG should be greater than 1.00. An EG/SG of less than one is a red flag. Unlike P/E-based measures, the EG/SG model can even be adapted to companies that have no earnings because it can measure how effectively management is using sales growth to shrink their losses, which will allow you to predict how quickly the company can achieve breakeven and begin generating profits.

Miscellaneous Valuation Models

There are many valuation measures besides price-to-earnings, price-to-sales, and price earnings-to-growth ratios.

Price-to-Book Ratio (P/B)

In his book *The Intelligent Investor*, Benjamin Graham[11] popularized the price-to-book ratio. It is calculated by dividing the stock price by the tangible book value per share. Tangible book value is the value of hard assets like buildings, land, and inventories minus the amount of debt owed by the company. This value, when divided by the shares outstanding, yields the book value per share (BVS). You then divide the BVS into the stock price to get the price-to-book value ratio (P/B). A P/B of less than 1.00 indicates the liquidation value of the company is greater than the price of the stock. Logic suggests that such a stock is underpriced and provides the stockholder protection against bankruptcy. Don't believe it!

There are two things wrong with P/B. First, if a company goes bankrupt stockholders usually get nothing. By the time the lawyers, creditors, and management take their cuts, nothing is left for the small investor. The second reason it is useless is especially important to retirees: Bankruptcies take time—years and years. Retirees can't afford to wait. You can find better ways to invest than buying the stock of low P/B companies.

Price-to-Cash Ratio (P/C)

Another valuation method that is equally precarious is the price-to-cash ratio (P/C). It is similar to the P/B, except you only use one type of asset in the calculation. It is calculated by dividing the price of the stock by the amount of cash or cash equivalents per share a company has on hand (Price ÷ [{Cash + Cash Equivalents} ÷ Shares Outstanding]= P/C). The amount of cash in a company could be a prelude to an acquisition or an unexpected dividend—but that is pure conjecture. Unless you have inside information on how the cash will be used, P/C is another measure offering few insights other than the company is generating more money than it knows how to reinvest.

Price-to-Cash-Flow Ratio (P/CF)

The P/C should not be confused with the P/CF (price-to-cash-flow ratio). The P/CF can be a very useful valuation method. The P/CF measures how much cash a company is generating, and is a way to determine how safe your investment is. It is calculated by dividing the price by the free cash flow per share generated by the company's operation (Price ÷ [Free Cash Flow ÷Shares Outstanding] = P/CF). The term *free cash flow* means the amount of cash left over after necessary capital expenditures to maintain operations are made.

The P/CF is especially useful if you are considering investing in companies not generating a profit. Such companies may offer significant potential for future earnings, but before they can realize that potential, they must survive their present misfortunes or growing pains. Using P/CF can help you determine whether they are generating sufficient cash to pay their bills, but be sure the cash flow is from operations. If it is from asset sales or borrowing, you may not be buying a viable business—you may just be buying into a Ponzi scheme (or pyramid scheme).

The Warren Buffet Model

Before we leave stock market metrics, let's look at a variation on the growth/valuation model that is reportedly used by the highly successful investor Warren Buffet.[12] Mr. Buffet compares the company's earnings growth rate to the growth rate of the company's stock price. The calculation is stock price growth (SPG) divided by EPS growth, which I will call the price-growth-to-earnings-growth ratio (SPG ÷ EPS growth = PG/EG). Both the price and earnings growth rates are annual numbers based on 3–5 years of historical data. PG/EGs above 1.00

indicate that stockholders are bidding the price of the stock up at a faster rate than the company is increasing its earnings. It is an interesting observation that attempts to capture the market's attitude toward a particular stock. It seeks to identify growth stocks with increasing P/Es, which is one of the key attributes of a ten-bagger.

What You Have Learned

These are just a few of the valuation methods you will discover on your journey through the various stock exchanges. Each is designed to serve a purpose; none should be used in isolation. They should not be treated as buy or sell signals. Valuation ratios like price-to-earnings, price-earnings-to-growth, price-to-sales, and earnings-growth-to-sales-growth should be viewed as invitations to peek into the inner workings of the company. If you are led to an investment opportunity after you take that peek, the valuation has served its purpose. That is all you should ask of it, and all you should expect from it. Let's review.

- In order to make valid comparisons, the market analyzes companies on a per-share basis.
- Dividends provide a certainty of returns. They are measured using yield and payout. The yield is the amount of the dividend divided by the current price of the stock. It is analogous to interest rate or return on investment. Payout is the percentage of the total amount of earnings paid in dividends.
- Growth is one of the most important reasons to invest in the stock market. With growth, your personal yield can be higher than the current yield. Personal yield is calculated by dividing the current dividend by the price you paid for the stock (not its current price).
- Early stock valuations focused on the dividend stream. Today, experts agree that valuations should be based on the total earnings of the company.
- The past performance of a company is not the sole determinate of its price. Other factors like market attitudes, future growth, and alternative investment opportunities must be considered.

- The price-to-earnings ratio (P/E) was developed to compare the market attitude toward various companies. High P/Es indicate the market is willing to pay more for a dollar of profit earned by the company. The reason for this could be the company is growing, its earnings are stable, and or its financial situation is secure.

- Since so many unknowns are built into the P/E, you should only use it as an invitation to study the company further.

- You must carefully scrutinize other stock market measures like the price-to-sales ratio (P/S), price-to-book value (P/B), or price-to-cash flow (P/CF). They are generally used to measure the company's potential for profit. They provide a means of comparing unprofitable companies where a P/E cannot be calculated.

- As a small investor, you should avoid companies that have earnings-growth-to-sales-growth ratios (EG/SG) below 1.00. Unless management has provided a well-thought-out explanation, EG/SGs below 1.00 indicate that the company is failing to achieve operational and financial leverage, which enhances profitability.

- Market metrics alone cannot pick winning stocks or avoid market scams; they simply point you toward strong stocks. Your common sense, analytical skills, and exhaustive research will help you uncover the winners and avoid the losers.

CHAPTER 9
Your Guide to Investing

As an investor, your focus will be on the performance of the company. Your goal is to find a company offering good future prospects. In the stock market, you are always buying the future; the past and present are simply clues to what the future might hold. Picking companies with a profitable past increases your confidence that you made a sound investment decision.

The investor recognizes the market influences price, but that influence is short term. Investors are interested in the long term. They analyze the company's fundamental metrics such as earnings, sales level, growth, and debt load to determine a stock's value—which is why we've spent so much time discussing these things. Investors buy stock in the same way Main Street buys companies, with one eye firmly fixed on the future and the other on past performance.

The guiding principle of stock analysis is that earnings drive price. Companies with high earnings will have high stock prices. Those with low earnings will have lower stock prices. However, earnings per share is not the only metric in the game. The price of a share of stock also depends on growth potential and debt load.

If this level of mathematical rigor is beyond you or you simply lack an interest in the inner workings of an operating business, investing is not for you. Serious investors are businesspeople. They don't have to be Harvard MBAs, but they do enjoy delving into the inner workings of a company, for it is in those inner workings they will find the future value of a company and its stock.

This is a good time to revisit your self-assessment in Appendix A to see if you have the aptitude, interest, and willingness to be an investor. There is no doubt investing is the most mathematically challenging of the three approaches to the market. If you don't have the personality for it, play a different game. If you dive into investing unprepared and uncommitted, you'll take shortcuts, make mistakes, and miss opportunities.

However, if investing fits you, this chapter will get you started with what you need to know—it will provide the basics. Let's begin with the fundamental metrics used to analyze the performance of a company.

The Fundamentals

There are three score cards used to monitor a company: income statement, balance sheet, and cash flow analysis. In Chapter 6, we discussed those score cards, and we will use the same score cards presented in Table VII and Table VIII to build our investment analysis. From these score cards, you will want to build a profile of the key performance ratios for the company. Again, the performance ratios were described in Chapter 6, Table IX. They are reviewed in Table XIII with the actual ratios for Company XYZ included. They are the pulse points of the company. They provide clues as to how healthy the company is and how effectively and efficiently the management is using the company's assets to generate sales and profit growth.

TABLE XIII
Common Performance Ratios for Company XYZ

Performance Measure	Calculation	XYZ
Sales-to-Assets	Sales ÷ Total Assets	1.68
Return on Sales	Net Income ÷ Sales	7.0%
Gross Margin	Gross Profit ÷ Sales	35.0%
Return on Assets	Net Income ÷ Total Assets	11.7%
Return on Equity	Net Income ÷ Total Equity	23.3%
Debt-to-Equity	Long-Term Debt ÷ Total Equity	0.67
Days Receivable	(Receivables ÷ Sales) × 365	43.8
Days Inventories	(Inventories ÷ Cost of Goods) × 365	33.7
Current Ratio	Current Assets ÷ Current Liabilities	2.0
Quick Ratio	(Cash + Receivables) ÷ Current Liabilities	1.4
Interest Coverage	(Pretax Profit + Interest) ÷ Interest Expense	5.4

Compare the ratios presented in Table XIII to the significance of those ratios presented in Table IX. Where has XYZ done a good job? Where does it need improvement? In areas where XYZ is weak, you can calculate a set of ratios for previous years to see if XYZ's management has been taking action to correct those weaknesses. Thus, if the sales-to-asset ratios for the two previous years were 1.0 and 1.25, respectively, this positive trend would reduce your concern over the low S/A of 1.68 in Table XIII. Most companies will report 3–5 years of past financial data, which will allow you to identify both positive and negative trends. These reports are found in their annual reports or on the Internet at sites like *www.reuters.com.*

Table XIII is just the beginning. From there, we will build a comprehensive review of the company's stock, and we will attempt to develop some insights into the market's past, present, and future attitude toward the company and its stock. We will then compare their attitude to ours to see if there is an investment opportunity. The opportunity may be inherent in the performance of the company, or it may be related to the dynamics of the market's reaction to the company. Let's use the data on Company XYZ to build that investment analysis.

Building an Investment Analysis

Before you invest in a company, you should analyze it from five different perspectives: business, earnings, growth, potential, and risk. Your objective is to evaluate past performance and project that performance into the future. Remember, all investing is forward looking. We analyze the past for only one purpose—to open a window on the future. In that regard, the most important criterion in our list is potential. A company with a rich past but a poor potential is a risky investment choice. However, a company with a rich potential but a lousy history can be equally risky if the management cannot get its act together. As important as potential is, we'll begin with business.

Business

The sales-to-asset ratio (S/A) is a good metric for determining the effectiveness of a company's business efforts. For Company XYZ, it is 1.68. A good rule of thumb is that a company should achieve $3 in sales for every $1 in assets. However, that is not carved in stone, and different industries have different S/A potentials. It's more practical to compare it to its peers. Peer-group data on all our metrics can usually be found on websites like *www.reuters.com*. For instance, the median S/A for all the companies listed on the various exchanges is 2.1, which is lower than the ideal.[1] However, more industry-specific S/As are available, which compare your company to its competitors.

The **gross profit margin** (GM) is another good metric. It identifies how effective the company is at converting sales into profits. Analysts measure this at the gross-profit level because gross profit is taken before the costs of management compensation, product development, financial structure, and marketing are deducted. For XYZ, it is a healthy 35 percent. Again, compare this number to its peers. Gross profits can range from 65 percent for drug companies to as low as 5 percent for distributors.

Our business perspective needs to include some stock market valuation metrics. A good starting point is the **price-to-sales ratio** (P/S). As we said earlier, this indicates the value the market places on $1 of sales. In the XYZ example, where we assumed 10 million shares outstanding and a $14 share price, the P/S is 1.40 ($14 ÷ [$100 million ÷ 10 million shares]). The median P/S for market-listed companies is 1.51. Yet, the average P/S for that same listing is 108. Such a large divergence between median and average indicates a great deal of volatility and extreme values at the high end. Thus, it's essential when you're comparing the stocks of different companies to make sure they're in the same industry.

Company size has a big impact on the value of the P/S. For instance, the average annual sales volume for companies with P/S values of 108 or larger is just $1.19 million, and the average P/S of those small companies is 3,387 with a median of 296. However, the average sales volume of companies with P/S values of 1.51 or less is more than $2.3 billion. Also, the larger companies' average P/S value is 0.55 with a median of 0.49. The larger companies appear to be more settled, less volatile, and closer to normal. It is important when making comparative judgments using P/S to limit your comparisons to similar size companies.

Investors are willing to pay more for $1 of sales if the company can convert that dollar into profits. For instance, the average P/S in the automotive industry is 0.54. In the drug industry, it is 9.76. Why is the market willing to pay $9.76 for $1 of drug sales and only $0.54 for $1 of car sales? Because drug companies earn $0.20 in net income on every dollar of their sales, while automobile companies only earn $0.02 on each of their sales dollars. The size of the sales is not the only thing affecting P/S; it is also the size of the earnings.

Earnings

One important earnings metric is return on total assets (ROA). This is similar to the interest on your savings account. It indicates the return earned on the total amount of money that has been invested in the company by stockholders, bond holders, banks, and trade partners. The ROA for XYZ is 11.7 percent, which compares well to your bank account at just 3 percent. Another useful profit metric is the return on equity (ROE). ROE measures the return on the shareholder's portion of those assets. For XYZ, ROE is 23.3 percent. Notice the magnifying effect of financial leverage on the ROE versus the ROA. This only occurs if the management is effectively using its debt and assets.

The most important aspect of profits is its effect on stock price. This leads us back to the gold standard of stock market metrics—the price-earning ratio (P/E). For XYZ, the P/E equals 20 ($14 ÷ $0.70). The inverse of the P/E is the return on the current value of the stockholder's investment in the company, which in this case is 5 percent ($1 ÷ 20 × 100 = 5\%$). The return on the stockholder's equity (ROE) is not the same as the return on the stockholder's investment (1 ÷ P/E). Equity is a reflection of past performance as measured by paid-in capital and retained earnings. Stockholder investment is a reflection of future performance and is calculated using stock prices and the number of shares outstanding. As such, it encompasses past performance, current performance, future performance, stock market liquidity, economic trends, personal investment objectives, and industry prejudices. More than any of those considerations, it represents future growth.

Growth

You cannot fully appreciate the impact of growth on the price of a stock without understanding the time value of money. Money loses value over time because of inflation. If someone offered to pay you $1 next year, what would you be willing to pay today for that promise? With prices rising 3 percent a year, if you gave them $1 today for $1 in a year, you would lose 3 percent in purchasing power. To break even, you would offer something less than $1—approximately 3 percent less, or $0.97. Thus, your payment is discounted for the effects of inflation. If you were promised ten years of payments, each of the ten payments would be discounted. That is the time value of money.

When you buy a stock, you are not buying what it has done, but what it will do in the future. And you must pay for it today. To determine what you should pay, you need to discount the future earnings of the company. In this case, the discount rate is not inflation; it is the return you think you can get elsewhere. Each person has a unique set of alternative investments, which means each investor will use a different discount rate to establish a price for the stock.

What is a fair price for XYZ's stock? The answer is in the calculation used to construct Table XI in Chapter 8. If XYZ is growing earnings 10 percent per year, the calculated value is $20.62. At $14 a share, XYZ is underpriced. Unless you can find some other reason for the market's pessimism toward XYZ, it would be a candidate for further study.

Potential

One area of further study is the company's potential to maintain or create the growth you have forecasted for it. Potential is the most elusive of the five analysis criteria. Sales, earnings, and past growth are historical facts—they are what was and what is. Potential is about what will be, and that is at the heart of the investment decision. Investors, traders, and speculators are all buying the same thing—future performance.

Potential is the most enjoyable and enlightening part of your stock buying and selling business. Assessing potential will draw you into new worlds and force you to overcome old biases. When you isolate a group of companies using historical metrics like sales, earnings, and past growth, the easy part is done. Anyone with a computer, online connection, and a good stock-screening tool can do it, but determining whether those metrics will continue into the future is the point where your stock-buying business will succeed or fail.

Where is the crystal ball that will help you see into the future? It is in you—your experiences, education, curiosity, and persistence. If you spot a company seeking to produce widgets, you need to understand the value of widgets: who would buy them, how many they would buy, and how often they would buy. Are there companies that make a better widget, a cheaper widget, or a simpler widget? Is there a growing demand for widgets or is the market stagnant or shrinking? Is this new technology, old technology, continually changing technology? At what stage in the life cycle are widgets? Is the company the market leader, a hungry second, or a perpetual also-ran? The answers to these questions combine to give you a sense of the company's potential and future performance.

Where do you find these answers? Everywhere. Newspapers are good sources, especially a national edition such as the *Wall Street Journal*. Magazines are another good source. There is a magazine for just about every subject matter, from medicine to technology to investing to banking to crafts to whatever product your company of interest makes. For instance, in business there are *Forbes, BusinessWeek,* and *Entrepreneur.* These magazines often include sections on innovations in the field of science and medicine. Television, radio, and word of mouth are other sources of information. If there is a buzz about a product or trend and your company is in the thick of it, there may be a long-term opportunity there. Most of this buzz can be found or confirmed on the Internet at websites like Yahoo! and Reuters. Most of the publications mentioned above also have websites carrying news, updates, and buzz!

When it comes to potential, look for competitive advantages such as distribution expertise (Wal-Mart), high capital costs (General Motors), government regulation (utilities), technology (IBM), personnel (Microsoft), etc. One unassailable competitive edge is a patent or a copyright. A company that holds a patent has a twenty-year (or more in the case of copyrights) exclusive right to profit from an innovation.

To get a better idea how companies can establish and maintain a competitive edge, read a book on marketing.[2]

Among the things that can inhibit a company's performance and make its stock a poor investment are government regulations restricting trade, competition suppressing prices and profits, and changing technology making a product obsolete. Another risk in any business is poor management. If you identify companies that are operating at low sales-to-asset ratios, meager profit margins, or generating stagnant sales growth, especially compared to their peers, approach them with caution. Until new management is installed, the future might reflect the past, which would not bode well for your investment.

When you study stocks, you are studying yourself, your neighbors, your friends, and your lifestyle. The more you study; the more you learn. The more you learn; the more you understand. The more you understand; the more success you will achieve as an investor.

Risk

There is always a risk that a company will go bankrupt. For the small investor, bankruptcy is bad, very bad. It doesn't matter what kind of bankruptcy it is—Chapter 7, Chapter 11, or Chapter 13—there are no good chapters when it comes to the small investor. Therein lies the problem. The market has a big influence on stock prices, and big investors, institutions, and hedge funds have a big influence on the market. Many experts claim that the market is efficient. They argue all the available knowledge is built into the price—the business, profits, growth, potential, and risk. Thus, there is no reason for the small investor to assess risk, because the market has already done that and built it into the price. Nonsense!

Big investors, institutions, and hedge funds have a different view of risk than you. They are not at that table to look after your interests; they are there to protect their own. In a bankruptcy, they are the first to know, first to sell, and first to get their share after management, banks, and lawyers have taken their chunk of the spoils. You must take care of yourself.

When it comes to risk, cash is more important than profits. There are three reasons for this. First, profits don't pay the bills, cash does.

Secondly, there are those pesky fixed costs. No matter where your business is on the breakeven chart, those fixed costs must be paid. Third, profits are single sourced. They are generated from operations—the making and selling of product. Cash can come from many sources—operations, banks, bonds, investors, asset sales, etc.

Our immediate concern is the short term, and the ability of the company to pay its current obligations—the current liabilities. They include such items as accrued employee wages, materials purchased on credit, and long-term debts due in the coming year. The cash used to pay these immediate bills comes primarily from the current assets. They include such items as cash, receivables, and inventories. These items are either cash or can be converted into cash within thirty to ninety days. By dividing the current assets by the current liabilities, you can calculate a current ratio (CR), which provides a simple metric for determining short-term risk. In our XYZ example, the CR is 2.0. A CR above 1.5 is acceptable.

Long-term viability of a company is the ability of the company to cover its fixed costs. Most references on the subject will focus on the ability of the company to pay the interest on its long-term debt. That metric is interest coverage, and the interest coverage at XYZ is 5.4. A 5.4 interest coverage is good; coverage below 2.0 is suspect; below 1 is dangerous.

Complicating the long-term risk analysis is leverage. The breakeven for XYZ occurs at 70 million units (refer to Figure 19). Below that point, the only cash available to cover the fixed cost must come from depreciation, borrowing, asset sales, or stockholders. A 30 percent decline in sales could force XYZ into bankruptcy. Thus, long-term risk is not simply a matter of interest coverage; it involves fixed cost levels, sales volatility, and profitability. These must be balanced to determine if a company is generating and managing sufficient cash to pay its short- and long-term obligations, even in a business downturn.

When it comes to risk, success can become failure. For example, Figure 23 is the breakeven chart for a company similar to XYZ. The difference is its fixed costs are very low, but its variable costs are higher, which reduces its incremental margin. In XYZ, the incremental margin was $0.37. In this new company, the fixed costs have been

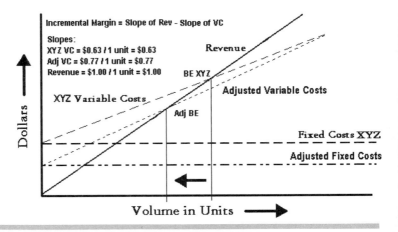

FIGURE 23: Impact of Lower Fixed Cost on Incremental Margin. Lowering the fixed costs can lower the breakeven point. However, if that is achieved by increasing variable costs, a company can grow itself into bankruptcy when its additional profits from growth do not cover the additional capital requirements of growth.

reduced from $26 million to $16 million and the variable cost has been increased from $0.63 to $0.77. This yields an incremental margin of $0.23. Every additional dollar of sales will deliver just $0.23 in additional profits.

On the balance sheet, receivables and inventories are closely tied to sales. At $100 in sales, the company carries $18 million in receivables and inventories. If the company were to double sales, it would create an additional $18 million in receivables and inventories. The company must finance this increase in assets.

The additional $100 million in sales will generate an additional $23 million in pretax profits. Assets are financed with after-tax earnings, but the after-tax increase in profits from the additional sales is just $14.6 million. This is an impressive 109 percent increase in net income, but it is not enough to finance the $18 million in current assets needed to support it. The balance sheet is out of balance. The company must reduce its current assets, borrow more money, sell more stock, work out an arrangement with suppliers, or file for protection under the bankruptcy act. The company has grown itself into bankruptcy; success has led to failure. That is the complexity of risk.

Investment Strategies

Once you have chosen investing as your game, you have three ways to play it. The first is dividends, where you focus on certainty of outcome and cash flow. The second is value, where you focus on the discrepancy between the price of a stock and its underlying value. The third is growth, where you focus on the future growth of earnings.

Dividend

The dividends paid by a company are primarily dependent on the company's performance. Therefore, a dividend strategy will tend to reduce investment risk because it reduces the impact of market attitudes. A dividend approach is touted as a retirement strategy. The reason is dividends provide retirees with an income. Investors in dividend stocks receive monthly, quarterly, or annual dividend checks. Their investment provides cash without the investor having to sell all or part of their investment.

Another reason many analysts recommend a dividend strategy to retirees is dividend-paying companies are usually more mature and settled, have proven track records, and operate in established markets. They are viewed as conservative investments, with less performance and price volatility than other listed stocks. Of course, the very maturity of these stocks means investors cannot expect much in the way of a long-term price bonanza. However, a well-managed company with just a 5 percent annual dividend growth rate can yield very impressive returns.

The dividend strategy is recommended for retirees with large nest eggs. A company like Verizon, which currently has a modest growth rate and a 4.75 percent current yield, could easily be paying a 14.85 personal yield in ten years. With a $250,000 investment, your annual income from dividends would rise from $11,875 at age sixty-two to $37,125 at age seventy-two. You could say goodbye to the concept of being on a fixed income. In addition, the price would also increase, which means your nest egg would grow from $250,000 to $776,500. All Verizon has to do is continue to grow at the historic rate observed in Table XV for large companies (12 percent).

The key point is that a dividend strategy, while conservative and income-focused, is still very rewarding; it is not a strategy to be taken lightly. You should use the same level of effort to select a dividend stock as you would to pick a value or growth stock. In fact, the best dividend stocks have a significant growth component. In that regard, if you have to choose between a high-yield stock (over 5 percent) with no growth prospects versus a low-yield stock (1–3 percent) with some growth prospects (3–9 percent), buy the low-yield modest-growth stock. In time, it will provide excellent yields as well as a significant price increase.

Value

The market is often described as rational or efficient. If this were true, there would be no such thing as value investing. Value investing is possible only because the market is neither rational nor efficient. Figure 11 illustrated the dynamics of value investing and the opportunities it provides.

The difficulty with value investing is establishing a value line. Since value is unique to the investor, market, and company, the value of the stock could be calculated in several different ways. One way is to do what we did in Chapter 8: Establish a Main Street value using earnings projections and the present value of those future earnings. While that may be the most accurate and rigorous approach, it is unique to us. It is heavily influenced by our personal assessment of the company's future and our chosen discount rate. In order for value investing to work, the market must recognize our value analysis and react to it.

A different approach is to use a valuation that is less personal and closer to the market's view of the company. You can do this in several ways. The first is to assume the value of the company is its price. Since we are defining value and price the same, the implication is there can be no gap between them and no such thing as a value opportunity, but the natural ebb and flow of buyers and sellers will still tend to move the stock price around its average. This average price becomes our value line. Thus, you have created a statistical valuation based on price rather than a performance valuation based on the company. When the price falls below the average, you have a value opportunity because you can expect the price, at some point, to return to the average. This is the same logic we used in the die roll of Figure 4, and is the basis for the Bollinger Band trading model, which will be discussed in the next chapter. Figure 24 illustrates an idealized chart of a growth stock that presents several short-term-value investing opportunities.

Another approach to establishing a value line is to convert price to a ratio that can be compared to itself or other companies. Depending on the profitability of the company, you can use either the price-to-earnings ratio or the price-to-sales ratio. This will allow you to establish a value line based on the market's unique view of the company versus its peers or the market as a whole. Figure 25 illustrates the market, industry, and company value lines for a company with a P/E of 8. The price line is arbitrarily drawn, but in practice, it would be the historical price movements presented on the company's stock chart. Note that Figure 25 is divided into historical and projected years. Past data is factual and certain; we're using it to establish a projection of how the market might price the company if the projected performance (the earnings per share) is realized. In Figure 25, there are three possibilities: The market could continue pricing the company on its current trend (P/E = 8); the market could price the company upward toward the industry value line (P/E = 16); or the market could price it further upward toward a general market poll of stocks like the SP500 value line (P/E = 20).

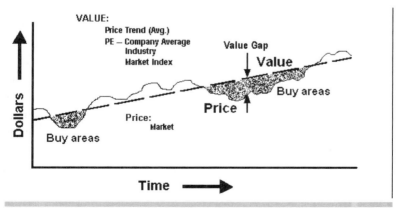

FIGURE 24: Value Opportunities in a Typical Stock Chart. As the price of a stock moves below its value line, a short-term investing opportunity is created. Several methods can be used to create the value line. These include the performance of the company, the moving price average, or a moving valuation average like price-to-earnings ratio (P/E).

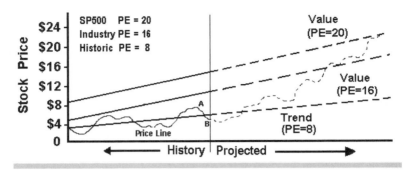

FIGURE 25: Using PE to Establish Value Lines. If a company is valued below the market (P/E of the SP500) or its industry (average industry P/E), an intermediate investment opportunity is created.

Figure 25 also illustrates how a focus on intermediate term value analysis can overpower short-term price fluctuations. In Figure 25, point B represents a short-term buying opportunity. Point A would clearly suggest a wait signal. If the market is in the process of revaluing the stock, point A is no longer a wait signal. In fact, it could be indicating the revaluation is underway, which would mean the stock's price would not cycle down to point B. Of course, at point A you don't know if the stock is moving to point B or is moving to a new valuation. These unknowns make the market interesting and challenging.

Of course, not all the companies you will analyze are as straightforward as the one depicted in Figure 25. Figure 26 illustrates a company with a trend line between the industry and the market value lines. The short-term value opportunities remain the same, but the longer-term valuation is unclear. The stock has three possible courses. Course B assumes the market will continue to value the company in line with its historical performance. Course A anticipates the company will be valued in line with its peers. Course C suggests the future value will match the overall market as described by the SP500. In situations like this, it is important to go beyond the numbers to discover reasons to support an upward or downward valuation.

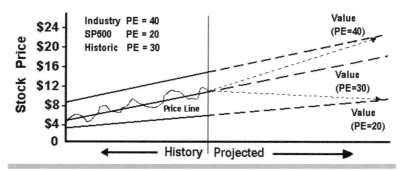

FIGURE 26: Choosing a Stock Valuation Standard. If the P/E of a company lies between a higher industry average and the lower market average (SP500), the stock could either fall to the lower average or rise to the higher average, depending on the performance of the company or the market's attitude toward the stock.

Growth

Since all investing is, or should be, forward looking, growth has a big influence on the outcome of any investment decision. The market is willing to pay more for a stock today because of its promise to earn more tomorrow. Table XIV compares a series of investment choices using various EPS growth assumptions and present-value techniques.

Table XIV illustrates two crucial attributes of high-growth stocks. The first is they carry higher P/Es than low-growth stocks. This high P/E occurs because investors have priced the stock based on future earnings. The second point is the high P/E is justified. For instance, stock F's price of $4.74 and P/E of 47.4 might lead the value or dividend investor to reject buying F. Yet, even if the market downgraded the stock over the next ten years from a P/E of 47 to 10, the price of F would rise to $28.90, which is a 20 percent annual return. If the stock held its P/E of 47, in year ten the price would be $136.99. Compared to the lower-growth stocks A, B, C, and D, F is a stellar performer.

Does the market actually price high-growth stocks higher than low-growth stocks? To answer that let's run a screen on *www.moneycentral.msn.com* to compare actual P/Es of various stocks to their growth rates. The result is divided into groups based on sales and is presented in Table XV.

TABLE XIV
Impact of EPS Growth on Stock Prices
Present Value Method, 10-Year Timeframe

Stock ID	A	B	C	C	E	F
EPS Growth (%)	0	5	10	20	30	40
Current EPS	$0.10	$0.10	$0.10	$0.10	$0.10	$0.10
Discount Rate	10%	10%	10%	10%	10%	10%
Present Value Per Share	$0.61	$0.78	$1.00	$1.66	$2.80	$4.74
Current Stock Price = PV	$0.61	$0.78	$1.00	$1.66	$2.80	$4.74
Current P/E	6.1	7.8	10.0	16.6	28.0	47.4
Current PE/G	NM	1.56	1.00	0.83	0.93	1.18
EPS in 10 Years	$0.10	$0.16	$0.26	$0.62	$1.39	$2.89
Stock Price in 10 Years P/E = 10	$1.00	$1.60	$2.60	$6.20	$13.90	$28.90
PE/G in 10 Years	NM	2.00	1.00	0.50	0.33	0.40
Potential Stock Price in 10 Years	$0.61	$1.25	$2.60	$10.29	$38.92	$136.99

It is clear that smaller companies (less than $500 million in sales) tend to, as a group, grow faster than larger companies. The market also tends to value these companies higher, as illustrated by their high P/Es and P/Ss. These smaller companies also have a wider range of three-year growth rates, as indicated by their growth volatility. This volatility makes it more difficult for the growth investor to compare individual companies to the group average. Not only is the small company group more volatile and less predictable, it is also less profitable. In the smallest group, 82.6 percent of the companies reported no or negative earnings, which means no P/E could be calculated. Thus, the valuation metric of P/S takes on greater importance in spite of the observation that the sales growth is more volatile. A good breakeven analysis would compensate for the volatility of the P/S.

Table XV also provides some guidance on where various investment strategies would be the most rewarding. For instance, dividend

TABLE XV
Stock Valuations by Company Size (Sales)

Annual Sales	3 Year Sales Growth % (Avg.)	3 Year Growth Volatility	Current Annual Sales Growth %	Price-to-Sales Ratio (P/S) Average	Price-to-Earnings Ratio (P/E) Average	Percent of Companies Not Profitable	Percent Paying a Dividend
$0 to $10 million	16.3	90	446	478	33.5	82.6	4.5
$10 million to $100 million	22.9	104	94	4.1	45.7	46.4	24.4
$100 million to $200 million	20.2	49	28	2.6	41.6	34.3	30.8
$200 million to $500 million	18.5	46	21	2.4	43.6	26.7	32
$500 million to $1 billion	13.2	22	19	1.8	51.9	21.4	40.9
$1 billion to $2 billion	13.2	17	17	1.9	53.5	13	53.8
$2 billion to $5 billion	12.7	20	15	1.6	25.9	17.8	62.6
$5 billion to $10 billion	12.1	21	16	1.5	22.3	13.2	71.6
Over $10 billion	8.5	14	14	1.3	18.9	6.2	81.9

investors would find many of their opportunities in companies with sales over $1 billion. You will usually find strong sales growth in companies with sales less than $200 million. These companies provide fertile ground for growth investors. From $200 million to $2 billion in sales, companies begin to transition from high growth to lower growth. They also become more stable and more consistently profitable. Note that the P/Es remain high in this group, which may indicate a tendency for the market to overvalue these companies based on past performance. Thus, value investing in this sales range may prove more risky because a price below trend may indicate a reversal of trend rather than a short-term value opportunity.

Growth can be a very rewarding strategy. In Figure 27, the stock chart of an idealized high-growth company is presented. Assuming the stock price matches the valuation, which in the long run it will, the rewards of owning a growth stock are impressive. Using PE/G as the valuation metric and setting it to 1.00, in the current year (year 0), the value of the stock would be $40 (EPS = $1, P/E = $40). In year five, the EPS rises to $5.38 and the value of the stock rises to $215.20. If you invested $5,000 in year 0, in five years you would have $26,900, which is a 40 percent per year return.

Not only is the reward great, the risk is low. Let's assume you were to purchase the stock at price point c, which is 50 percent greater than the stock's calculated value. This would set the P/E at 60 and the price at $60. That is a sizable premium. Yet, the value of the stock rises to $60 in a little more than a year. In five years the value will reach $215.20 and the annual return on your overpriced investment is an impressive 28 percent.

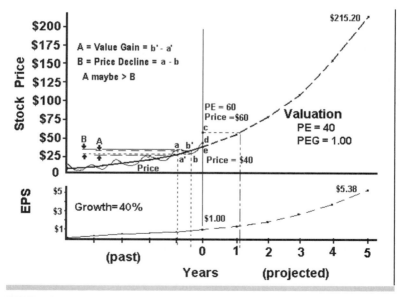

FIGURE 27: Idealized Stock Chart for a High-Growth Company. A high-growth stock can quickly outgrow its price volatility. It is this potential of a growth stock that allows growth investors to ignore the volatility of the stock's price. Thus, this growth stock can be purchased at points a, b, or d. Within one year, its value c will exceed all the buy points.

Of course, price doesn't exactly track value. In Figure 27, the actual price is depicted as a wavy line that follows the general trend of the valuation line. Thus, at any given time, the stock is either overpriced or underpriced with respect to its calculated value. The value investor uses these swings to help determine buy and sell points. However, the investor in high-growth stocks can usually ignore these price swings because the fluctuation in the stock's price is usually smaller than its growth rate. For instance, if the stock buyer were to avoid buying the stock at point a and wait to point b, the price of the stock would decline from point a to point b. This yields a price advantage of B (a – b). By waiting, the buyer loses value equal to A (b' – a'), which in a high-growth stock could be considerable. Depending on the volatility of the stock, the loss in value can be greater than the price advantage. In the long term, the growth investor may gain little or nothing for the wait. Thus, at the time of his evaluation (where EPS equals $1) there may be very little penalty if the buyer buys at point c, d, or e. Thus, market timing is not as critical to the growth investor as it is to the value investor.

The biggest risk the growth investor faces is a negative transition. In Table XV, there is a rapid decline in current annual sales growth in the $100–$500 million sales groups. This is a fairly common and intuitive observation. As companies grow larger, it becomes harder for them to maintain high growth rates. Figure 28 illustrates a stock chart of a company with a historical growth rate of 40 percent, which begins to transition to a growth rate of 20 percent. In this example, the valuations presented are based on a PE/G of 1.00, which means that the market recognizes the changing growth rate and has reacted to it by lowering its P/E for the company. Thus, the growth rates in year 2, 3, 4, and 5 are 35, 30, 25, and 20 percent, respectively. The P/Es are also 35, 30, 25, and 20 for the same years. The impact of that revaluation is depicted by the bottom valuation line, which yields a final price in year 5 of $73.71. This is only one-third of the originally projected price of $215.20. Yet, even with this drastic growth downturn, the stock purchased at $40 in year 0 would earn an annual return of 13 percent, which is still greater than the long-term average of the SP500 (10–12 percent).

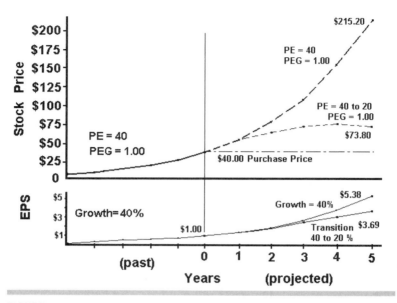

FIGURE 28: Price Chart of Stock with a Decreasing Growth Rate. The forgiving nature of a growth stock is illustrated in this chart. Even if the investor misses the growth projection by a factor of two, the future value of the stock will be larger than the purchased price of the stock.

Interestingly, the biggest opportunity for the growth investor is also in transition, except this transition is positive. Figure 29 illustrates a stock chart of a company with a historical growth rate of 20 percent, and then begins to transition to a growth rate of 40 percent. The valuations presented are based on a PE/G of 1.00. Thus, the growth rates in year 2, 3, 4, and 5 are 25, 30, 35, and 40 percent, respectively. The P/Es are also 25, 30, 35, and 40 for the same years. The impact of that revaluation is depicted by the upper valuation line, which yields a final price in year 5 of $147.60. This is almost three times the originally projected price of $48.80. The stock purchased at $20 in year 0 would earn an annual return of 49 percent. It is in this group of stocks you will find the ten-bagger.

This is not to say that a growth strategy is foolproof. It isn't. The market doesn't always react in a rational and linear way. It may overreact to a company with a disappointing growth decline, and this could

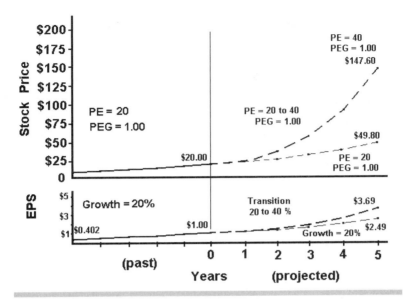

FIGURE 29: Price Chart of a Stock with an Increasing Growth Rate. The greatest opportunity for the growth investor is when she underestimates the growth of a stock. This is especially true if the market adds to the price growth by increasing its valuation by increasing its price-to-earnings ratio (P/E).

drive the price of the stock far below your calculated targets. There are no guarantees in the stock market.

Some Caveats

The vagaries of the market can be problematic, but if you're aware of them, you can take them into consideration.

Others' Opinions and Actions

First, is the basic dynamic of reason, recognition, and reaction. You are not in this game alone. Your analysis of a company and its prospects may be flawless, but other players must see what you see and have the resources and willingness to act on it. Unfortunately, in today's market, up to 80 percent of all trading is done by institutions like pension funds, mutual funds, and insurance companies. They operate within strict guidelines that often prevent them from seeing or buying your great find.

Metrics

Another vagary of the market is the metrics. The market raises havoc with the metrics. Since corporate earnings are reported on a quarterly basis, the earnings component of the P/E calculation remains fixed over a three-month span, but price changes daily. As the price fluctuates, so does the P/E. Thus, there is no fixed valuation because there is no fixed stock price. You are working with dynamic metrics that can only give you a broad understanding, not a precise definition. This can inform your investment decisions, but it cannot make them for you.

Another vagary of the market is its players. The market is populated with investors, traders, speculators, insiders, manipulators, and thieves. It is a witch's brew of self-interests and agendas. You cannot ignore their impact on your investment decision, and you cannot adequately predict it.

Many stocks you will study will appear overpriced, especially at the start of a significant price run-up. In the case of Hansen Beverage (Figure 1), the stock began its price rise almost one year before the company began to show significant performance gains. In a study of stocks with annual price increases of 100 percent, the price of the vast majority began to move six to twelve months before the performance of the company indicated a turnaround or a growth spurt. These pre-valuations indicate there are other players in the game—insiders, speculators, or manipulators—generally a signal to stay away. However, if you do your homework, there is no reason to stay away from these potentially profitable investment opportunities.

What You Have Learned

Smart investors understand the risks, rewards, limits of the metrics, dynamics of the market, and the nature of business. They combine all these understandings into a basic investment approach that also reflects their personalities, applies sound marketing techniques, and is cognizant of the business life cycle. It's great work and great fun, if you have the personality for it.

- Investors use past and future company performance metrics to predict future stock price moves and dividend flows.
- To be an effective and efficient investor, you must understand business and the performance metrics associated with business.
- A complete stock analysis consists of five perspectives: business, earnings, growth, potential, and risk.
- The key metric in the business perspective is sales. In order to be a business, a company must generate sales.
- Earnings drive stock prices. The key metric in the earnings analysis is price-to-earnings ratio (P/E). It allows you to compare one company to another.
- Without growth, there would be very little reason to buy stocks. The most important growth is growth in earnings. While past growth is an important observation, the key measure is future growth.
- Growth in sales is also important because sustainable earnings growth depends on sustainable sales growth.
- The potential of a company to safely increase sales and profits depends on its product development efforts, market position, management competency, structural advantages, and other tangible and intangible factors. Potential is the most important perspective in your analysis because it looks to those factors insuring your forecasts of future sales and earnings growth will be realized.
- Risk explores the ability of a company to pay its short-term and long-term bills. Two important metrics in the risk analysis are current ratio and fixed-cost coverage.
- It is important to go beyond the metrics to understand "the story." It is here you will understand why the company exists and develop your confidence in its metrics and ability to meet your forecasts.
- There are three basic investment strategies: dividend, value, and growth.

- The dividend strategy focuses on the certainty of immediate returns and cash flow. It is highly dependent on the performance of the company, which makes it less susceptible to the vagaries of the market.
- The value approach seeks to identify differences in the price of a stock, which is market-dependent, and the value of the stock, which is performance-dependent. The assumption in a value strategy is that any differences discovered will ultimately close, which creates an investment opportunity.
- The growth strategy goes to the heart of stock market investing. It seeks to find fast-growing companies that will exert upward pressure on their stock's price. The growth approach has a unique contradiction. Because it is dependent on a forecast of future earnings, it carries considerable risk. Yet, because of the power of compounding, it is the most forgiving strategy when it comes to incorrect forecasts.
- In spite of its mathematical rigor, investing is not an exact science. For your strategy to work, the market needs to recognize your reasoning and react to it the way you expect.

CHAPTER 10

Your Guide to Stock Trading

To make money in the stock market you must sell. In the absence of dividends, it is possible a company can develop, grow, mature, and die without delivering one penny of return to the long-term investor. Thus, the underlying strategy of the investor is to hop onto a growing company, bail when it matures, and then hop onto to a different growing company. If a company has unusual staying power with modest growth prospects, the investor can revisit it for value and dividend opportunities. The timeframe for these buy-and-sell decisions is years or even decades. This timeframe is one of the key differences between an investor and a trader.

Investing and trading are different in other ways. They are based on different philosophies, focus on different dynamics, and are favored by different personalities. From your point of view, personality may be the most important determinate, but to better understand trading, let's explore its philosophy and the dynamics.

The Trader's Reasoning

In the short term, stock prices are moved primarily by the market's attitude toward the stock, but we can never know all the factors that contribute to the market's attitude. Thus, it makes no sense to try to buy stocks based on an unknown. This is the trader's main point.

The trader's job is to recognize that the market is reacting to some news. He could care less about what that news is; he is only concerned with the market's reaction. He can never know all the market knows, but he can see what the market is doing. John Magee, a famous trader, reportedly stated that he could be locked in a room with nothing but a stock chart, and he could determine which direction a stock's price was going.[1]

It is clear there are opportunities in trading. What is not clear is whether these opportunities deliver reasonable returns. By *reasonable*, we mean returns that compensate for the additional risk you take when you abandon the market average (reference Figure 8). There are many studies indicating trading is a losing strategy. However, it is estimated that as many as 20 percent of market players have decided to take the risk and consider themselves traders. If you decide to trade, you are not alone.

As a small investor who is not privy to the rumors and inside information of Wall Street, you are at a great disadvantage. The computer can relieve some of that disadvantage. You can fill your morning e-mail inboxes with news alerts in hopes of scooping an inattentive market, but the reality is you will always be a step behind the insiders. Trading offers the opportunity to see what they see, when they see it, because the news is in the chart, not on the newswires.

As we've said earlier, if you lack the patience, interest, and mathematical skills to slog through the financial statements of a dozen companies, investing is not your game. This doesn't preclude you from the market, because traders spend very little time or energy dissecting the inner workings of a company or the markets they serve. They spend their time dissecting the inner workings of a stock's chart. This is why traders are sometimes called chartists. They believe that the charts reveal what the in-crowd is doing, even before they admit they are doing it. Charting levels the playing field.

Reading the Stock Chart

Figure 30 is a stock chart. The top graph tracks the movement of a stock's price over a specific timeframe (price chart). The bottom part is a record of how many shares were traded in that timeframe (volume chart). The usual timeframes are days, weeks, months, or years. These timeframes are further divided into trading periods, which can be minutes, hours, days, weeks, or months. The stock chart in Figure 30 encompasses a one-year timeframe and is divided into weekly trading periods.

The price chart in Figure 30 is a candlestick chart because each trading period is depicted by a bar with a line extending from each end, like a candlestick. The top end of the line represents the highest price paid for the stock for that trading period; the low end of the

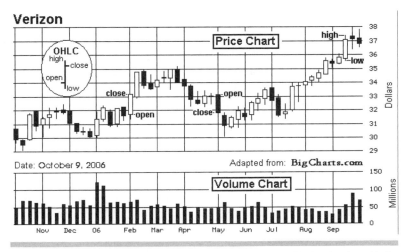

FIGURE 30: One-Year Weekly Stock Chart for Verizon (VZ). Trading begins with the stock chart like the one developed above for the Verizon Company.

line is the lowest price. One end of the bar is the opening price for the trading period and the other end of the bar is the closing price. When the opening price is less than the closing price, the bar is hollow. If the opening price is greater than the close, the bar is solid. This allows traders to quickly spot up or down trading periods. There are chart styles other than candlestick. One of the most popular is the Open-High-Low-Close (OHLC). The only difference between a candlestick chart and an OHLC is how the trading period is depicted. An example of an OHLC trading period is presented in Figure 30 for comparison.

From the price chart, we can quickly track the price movements of a stock. Figure 30's price chart is for Verizon (ticker: VZ), and it can be constructed from data found on the Internet. Over the past year, the stock's price has moved from $30 to approximately $37, a 23 percent gain in price, plus an additional 4.43 percent dividend payment. For an investor, a 27.43 percent return on investment is an impressive achievement. Over the same timeframe, the SP500 provided a 13.6 percent price increase and the Dow increased in price by only 14.5 percent, with another 2.61 percent in dividends. (The SP500 doesn't report a dividend yield.)

The Basic Charting Model

Using the power of hindsight and an ideal trading scenario, the potential trading profit in Figure 30 is illustrated in Figure 31. There are ten buying opportunities on the chart. These are defined as weeks where the stock's price opens higher than the previous week's close. The sell points are defined as weeks that the stock's price closes lower than the previous week's close. These buy-and-sell points are signals. If you buy and sell at those signals, the total return over the entire year is 76.9 percent. Clearly, trading is a potentially attractive strategy—in the ideal.

However, we must adjust the ideal for trading costs. Remember, this was one of the criticisms of trading. If we deduct a trading cost of $50 for each buy or sell transaction, the overall return for the year is 26.9 percent. To reduce these costs, it is important to have computer access to discount trading sites. Many of these accounts charge transaction fees as low as $10 per trade. With trading costs of $10, the overall return is 66.9 percent.

Another consideration is the size of the transaction. Transaction costs are usually fixed over a trading volume up to 1,000 shares. Buying

FIGURE 31: Stock Chart Illustrating Buying Opportunities for a Trader. A simple trading regimen is presented. Stocks are bought when their price opens above the previous week's close. They are sold when their price closes below the previous week's close. This simple trading plan delivered a 76.9 percent return over the length of the chart.

100 Verizon shares required an original investment of $3,000 plus the $50 fee. The above analysis was based on that $3,050 transaction. However, if you were trading 100 shares of a $10 stock with a similar chart, the total transaction would only be $1,050, and the overall result for the year would be a 73 percent loss. Thus, each trade has a breakeven point depending on the size of the transaction (fixed) costs. In the Verizon example, the breakeven point for a $50 fee transaction is $2,000.

Up to this point, we have focused on the ideal, which we created with the benefit of hindsight. Let's move into the real world—the world where we are not betting on what was, but on what we hope will be. To do that, we simply apply our basic charting model as if we didn't know what was going to happen. If we apply the buy and sell rules in this manner, we will identify eight additional transactions. These are depicted in Figure 32 with a circled "F."

What is the significance of the added transactions? These are the transactions that failed. They are trades that went down when they should have gone up. In the ideal (Figure 31), we made ten trades and each was a winner, for a confidence level of 100 percent and a risk

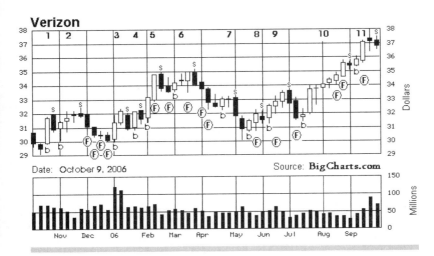

FIGURE 32: Stock Chart Illustrating Failed Trades. Without the benefit of hindsight, the simple trading regimen of the previous chart would dictate eight additional trades. These would be losing trades. Adjusted for transaction costs, the return on this trading model would be 40.84 percent.

factor of zero. In the real world, following the rules, you would have potentially made eight more transactions, all losers. Your confidence level would collapse to 57 percent. This points out the need to test your trading model on past data before you begin to trade.

The drop in confidence level indicates that in the real world this is not a very effective trading model, but how efficient is it? Let's do the complex math to see how we would actually fare in dollars and cents. We will limit the analysis to online trading with a $10 transaction cost and a $3,000 initial investment. In the ideal, the overall return was 66.9 percent. In the real world, the overall return decreases to 40.84 percent. How can a trading model with such a low confidence level provide a market-beating average of 40.84 percent? Simply put, the winning trades are bigger than the losing trades. We saw a similar outcome when we analyzed ten-baggers in Table VI, Chapter 4.

For now, it would appear that trading is very profitable. If you are disciplined and agile, you can increase the return on a rising stock from 23 percent to 40.84 percent. What if the stock price is not rising? In 2006, which was a bull market, only 57.3 percent of listed stocks increased in price, while 39.6 percent declined and 3.1 percent were flat. This means

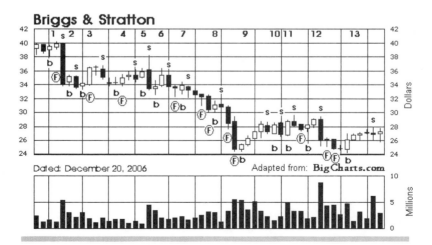

FIGURE 33: Trading Declining Stocks. Even with a declining stock, trading can be a profitable strategy. Using our simple trading model, the method applied to this chart yields a 59.85 percent return over the length of the chart.

that you only have a 57.3 confidence level the stock you are trading will increase in price. What happens if you are betting on one of the losers?

Figure 33 presents the stock chart for Briggs & Stratton (BGG). Its price declined from $40 to $28. Using our trading model, we can identify twenty-four trades, thirteen of them positive. This gives a 54.2 percent confidence level. This is lower than your confidence level on the Verizon chart. What about the returns? The overall return is 59.85 percent. Trading would appear to be good with both bull and bear stocks. So why isn't everyone trading?

One answer is illustrated in Figure 34. In Figure 34, the weekly candlestick is compared to the daily candlesticks that comprise it. These were taken from the November 2006 readings on the BGG chart. In the first week of November, there was a failed trade because the week opened higher than the previous week's close (PWC), which triggered a buy signal. However, the price then declined until it fell below the PWC, which triggered a sell signal. This caused us to lose money on the trade. Since we were using the PWC as the trigger point, once we completed the failed trade in week 1, there were no other trading signals since the price stayed below the PWC.

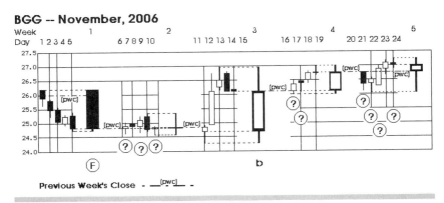

FIGURE 34: Daily Buy and Sell Signals. Each weekly period is made up of a series of daily periods, each with its own open, high, low, and close price. Trading regimens can be created using different charts (daily, weekly, and monthly) to identify buy and sell signals. For instance, a trader could buy based on a weekly signal but sell based on a daily signal.

In week 5 we see a different situation. We already own the stock based on the buy signal in week 4. Week 5 opens at the PWC and promptly heads downward (day 20). It is a clear sell sign. Yet, when building our model, we only back tested against the weekly candlesticks, and week 5's candlestick is bullish. There was no sell sign apparent at the weekly level. The daily charts gives a very different set of buy and sell signals. In week 5, we would sell on day 20, buy on day 22, sell and buy on day 23, and hold on day 24. While a look back on the week indicated that we would simply hold an already-owned stock, the daily chart suggested a minimum of two additional trades.

When we analyze the month of November for BGG, we see the following returns: Investing is 3.4 percent, weekly trade 5.3 percent, and daily trade 3.6 percent. Daily trading diminished the effectiveness and efficiency of the outcome, but not enough to destroy the advantage of trading over investing. It does offer some clues as to why investors disparage trading.

First, many investors simply can't psychologically absorb so many losing trades, even though the final outcome may be positive. Also, the key to trading is agility, which means it is done on a weekly, hourly, or even minute-by-minute basis. Traders are quick to pull the trigger at the first sign of opportunity or trouble. Investors see all this hyperactivity as counterproductive. It simply adds volatility to the market and anxiety to their market endeavors. Finally, all the chart watching is too intense and hectic for most investors.

In Search of a Better Charting Model

Rules are at the heart of the trading approach—rules designed to increase the effectiveness and efficiency of the trading model. Let's attempt to improve our Verizon model by adding a six-week moving average to the chart. A moving average (MA) is simply the average of some fixed number of past periods, in this case six weeks. In Figure 35, it is drawn as a continuous line on the price chart. Our new rule is to buy when the price closes above the MA. This is a breakout. The sell signal will be when the price closes below the MA. Under this rule, seven trades have been identified. Five were losing trades, which provides a confidence level of just 28.6 percent. The total return for all six completed trades was 1 percent. While it has reduced the number of trades, it clearly needs something more to make it a viable trading strategy. That something is volume.

Analyzing price movements is just half of the equation; volume is the other half. Since the stock market is like an auction, price must be analyzed in the context of volume. If there are more buyers at the auction, the price will rise. If that increase in price corresponds to an increase in volume, it is assumed that most of the volume increase is buyers. Since buyers come to the auction for a reason, even if we don't know what that reason is, it is a signal that the stock is going to continue to increase in price. Thus, an increase in price that corresponds to an increase in volume would be a strong buy signal. Further, this would be an especially strong signal if it were to reverse a trend, since that would indicate a change in market attitudes toward the stock. Since the MA is a form of trend line, we can combine volume, price, and trend to formulate a new trading rule. The rule is, when the stock's price rises above the MA on increased volume, we buy.

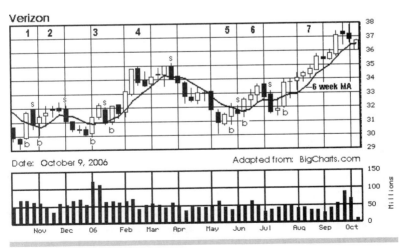

FIGURE 35: Trading Model Using 6-Week Moving Average (MA). Traders can also add a technical indicator to the stock chart. The moving average (MA) is a simple one. Moving averages can be calculated for any number of periods. The greater the number of periods used to calculate it, the less volatile the average. As the price crosses the MA, the trader will buy or sell depending on the direction of the price movement.

Buying is only half the trade. What about selling? Let's keep the old rule; when the stock price closes below the MA, we sell. We will sell regardless of volume. The only thing left to do is define increased volume. There is no magical number. For our example, we will use a volume that is at least 10 percent higher than the average of the last three trading periods. This new trading strategy is illustrated in Figure 36.

The new trading strategy delivers just three trades. Two of the trades are positive and one is negative—a 66.7 percent confidence level. The total return for the three trades is 14.4 percent. This is an improvement over the previous model using MA, but it provides a lower return than our investment strategy, which delivered 27 percent. There is obviously more to do here.

Technical Indicators

In the last example, using basic charting techniques and variables, we were only able to achieve a 67 percent confidence level and a 14 percent return on investment. In order to prove that a chart-focused strategy is a viable alternative to investing, trading has to consistently outperform

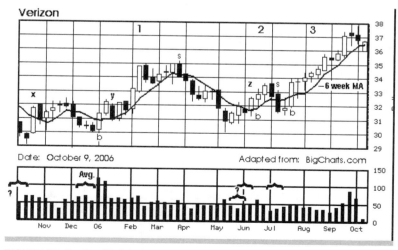

FIGURE 36: Trading Model with Price, Volume, and Trend. Besides price, the volume of shares traded is an important consideration when trading stocks. When a buy signal occurs on the price chart, many traders will look to the volume chart for confirmation. If the volume of shares traded increased, the buy signal is considered more compelling.

the long-term return of the market. To do that, traders would have to create new and more accurate buy and sell signals. Unfortunately for them, since they are chartists, they only have two variables with which to work—price and volume. Yet, they have not let that deter them.

Chartists have amassed a large number of indicators based on price and volume. These are technical indicators, and their application is technical analysis. A few examples of these indicators are money flows, on-balance volume, moving-average convergence-divergence (MACD), Bollinger Bands, etc. They are all mathematical manipulations of price and volume used to establish better buy and sell signals.

Figure 37 illustrates the Verizon price chart with a six-week MA included, as well as Bollinger Bands.[2] Bollinger Bands represent the outer limits to which a stock's price might fluctuate. They are similar to a statistical distribution around a mean that we discussed in previous chapters. When a stock's price crosses a Bollinger Band, we expect (for statistical

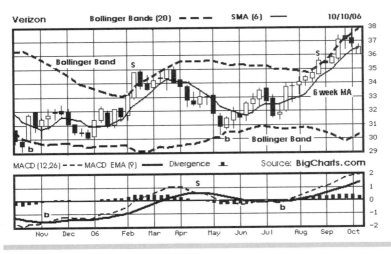

FIGURE 37: Trading Models Based on Technical Indicators. Other technical indicators can be added to the stock chart and used to identify buy and sell points. On the price chart are Bollinger Bands, which mark the outer limits of the stock's price variation in the same way a normal curve marks the outer limits of a population's attribute. Whenever the price reaches these bands, it is expected to reverse direction and return to the middle of the range created by the bands. Below the price chart is a MACD (moving-average convergence-divergence), which consists of two MAs based on two different numbers of periods. When the two MAs cross, a buy or sell signal is given.

reasons) it will reverse direction and head back toward the mean. Thus, the Bollinger Bands provide a buy signal at the lower band and a sell signal at the upper band. There are two buy signals on the chart and both were followed by an increase in the stock's price. However, the first sell signal appeared six weeks before the stock began to turn down. The same appears to be the case with the second sell signal. However, in both sell cases the stock price did begin to decrease within weeks of the signal. The overall return for this system was approximately 31 percent.

The MACD is plotted below the price chart.[3] The MACD is a very complicated indicator based on two different moving averages. When one MA (the dashed line) crosses the other MA (the solid line), it triggers buy and sell signals. This MACD provided two buy signals. The first occurred around the sixth week at a price of about $31.50 and culminated with a sell sign at about $32.50, a 3.2 percent return. The second buy sign occurred at $31.80 and is still active, with the stock price at $36.60, a tentative return of 15.1 percent. The overall return on the MACD is presently at 18.7 percent, depending on when the next sell signal develops.

Note that both the Bollinger Bands and MACD provided 100 percent confidence and positive returns with this chart. Note also that technical indicators tend to slow the process. In our earliest examples, speed was the key. With technical indicators, the focus shifts to accuracy. You perform fewer trades, but they are more likely to be positive. You will want to try many of these indicators yourself. The Internet has made it easy to do. Just log on to a stock-charting site like BigCharts.com. There you will be able to open a price and volume chart for a company and add a variety of technical indicators to the chart. By analyzing the price movements in comparison to these indicators, you can develop your own mix of indicators and confidence levels for their buy and sell signals.

We have been looking at just one approach to charting—the search for a trend. Our reason has been that once a trend has started, for whatever reason, it will continue until some other factor comes along to reverse it. By coupling price moves to sales volume, traders hope to confirm a price move is a trend rather than a random occurrence. They add technical analysis to the mix to refine their observations and create a timely signal. However, trend analysis is not the only approach to trading.

Chart Patterns

Chartists look for patterns in the price chart that may give them clues to how the market is acting. This is as close as they get to cause-and-effect logic. Technical analysis is all about manipulating price and volume in the hopes of finding the one number that screams buy or sell and does it with a confidence of 80–100 percent. But chart patterns are different; they tell a story—a story traders hope will lead to stock market profits.

The first of these stories is the trend. There is a saying in the stock market: The trend is your friend. A trend is represented by a straight line connecting a series of increasing lows (an uptrend) or decreasing highs (a downtrend). Figure 38 shows three trend lines. The first is the uptrend A–B. The second is downtrend C–D. The third is another uptrend, E–F. The logic behind trends is simple: The market responds en masse. Thus, once a stock begins to increase in price, other buyers are attracted to it, which further pushes the price higher. This creates a momentum in the stock, which will not be broken until some event

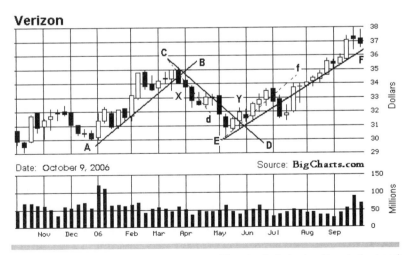

FIGURE 38: Stock Chart with Trend Lines. The simplest chart pattern is the trend line. You can create an uptrend line by connecting the lowest points on the price line. Downtrends are created by connecting the highest points on the price line. When the price line breaks an uptrend line, it is a sell signal. When the price breaks a downtrend line, it is a buy signal. However, in some charts it is difficult to determine the actual trend line (compare C–d to C–D and E–f to E–F).

curtails the flow of buyers to the auction. The chartists will never know what that event is; they only know it breaks the trend, as it did at points X and Y.

Trends are used to create buy and sell signals in the same way we used the moving average. If a stock price breaks through a downtrend line, it is a buy signal (point Y). This is especially true if it does so on increasing volume. If the stock price falls through an uptrend line, it is a sell signal (point X). Again, the signal is strengthened by volume. In Figure 38, there was a strong sell signal at point X when the price broke the uptrend line A–B. The slight increase in volume confirmed the sell sign.

Another chart pattern used by traders is support and resistance. Figure 39 shows a support line at the $30 level. The logic is the market will not let the stock fall below $30. Once it reaches that value, a sufficient number of buyers appear to support the price and even raise it. The opposite of support is resistance. When a stock's price reaches resistance, a sufficient number of sellers are drawn to the market. This prevents the price from rising further or even reduces it. There's a

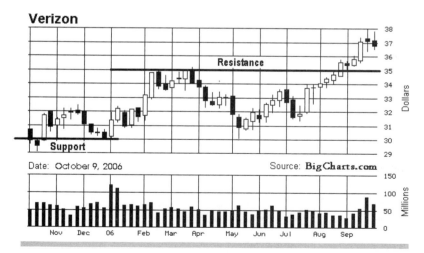

FIGURE 39: Stock Chart Illustrating Support and Resistance. When a stock's price repeatedly falls to a point and reverses direction, it is said to have support at that point. When a stock's price repeatedly rises to a point and reverses direction, it has resistance at that point. Breaking through support is a sell signal; breaking through resistance is a buy signal.

resistance line for Verizon at the $35 level. As you might expect, when a support line is broken, it is a sell signal. Breaking a resistance line, as was done at the end of August 2006, is a buy signal. Traders view this as an indication the market has re-evaluated the stock's worth.

While trends, supports, and resistances are the basic chart patterns used by traders, they are by no means the only ones. Chartists read stock charts like fortunetellers read tea leaves. They see in that swirling mass of prices a wide variety of meaningful patterns. There are tops, double tops, triple tops, flags, cups and handles, bottoms, double bottoms, and triple bottoms, just to name a few. There are enough to fill a book—in fact several books. I will leave it to you to find out more about these various patterns by reading one of those books.

Trading Short

When you buy a stock, you own it with the hope it will increase in price. The increase in price is your return. Buying and owning stocks is taking a long position. But what if you spent months analyzing a stock and discovered it is destined to decrease in price because of a sell signal, poor profit report, or adverse news? Is all your hard work wasted? Not necessarily.

The way to make money on a stock decreasing in price is short-selling. When you short-sell a stock, you borrow it and sell it at today's price. After the price drops, you buy it and replace the stock you borrowed. For instance, if a $1 stock was expected to drop to $0.75, a short-seller would borrow a share and sell it for $1. After the stock dropped to $0.75, she would buy a share and give it to the person she borrowed it from. The short-seller's profit is $0.25 ($1 received when she sold the borrowed stock minus the $0.75 she spent buying the replacement stock). Of course, it is not as simple as that in practice because there are various transaction fees, but that is the basic short-selling model.

Short-selling is a way to make money in a down market or from companies in trouble, but it has problems.

1. You must open an account that supports short-selling.
2. You must learn how to do it.
3. You could lose more than you invested.

Let's look at the last point. A buyer owning a $1 stock has limited his loss to $1. On the upside, the stock could rise 50, 100, or even a 1,000 percent. A short-seller creates an opposite scenario. His upside is limited to $1, since the stock can only lose 100 percent of its value. However, if the stock rises 50, 100, or 1,000 percent, the borrowed stock must be replaced with stock that could cost $1.50, $2, or $10. At $10, the short-seller would lose $9 on a $1 investment. High risk and limited reward is the exact opposite of what we are striving to achieve.

Short-selling is beyond the scope of this book, and beyond my interest as a market player. I do not recommend it for a retiree, especially one just starting out. If the market turns down, stay disciplined. Honor your sell signals and then wait. Be patient. The market will turn up again. Leave the short-selling to the professionals.

The Advantages of Trading

One of the biggest advantages of trading is immediacy. It focuses on the reaction phase of the stock market dynamic. This provides for immediate returns. There is no waiting for a lethargic market to catch up to your exhaustive analysis, and the potential rewards of the trade are often greater than the underlying performance of the company, as was illustrated with the Verizon example (Figure 31).

Another advantage is the discipline inherent in the trade. Technical analysis and charting allows traders to distill the complexities of company performance and market attitudes into a systematic, even rote, strategy. This also gives traders a sense of control. For some people, control is the most important issue in their lives. As an investor and speculator, you relinquish control to the vagaries of the market and the competence of corporate managers. Traders are not dependent on the whims of the crowd; they are betting on them with the confidence the metrics of technical analysis and chart patterns will reveal the crowd's direction. Even when their metrics fail, their sense of control remains intact—they have not been duped. They have simply failed—to see, to react, to decide. It is all about their actions, which is the essence of control.

Of the three stock market strategies—investing, trading, and speculating—trading provides the highest potential rewards. This was illustrated in the Verizon chart. With Verizon, the speculative and investment reward was 27 percent (price and dividends), while the trading reward was 66–70 percent.

Finally, trading is the perfect strategy for people who need to grow their nest eggs, but have neither the patience needed to invest nor the desire to take on the risks of speculation. Trading provides them with a disciplined regimen of buy and sell signals. For the average trader, disciplined decisiveness is a key personality trait. Without the correct personality, you run the risk of second-guessing the signals and missing the trade. Once again, the key to successful trading is you.

The Disadvantages of Trading

As seductive as trading appears, it is riddled with flaws and caveats. The first, and most critical from your perspective, is that most technical indicators and chart patterns lack confidence; most range between 50–60 percent. Sometimes you will sell at a loss. Traders must take these failures in stride.

Another problem with trading is some of the simplistic axioms underlying the system. Though the trend is your friend, in reality, by the time you spot it, it may be time for it to reverse. Often, trends are more after the fact than predictive, and the stock market is always about what is going to happen, not what has happened. While it is true one can extrapolate past performance into the future, it is equally true all trends end, some sooner than others, and no one knows when that end will come.

The same is true on the volume chart, where traders interpret an increase in shares traded as an increase in buyers or sellers. In the era of big institutional investors, this is not always true. For instance, over a three-year period, the number of Hansen Beverage shares traded each month increased tenfold, but the number of recorded shareholders actually decreased over the same period. There were no more buyers at the auction; there were the same number of buyers buying more stocks.

Trading is self-fulfilling and prone to manipulation. The early players in the game make money; the latecomers lose. For example, a group of traders could, with the purchase of a stock, trigger a buy signal. This brings more traders to the game, which pushes the stock's price higher. The original buyers sell when their preset profit target is reached. (The trend is not their friend.) This triggers a sell signal. Other traders, responding to the sell sign, now begin to sell. The market manager, not wanting to be stuck with high-priced stocks—remember, they must buy when the market is selling—quickly lowers the price. The early buyers and sellers, by design or by happenstance, make money. The latecomers are left with a failed trade.

The example above highlights the influence of the market manager, whom we discussed in Chapter 2. Market managers can send false trading signals. Because they have responsibility for the stock price and their stock inventories, they must manage both. For instance, a market manager with a small inventory of stock might not want to deplete it in response to a rash of buyers. He maintains a list of customers in a book[4] who want to sell their stock for a certain price. When this price is lower than the current price, it is a stop-loss order. Rather than sell his own stock, the market manager can lower the price and execute the stop-loss orders. What the trader sees is an increase in volume and a drop in price—a sell signal. The reality is there is an increase in buyers—a buy signal.

Therein lies the fundamental problem with trading: The test of any stock market system, axiom, signal, metric, or calculation should be in how well it predicts the future. Traders base their entire fortune on the manipulation and interpretation of current data. Yet, with the exception of Bollinger Bands, there is no real linkage between what the price is doing today and what it will do tomorrow. There is no cause and effect.

What You Have Learned

If you have no interest in business and no desire to suffer the wiggles and waggles of the stock market, trading is your game. It is there you will use those wiggles and waggles to your benefit. All you have to do is play them with decisiveness and discipline. Trading offers high potential, but it is not a guarantee. You will have to limit your losses and ride your winners for all they are worth. This is the key to successful trading. If you can master it, you will join that 20 percent of traders who swear there are vast riches in those ups and downs. The following review will give you a firm foundation on which to build your stock-trading business.

■ Trading allows people not interested in the dynamics of business or without the patience to weather the market's shifts a way to make profits in the stock market.

■ The basic philosophy behind trading is the small investor can never know what the market is thinking; she can only observe what the market is doing.

■ Trading methodology is built on three premises:

1. Current price activity is predictive of future price activity.
2. A trend will continue unless it is disrupted by a significant event.
3. People are creatures of habit, which shows up as patterns in the stock chart.

■ Technical analysis is an attempt to clarify the relationship between current price activity and future price activity. Technical analysis provides an indicator that gives clear buy and sell signals.

■ Analysis of trends and chart patterns is also designed to provide clear buy and sell signals.

■ All technical analysis and chart studies are manipulations and observations of just two variables: price and volume.

■ You must measure trading, like any other business activity, for effectiveness and efficiency.

■ Most technical indicators and chart patterns achieve effectiveness levels, as measured by the confidence a trade will deliver positive results of 50–60 percent. However, the efficiency of the simplest trading regimens, as measured by the overall return on investment of a series of trades, can easily exceed the average long-term return of the SP500. This efficiency has been observed with both bullish and bearish stocks.

■ The key to successful trading is process management. You must limit your losses and maximize your returns. You can do this by establishing decisive and quickly implemented buy and sell triggers. The strategy is to sell your losers and let your winners run.

■ Technical analysis and pattern interpretation are useful in confirming these buy and sell signals. Unfortunately, they tend to slow down your reaction time and decrease the number of trades performed. This may improve your confidence level, but often it decreases your overall returns.

CHAPTER 11

Your Guide to Speculating

If investing is the playground of the patient thinker and trading is the arena of the agile disciplinarian, speculation is the field of dreams. This is where visionaries and gamblers come to play. Speculation, no matter how you phrase it, is gambling, and there are only two ways to win. One is with blind luck; the other is with reasoned luck. Here, we strive for reasoned luck.

Are You a Speculator?

Speculators play the game at different times and places than investors and traders. Figure 40 compares the various stock market strategies to the life cycle of a business. In the early stage of a company's life, the dominant investment strategy is speculation. These are the innovators; they have very little past performance to extrapolate. As a company's product begins to gain acceptance in its market and enters its growth stage, speculators begin to fade from the scene and growth investors come in. As

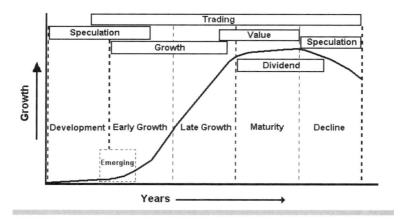

FIGURE 40: Stock Market Strategies for Various Stages in the Life Cycle. Various stock market strategies are compared with the various stages of a company's life cycle.

growth subsides and the company begins to mature, the growth investors give way to value investors. In maturity, where growth has slowed, investors look toward dividends for a greater portion of their returns. As the company declines, it may retain some dividend investors, attract some short-sellers, and renew the interest of some speculators looking for a turnaround. Throughout the life of the company, as soon as the price of the stock can support a trading strategy, traders trade.

Figure 41 illustrates how people adopt new ideas, products, or opportunities. It suggests in a population of consumers or investors, there are five distinct personalities, which form five attitudes toward new innovations or ideas. The smallest group is the innovators. They are the first to adopt an idea, even before it is proven. Early adopters follow the innovators into the market as soon as there is some confirmation that a product, company, or idea is viable. The early and late majorities represent most of the players. These majority entrants are usually, at the early stage, more deliberate than adopters and, in the later stages, more skeptical. The final group is the more tradition-bound laggards. Laggards are beyond skeptical; they are suspicious and even resistant to new innovations or ideas.

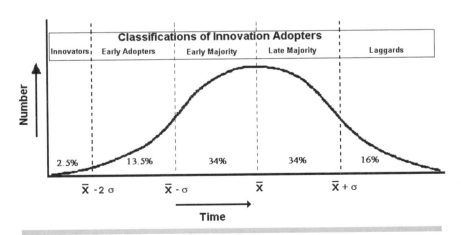

FIGURE 41: Time Required to Adopt a New Innovation or Idea by Various People. When a new product, service, or idea is marketed, it is embraced by the public according to the adoption model. In the beginning, very few people will accept it. After it is proven, the majority will begin to accept it. Finally, in the end, just a few laggards are left. The superimposed normal curve indicates the percentage of the population represented by the various adopters.

The adoption model[1] suggests speculators are among the innovators. To be a good speculator, you should have some intuitive ability to spot trends, good ideas, attractive products, or social shifts. The job of the speculator is to guess or see which of these changes can be converted into a commercial opportunity, and to spot which company has the best chance of making the conversion.

Figures 40 and 41 add another dimension to our understanding of the stock market: The game you play depends on who you are. That, in turn, dictates where you will look for opportunities. If your personality fits the speculation profile above, you should focus your attention on the early stages of a company's life cycle; there you will find emerging opportunities. The companies may not have strong performance records, but they will have products and be in markets offering a great deal of potential. Thus, successful speculation melds your visionary abilities with your ability to spot eventual winners from a pile of soon-to-be losers.

Learning by Example

Most speculations, at least ones offering the biggest rewards, are found in emerging companies, markets, and technologies (ECMT). Here there is very little historical performance to support your bet. It is all about where you think the company, market, or technology can go. The most recent example of an ECMT is the Internet. In the 1980s, the Internet was a new concept. It was more a technical curiosity than a commercial opportunity. Yet, there were entrepreneurs who understood its commercial value, and there were speculators who shared their vision. Both made lots of money speculating on its potential. The Internet is not the only example. In the 1880s, there were the railroads. Radio dominated the twenties and thirties. TV followed radio, and computers followed TV. Each was a golden opportunity for those players who had the vision and courage to place the earliest bets.

Not all speculations are visionary; some are routine and predictable. The American economy is cyclical—it goes through periods of expansion and contraction. The stock market is fluid; money flows from one industrial sector to the other. These cycles and flows provide speculative opportunities. A good example is the stock market decline in 2000–2003. Historically, during these declines, investors seek refuge in defensive stocks such as gold, utilities, and consumer necessities. These stocks hold their value in a recession. Unfortunately, that tried-and-true approach was contrary to the advice touted by many experts. The professionals lamented the demise of gold; in the age of technology, gold was passé.

Figure 42 is a ten-year stock chart of the SP500 compared to Newmont Mining, one of the largest gold producers listed on the stock market. As the SP500 began its decline in 2000 with a price drop below its uptrend line, Newmont Mining was just completing a multi-year downtrend and heading lower. However, as the downturn in the SP500 became clear, it also became clear the market did not agree with the professionals. It may be true there are sizable numbers of players who no longer look to gold for protection, but as Figure 42 illustrates, there is still a significant number that do. Enough to double the price of Newmont Mining while the SP500 was in decline.

What makes this a speculative play is apparent in Newmont's chart. Its recent price downtrend offered no encouragement, and its EPS

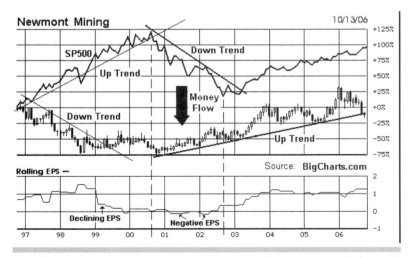

FIGURE 42: Money Flows into Defensive Stocks. A defensive stock's price will increase when the rest of the stock market is declining. There are many different reasons that money is attracted to these stocks during downturns, but whatever the reason, as money flows into them, their prices rise. This can occur regardless of the underlying fundamentals of the company they represent.

went flat after a major one-year decline. There was no performance on which to base a buy decision. A move to gold would have to be done without performance and contrary to the prevailing professional wisdom. Yet, history suggested gold was where the money would flow in spite of the pronouncements of the experts. It would require an immense amount of speculative courage and faith in historical precedents to ignore the experts.

This is what speculators do, and they are often rewarded for it. While the SP500 declined 30 percentage points, an equivalent investment in Newmont Mining was gaining 100 percent. Additionally, as the economy recovered and gold prices began to rise, Newmont's EPS began to rise. The speculator was in on the ground floor of that additional bump in Newmont's stock price. By the time the SP500 was in full recovery (2006), Newmont had already increased in price fivefold.

Newmont actually illustrates two speculative opportunities. First, Newmont benefited from the effect of money flows on stock prices. Figure 43 illustrates the expected impact of money flows on the overall market. As money flows out of the market because of an event like a recession, prices decline below their trend line. When the economy begins to recover, money flows back into the market and prices

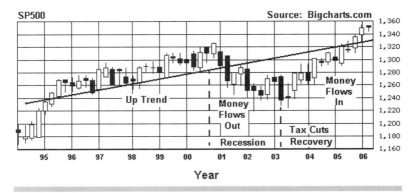

FIGURE 43: Impact of Money Flows on the Overall Market. Money flows can impact the entire market. A recession can cause money to flow out of the stock market and into bonds or CDs. This will drive stock prices down. When the recession is over, money flows back into the stock market, which pushes stock prices higher.

rebound. When the money flowed out, it had to go somewhere. It could flow into money markets, bonds, a coffee can, or a defensive stock. Newmont, being a defensive stock, became that "somewhere." This pushed its price higher. Normally, when the recession was over, money would flow back out of the sector, which would lower prices back to its previous trend line. However, as illustrated in Figure 44, if the recovery adds additional profits to the sector, or to select companies in the sector, the money flowing out of that sector will be slowed or reversed, which maintains the price uptrend. In the case of Newmont, the profit boost was caused by an escalation of commodity prices in materials like oil, copper, steel, and gold.

Of course, not all your speculations are as routine as a money flow triggered by a business cycle. Some opportunities are off the beaten path or embedded with a bunch of also-rans. That is the case with Hansen Beverage. Hansen is a beverage company that makes and distributes nonalcoholic beverages. There are twelve nonalcoholic beverage companies listed on the various stock exchanges. Yet, with very little performance history to point the way, Hansen's stock took off. Why? Over the five years of its stock rise, Hansen's sales grew 37 percent per year

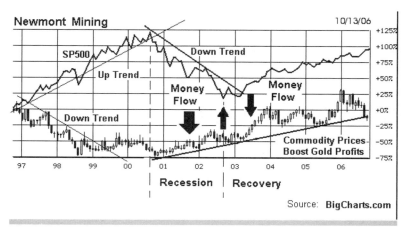

FIGURE 44: Effect of Money Flow and Secondary Profit Boost. Some stocks will benefit from rising prices. Newmont Mining is a good example. Rising gold prices boosted their profitability, which made their stock attractive to investors as the recovery proceeded.

while the nonalcoholic beverage industry grew only 7 percent per year. Hansen's EPS during that period also outpaced its industry, 69 percent versus 17 percent. However, as Figure 45 illustrates, the stock's takeoff preceded the performance of the company by six months. Clearly, the speculators knew something that investors didn't.

What they knew and when they knew it would make a great exposé, but that wouldn't help us. Those in the know are part of an insider web that hears things. Based on what they hear at their listening posts, they make their bets. To this game we will always be latecomers, but being latecomers in the speculation game sometimes means you are perfectly timed for a growth investment game. As we can see from Figure 45, one of the largest price moves occurred during May 2004. This occurred with a massive volume increase. Prior to that point, starting in July 2003, it was clear someone was buying this stock. Their activity was enough to put it on the investors' radar screen.

As speculators, by mid-2003, we don't know what lies ahead for Hansen, but the current performance is clearly taking this company

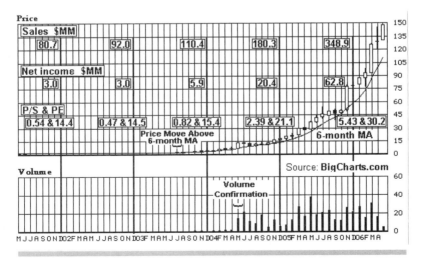

FIGURE 45: Hansen Natural Corporation (HANS) Five-Year Monthly. The stock price of Hansen Beverage begins its rise in mid-2003 and confirms in mid-2004. However, its annual profits do not show significant growth until the end of 2003 and its sales growth does not accelerate until the end of 2004.

beyond its historical pattern. Sales growth has accelerated from 14 to 20 percent. Profits are on track to double in one year. This is a company experiencing tremendous economies of scale and leveraging its sales into strong profit growth. We may not know the future, but by August 2004, the market, with its massive volume and price increase, has declared Hansen to be a good bet. As an investor, you may still want to wait, but as an out-of-the-loop speculator, with a bit more investigation into the underlying causes of this growth, it is time to buy.

What would that bit more investigation have uncovered? Hansen is in the business of making healthful, natural sodas and juice products. Organic and health foods were and are the "in" thing. The rise of organic grocery stores like Whole Foods and Trader Joe's were providing Hansen with a growing retail outlet for their products. Was it a good bet? Based on the early movement of its chart, many speculators said, "Yes!"

Let's look at a very different example—Ampex Corp. Ampex is a technology company that holds several patents in the digital camera field. As indicated by its chart in Figure 46, it had a tremendous price run-up between October 2004 and January 2005. However, there was no performance record to support such a large run-up. In fact, the failed price run-up in 2003, which was well supported with a volume increase, would raise a major red flag for any out-of-the-loop speculator. Given the performance data presented is not made public for two months after the company closes its books, the $46 million net income for 2004 would not be officially reported until February 2005, after the stock had already closed at $50. So how did the speculators know? There where clues, but they were not in the chart. They were in the newspaper.

In May 2004, Ampex reported that it filed an infringement lawsuit against Sanyo. By July 2004, Sony was also in Ampex's crosshairs for violating one of its digital camera patents. In October 2004, Ampex settled with Sanyo and signed them as a licensee. In October, Ampex also signed Canon as a licensee and filed an infringement suit against Kodak. This was the crack in the floodgate, and all a speculator might need to buy into the stock. If he did, he would have been richly rewarded. A $5,000 purchase of Ampex stock at the October 2004 open ($1.85) would yield, within four months, a $135,243 payout based on the January 2005 close.

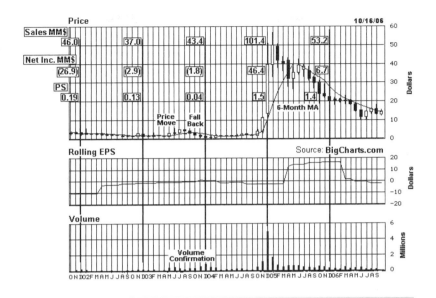

FIGURE 46: Ampex Corporation Five-Year Monthly. The clue to Ampex's stock rise is not in the chart or in the fundamentals. It is in the newspaper. A comparison of this chart to news releases by the company provides the reason behind its phenomenal price increase.

The Ampex example illustrates three points about speculation that should be emphasized.

First, speculation, like trading, is a buy-to-sell strategy. As value investors recognize, the market often overreacts. In the case of Ampex, the market drove the price up only to drag it back down after its peak. Speculative opportunities rarely settle at their peak prices. Thus, speculators will maximize their returns by setting reasonable sell guidelines, then stick to them. Those guidelines can be formulated around either chart or performance metrics or a combination of the two. In the case of Ampex, using a sell point of a 10 percent fallback penetrating the six-month moving average would have triggered a sale in April 2005 at $32 per share, which would have yielded a payout of approximately $87,000 on a $5,000 investment.

Second, there is a considerable lead time between the movement of the stock and an uptick in the company's performance. The big jump in EPS for Ampex does not occur until April 2005—six months after the stock began to rise. There is little in the 2002 and 2003 performance metrics to confirm the price move. (A similar lead time was observed with Hansen.) Speculation is all about potential. The clues to the success of a speculative stock are in its potential, which brings us to the third point.

Speculators don't have to be business or technical analysts. Their opportunities are not found in the company's financial statements or its stock chart. They are found in newspapers, magazines, technical journals, and the local mall. Good speculators are aware of their surroundings. They need to see trends, spot new products, identify growing needs, and embrace new ideas. Cynics, naysayers, and critics make lousy speculators because they too often see why something can't work rather than looking for what and who can make it work. Speculation is a can-do strategy.

Splits and Reverse Splits

One difficulty with buying Ampex in 2001 and 2002 was its extremely low price. Prior to June 2003, the highest price recorded on our chart (Figure 46) was $0.50 a share, with a low of $0.05 per share. During this time, a block of 1,000 shares would cost $50–$500. This is well below the transaction size needed by traders to achieve breakeven with any reasonable trading model. Thus, traders were locked out of the market for Ampex stock. Without a strong performance history, investors were also precluded from buying the stock. The only buyers for Ampex in 2001 and 2003 were speculators and insiders. This is a problem with many penny stocks; they are priced too low to be attractive to traders or investors, which (as we know from our adoption model) is where most of the buyers are, and to move stock prices up, you need buyers.

This creates a Catch-22. You need buyers to increase stock prices, but buyers won't come until stock prices increase. The way out of this loop is illustrated in Figure 47. It is the reverse stock split.

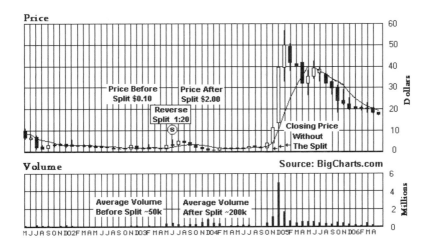

FIGURE 47: Impact of a Reverse Split (AMPX). The reverse stock split in mid-2003 positioned Ampex for its eventual big price rise in 2004. By increasing the stock price from $0.10 a share to $2 a share, the split made the stock attractive to traders, which boosted the average shares traded from 50,000 shares a month to 200,000 shares a month.

In a stock split, a company issues new stocks for its old stock. For instance, a 2-for-1 stock split gives the current stockholder two shares of new stock for each share of her old stock. Theoretically, this does not affect the value of her holdings, since the new stock is priced at half the old stock. Thus, before the split, a shareholder might own 100 shares of XYZ Company at $14 a share; after the split she owns 200 shares of XYZ Company at $7 a share.

The primary reason to split a stock is to make it easier to buy and sell. As a retiree considering a stock purchase, you would be more likely to buy 100 shares of a $5 stock than one share of a $500 stock. And what is more likely for you is also more likely for a million other investors and traders. So lowering the price of a stock will bring more buyers to the auction, which will, ironically, raise the price of the stock.

A reverse split is simply the opposite of the split described above. It delivers one new stock for several old ones. A 1-for-20 reverse split, as was the case with Ampex in June 2003, effectively raised the price of their stock from $0.10 to $2. The impact on Ampex was tremendous, as illustrated in Figure 47. Besides the obvious price increase, the average volume of shares traded jumped from 50,000 per month to 200,000 per month. Now a 1,000-share trade was well above the trader's breakeven, and investor's could buy the stock with some confidence there would be enough activity to bring it to its calculated value line.

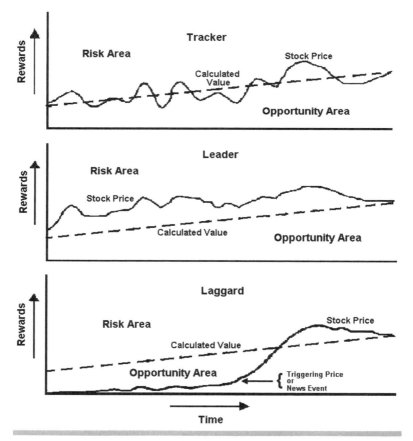

FIGURE 48: Stock Price to Company Performance Profiles. There are three types of stock in the market. The tracker occurs when the stock's price oscillates around its value. This is usually a stock closely watched by analysts, who buy and sell the stock at the first sign of strength or weakness. Leaders occur when speculators bid the price of a stock up in anticipation of future performance. Laggards occur when buyers lose confidence in a stock, anticipate a downturn in the company's performance, or find the stock too cheap or expensive to trade.

Figure 48 illustrates three possible stock-price-stock-value profiles. The tracker is when a stock's price oscillates around its calculated value line, providing long-term growth and short-term value opportunities. This is what one might expect from a rational market. The leader is when speculators and growth investors have driven the price above its value in anticipation of even more growth. These overpriced stocks are the result of irrational exuberance. The laggard is when a stock's price has been suppressed by adverse news or fails to keep pace with the company's performance. Laggards are the source of many of our two-, three-, four-, and ten-baggers. An upward price pressure builds in the laggard until it is released by some triggering event. Once that triggering event occurs, traders and buyers rush into the stock, driving the price up and releasing the pressure. In the case of Ampex, that triggering point was reached first with a reverse split in June 2003, then with the positive news releases in October 2003.

Types of Speculative Opportunities

There are five types of speculative opportunities in the stock market. They can be divided into two groups. The first group comprises the three visionary opportunities: emerging technologies, markets, and companies. The second group comprises the two cyclical opportunities: economic and company.

Visionary Opportunities

Visionary opportunities are those opportunities with no historical performance foundation other than the fact they always occur. The innovation of the railroad was followed by the innovation of the radio, then television, then computers, then the Internet. We don't yet know what will follow the Internet. It could be biomedicine, nanotechnology, or a yet-to-be-discovered breakthrough. What is known is something will follow.

Emerging Technology

This is a scientific advance or series of advances that promises to have broad social and commercial implications. The Internet is a prime example. It promised to be a boon to the American consumer.

To maximize the profit potential of an emerging technology, one needs to understand its true implication and commercial potential. To those speculators who saw the Internet for what it really was, it was a boon. To those that believed the hype and bet on the hype, it was a bust. For example, the Internet is not a replacement for the bricks-and-mortar retail sector. It is a public forum, a meeting place, and a wellspring of information. The difference between these two views of the Internet was the difference between success and failure. Those who bet on Internet retailers found American consumers uncooperative. Most people didn't do their shopping online, and those that did, tended to buy from companies they trusted like JCPenney, Sears, or Wal-Mart.

Speculators who saw the Internet for what it was and would be—an information highway and community forum—recognized a business model that would generate profits. Money would be made on the Internet by selling exposure. Companies like Yahoo! and Google, companies that deal in information and sell exposure in the form of advertisements, were the big winners. It is a magazine model where readership is their ticket to profits. Speculators who bought the information highway rather than the online mall were the big winners.

Emerging Markets

There is a rising need in the marketplace satisfied by the development of a family of products or services. Dell's development of a mail order, made-to-order computer marketing service is an example of an emerging market. Emerging markets often lie dormant until an innovative entrepreneur recognizes and capitalizes on them. Unlike emerging technologies where the number of players at the inception of the technology is large, emerging markets often begin with just a single innovator. The innovator is often followed by copycat companies seeking to do it better, different, or cheaper. To the extent the followers succeed in positioning themselves shrewdly in relation to their competitors, they will also survive and prosper.

Emerging markets are much harder to spot than technologies. There is no way to determine which company will discover that magic niche.

Emerging Company

An emerging company significantly increases its market share in a settled market or technology. Hansen Beverage is a good example of an emerging company. The nonalcoholic beverage industry was growing at 7 percent per year and dominated by two players, Coke and Pepsi. Hansen, a company that had been in existence for decades, began a sales spurt that propelled it to new heights of sales and earnings. Its stock responded with a fiftyfold increase in price.

As difficult as it is to spot a winner in an emerging market, picking one in a settled market is more so. Since the industry is mature, as a whole it will only provide average or below-average rewards. Finding another Hansen is a difficult task for an outsider.

Cyclic Opportunities

A good speculator knows history. One type of speculator, a cyclical speculator, specializes in this. Cyclic speculators understand and monitor the ebbs and flows of the business community. These ebbs and flows create speculative opportunities at both the economic and business level.

Economic Cycles

Our economy goes through periods of expansion and contraction as consumers satisfy their material needs and then cut back on purchases to pay down debt or increase savings. These economic cycles cause the Federal Reserve to increase and decrease interest rates in order to control money supply, which acts to encourage or restrain economic growth. These shifts in interest rates affect the returns on corporate bonds, which make them more or less attractive to stock investors. If the interest rate becomes high enough, money will flow out of the stock market and into bonds. This outflow of money reduces the prices of stocks. When the interest rates are declining, money moves out of the bond market and into stocks, increasing stock prices. Speculators, aware of this cyclical effect, anticipate the flow to increase their returns.

Company Cycles (Turnarounds)

The field of company revitalizations or turnarounds is another speculative area where the knowledge of history and a little business sense can be used to identify speculative opportunities. While these are not really cyclic in nature, they do occur on a routine basis. Newmont provided an excellent example of a turnaround. Since Newmont produces and sells gold, as the price of gold increased on the world market, Newmont's profits increased, since the cost to mine the gold was not affected by the price run-up. This dramatically increased their profits.

These revitalizations can also be sparked by divestitures, acquisitions, and bankruptcies. Revitalizations are complex opportunities best suited to professional investors who take controlling positions in the stock. A good overview of these and other types of opportunities can be found in Joel Greenblatt's *You Can Be a Stock Market Genius*.[2]

The Search for the Speculative Opportunity

The key to speculation is discovering the undiscovered. In any given year, the stock market will produce 300–500 speculative opportunities—stocks that double in price within a year. Some of them double for multiple years, as was the case with Hansen Beverage. Others, like Ampex, can more than double in just a few months. Opportunities like Hansen and Ampex are hard, but not impossible, to find. The key is to know where to look.

One of the first places to look is where you used to work. This is your area of expertise and one of the few areas where you were the insider. For instance, if your old company had difficulty holding market share against a particularly aggressive and innovative competitor, investigate that competitor. Is it publicly traded? Is its stock underpriced compared to its performance or its potential? The same investigation should be undertaken for vendors that solved sticky problems within your company. Does their solution have broader applications? Are they now seeking to capitalize on those broader applications? Also, remember your company's customers. Was and is their business growing? One of the first people to know how successful a company is or can be are those people selling to or buying from them. Do not underestimate the opportunities, experiences, and expertise that surrounded you in the workplace.

You also have interests. Hobbies, science, politics, and government are all good sources of information. If you were a professional, you are probably still reading technical journals. Those journals are a source of innovations, some that may be on the threshold of commercialization. If you are a hobbyist, you may find your hobby is becoming the latest fad. The large influx of participants in your hobby may give you a sense of being a trendsetter, but why not also let it give you a speculative opportunity by being the first to spot who profits from the influx and then investing in that company's success.

Retirees, even those with modest means, are often travelers. Make these trips part of your stock market experience. Whenever you travel, remember to take a small notebook to record investment ideas for further investigation.

Fads and trends can provide speculative opportunities. While others are out buying Cabbage Patch dolls and pet rocks, you need to be checking out who makes them. The stock market is about reason, recognition, and reaction. If the market has yet to recognize the trend or react to it, that is your opportunity. This is not to say you can't buy the doll or the rock. You can, but remember, you are in the stock buying and selling business, and you need to put business before pleasure.

One of the biggest phenomena in the American economy is the franchise. The basic success model for the franchise is to become a local success, expand that success regionally, then nationally, and finally globally. If you spot a growing franchise in your area, investigate it. Is it publicly traded? Is it a tracker? A leader? A laggard? Speculating on a growing franchise is tricky. Franchises can exhibit tremendous growth by opening new outlets; newness often draws customers, but the real success of a franchise is in its ability to retain and grow the customer base after the first spurt of business. However, you are a speculator, and that initial spurt defines your success. The ability to grow same-store sales is the investor's worry and your signal to take profits.

You can find speculative opportunities everywhere. National companies start as local companies. A local winner with a unique product and a growing loyal customer base is a good candidate for a speculative play.

This is especially true if they are implementing a plan that will take them national or global. Even an existing national chain can provide speculative opportunities if it has revitalized its product offering or improved its commercial image. As a customer, you are often the first to know if these company spruce-ups are working. When you enter your local mall or shopping plaza, keep your eyes open for stock bargains.

Blind Luck

The above examples of speculative opportunities are based on your personal investigative prowess. These are the purviews of the visionary and the extrapolator. What about our third speculative personality, the gambler? Gamblers seek big returns with very little effort, but this book cautions against relying on blind luck and encourages you to make your own luck—reasoned luck. I caution you against certain sources of speculative ideas that are the gambler's mainstay. It's not that they never succeed; it's that they are out of your control and offer very low confidence levels.

One of these is the boiler-room stockbroker. These people call you on the phone with their latest recommendation. They claim to want to build a relationship with you, but all they really want is for you to play their game. Don't take the bait. If they call and pitch you, hang up.

The tipsheets are another dangerous speculative source. Companies produce them in an attempt to increase the stock's price. Are these tipsheets worth anything? To the extent they bring a stock to your attention, they are a valuable source of speculative leads. However, be very careful to do your own investigation before you buy one of their recommendations. They may have uncovered a diamond in the rough, but it is up to you to make it sparkle.

Most tipsheets focus on penny stocks. The great appeal of a penny stock to the speculator is its low price. Since many of these stocks represent smaller companies with high potential growth rates, their cheap price and upside potential are extremely seductive. However, keep in mind, the failure rate (bankruptcy) of these small companies is high. Speculators who deal in penny stocks just because they are penny stocks could find themselves being penny-wise and pound-foolish.

If you decide to invest heavily in penny stocks, there are some things to keep in mind:

■ The company you speculate on should be profitable or have a strong prospect of profitability. To determine this, focus on incremental margin as a measure of the long-term profit potential of the company and the validity of its business model.

■ Explore why the company is listed. In many cases, small companies are listed so the owners can cash out. Such a cash out is not necessarily to your benefit, especially if the owners that built the company are moving on to more fertile opportunities. You end up owning a company with no growth prospects and insufficient profits or cash flows to provide a dividend payout. It is a dead investment with a high risk of loss and a low likelihood of return.

Finally, you can find insider trading to be a big source of speculative opportunities. Insider trading is buying company stock based on information about the company not released to the general public. As outsiders, we rarely hear the rumor. However, if an engineer in their R&D laboratory discovered a new product with the potential to revitalize a maturing company, and he divulged that to his wife, who told a neighbor who bought the stock, that's an insider trade. The Securities and Exchange Commission (SEC) has outlawed the practice, but they can't stop the rumor mill, and if you innocently hear something, it's up to you to act on it or not. Just remember, not all rumors are true. You might want to wait for the public announcement.

The Speculative Advantage

The number one reason to be a speculator is the high upside potential. To fully capture such huge rewards, you need to be in before anyone else spots the opportunity. Figure 49 compares the profile of a ten-bagger with the new product adoption model presented in Figure 41. The speculators are the innovators. They are in before the price is driven up by the traders in the early adoption stage and the investors of the early and late majorities.

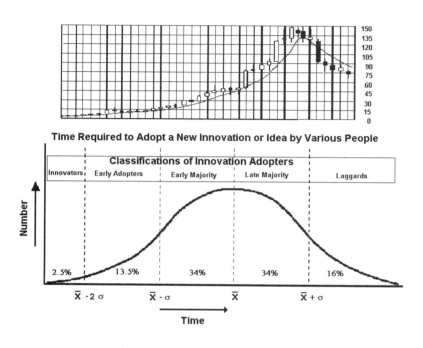

FIGURE 49: Stock Chart for a Typical Ten-Bagger. The chart of a ten-bagger is compared to the adoption model. As more and more investors recognize the opportunity, the price of the stock rises. When most of the buyers for the stock are satisfied, the price begins to decline.

Of course, speculators lose too, but they can afford to lose. Even if they are prone to Type I errors 90 percent of the time, speculators can make a good living. A speculator who invests $100 in ten different stocks and limits her loss in any one stock to 50 percent, will earn $1,450 in three years if she hits just one ten-bagger, a 13 percent annual return. If her nine losers simply stagnate rather than shrink, the value of her stocks will equal $2,000, a 28 percent return. Speculation with just a 10 percent confidence level and a strict loss-prevention rule can deliver a full range of annual returns from the market average up to 100 percent. The speculator has plenty of room for error.

Another advantage of speculation is it requires very little business or stock market expertise. Unless you are dealing in corporate turnarounds, most speculative opportunities are intuitive. It is a bet on your vision of the future and how a particular company fits into that future. Anyone can do it. All you need is some common sense, with an eye for innovation and a sense of what works.

Finally, speculation requires minimum attention. Once a speculative stock is purchased, it becomes a wait-and-see game. Other than monitoring a downturn and cutting your losses, a speculative buy requires little work. Thus, it is an excellent strategy for dabblers— people who are not going to spend hours a day or even hours a week watching the latest moves of their stock's price.

The Speculative Downside

One of the biggest flaws in the speculative strategy is there is no company history on which to base a decision. Companies can lumber along for years and then suddenly burst onto the scene as a speculative success story. Refer back to the Hansen chart (Figure 45). Note that in the years prior to its big price move, there was very little volume or price movement in the stock. With no growth in the net income 2001–2002, there was very little reason to expect a beverage company to take off as Hansen did. In early 2003, getting in on the ground floor with Hansen was a very risky move.

Transaction costs are another obstacle. A recent study of ten-baggers found that the average price of these stocks before their move was just $0.87. With a $50 brokerage fee, 100 $1 stocks must double in price to reach breakeven. Since more than half the ten-baggers start their run-ups under $1, for the very small investor, the first year of a ten-bagger's gain goes to pay the transaction costs. Of course, using a discount brokerage firm or Internet stock-trading site will reduce this obstacle.

Another disadvantage is that speculative stocks are psychologically taxing because there is no clear sell point. Referring to Figure 46, selling Ampex at the first pull back in 2003 would net a return of 100+ percent, but it would have lost additional gains of 600 percent. In 2005, holding until the price closed below the six-month moving average cut almost 40 percent from your peak earnings. Even though your overall gain was a tenfold improvement, a sale in April 2005 might leave you with a bitter taste and a sense of failure.

Finally, speculation requires vision and the courage to stand behind your vision. This can be exceptionally difficult for retirees who are not plugged into the latest technologies. It is in these technologies, fads, and trends that most speculative opportunities are found. Spotting them is difficult for the average speculator. It is exceptionally difficult for those players who have a natural aversion to the new and unproven and an attachment to the old and proven. Before you can successfully speculate, you must do more than tune into the modern world; you must embrace it.

Eight Rules for Profitable Speculation

Speculation can be made profitable by following eight simple rules:

RULE #1: Sell your losers and let your winners run. By adhering to this strategy, it is possible to achieve above-average returns with only a 10 percent success rate.

RULE #2: Establish your sell point before you buy and stick to it. Don't second-guess yourself in the heat of battle. Sell the losers and move on. With almost 400 ten-baggers in play at any one time, there will be plenty of new stocks to buy.

RULE #3: Don't let what you could have had interfere with what you did achieve. If you sell too soon, forget it. If you sell too late, forget it. Just remember how much money you made when you sold, not how much you could have made by not selling.

RULE #4: Rely on your own vision. Don't buy what some tipster sees unless you see it also.

RULE #5: Perfect your vision by taking an interest in tomorrow, not yesterday. If that means hanging around your grandchildren more, do it. It will be good for them and profitable for you.

RULE #6: Don't let your political biases get in the way of your investing strategies. You may hate the rich, or Republicans, or Democrats, but if they cut taxes, embrace the change and seek out companies that will benefit from the cut. One of the biggest obstacles to intelligent decision-making is prejudice. Forget your biases and focus on your opportunities.

RULE #7: Don't buy a speculative stock before its time. As a retiree, time is precious. The time to buy Ampex was not in 2001 or 2002. Retirees don't have the time to buy and wait. Better to put your money to work somewhere else while you watch. As soon as you spot a triggering event, make your buy. You may lose a few dollars, but the time saved will be well worth it.

RULE #8: Remember, in speculation you must lose some to win some. Often, you will have more losers than winners. However, it is the size of the winners that makes speculation a winning strategy, which brings us back to Rule #1.

Some of these rules can also be applied to investing and trading. For instance, rules 1, 3, 4, 5, and 6 are helpful guides to investors. Rule #8 is especially important when it comes to trading. Rule #3 applies to just about everything you do in life.

What You Have Learned

As a speculator, you will want to keep the following points in mind as you search the stock market for opportunities. There is more to learn, and that learning will accompany your doing. Experience is a great teacher. The following review will give you a firm foundation on which to build that experience.

- The basic stock market strategies of investing, trading, and speculating can be related to each stage in the business life cycle.
- The basic stock market strategies also conform to the consumer adoption model. Speculators are innovators. Traders and investors tend to join the adoption process in the middle and later stages.

- There are five speculative opportunities in the stock market that can be divided into two groups.

    1. Visionary opportunities found in emerging technologies, markets, and companies.
    2. Cyclical opportunities found in economic cycles and company turnarounds.

- Many speculative opportunities cannot be discerned by studying the past performance of a company. Their price movement often begins six to twelve months before they are confirmed by the company's performance. Look to newspapers, magazines, and your local area's business activities for speculative opportunities.

- Stocks can be grouped into three distinct profiles: trackers, leaders, and laggards.

- Trackers are stocks with prices that oscillate around the calculated value.

- Leaders are stocks with prices significantly and persistently higher than the calculated value.

- Laggards are stocks with prices significantly below the calculated value. They contain a high upward potential that can be unleashed by a triggering event like a stock split.

- Stock splits are used to change the price of a stock to make it more attractive to stock buyers. A normal split lowers the price of a stock. A reverse split increases the stock's price. Both are designed to move the current price of the stock into a more tradable range.

- It is important to sell speculative stocks after they have made their move.

- Don't buy too soon. Wait until the trigger point is reached, and then check the trading volume to see if the trigger released a significant pent-up demand for the stock. This is especially true for laggards.

CHAPTER 12
Putting It All Together

We now know what we need to do and how to do it; but knowing is not doing. To be confident in our investing, we must leave the comfort of School Street and take a walk down Wall Street. In this chapter, we open for business and make our bet. We'll start with a plan.

The Plan

Our plan will be built around an average retiree with an average size nest egg and little or no experience in the stock market. At the strategic level, the plan should take up no more than a single page. Attached to that strategic plan summary will be the action plans necessary to implement it. These should also be no more than one or two pages. Let's build a five-year plan according to the guidelines proposed in Chapter 7.

The Goal

THE GOAL: To create a retirement income of $40,000 per year, which is just above the current national average.

How SMART is this goal? To answer that we will need to do a self-assessment and resource inventory.

The Self-Assessment

The first question is, "Who am I?" After completing the personality profile in Appendix A, you conclude that you are emotionally and psychologically suited to be an investor.

The Resource Assessment

We'll start with your financial resources. In this example, your nest egg is $25,000—that is your capital base. Since your goal seeks to create an income stream, you will need to determine how much of the goal is already satisfied by your present or anticipated income.

From Social Security, you can expect $803 per month or $9,636 per year. From your previous employment, we'll assume you have a modest pension of $450 per month for an additional $5,400. The total annual income from those sources is $15,036, which is $24,964 short of your goal. Using five years as your planning horizon, your plan must overcome that shortfall using your modest capital base of $25,000, a daunting task.

Another resource area to explore is technology. In this example, since you are investing, daily monitoring of your stocks will not be critical. You can use the computer at the local library. While at the library, you will also use their resources to increase your knowledge by researching companies, markets, technology, and economic trends.

Fully invested at a 12 percent annual return, your nest egg will grow to $44,050 in five years. Continuing to invest that new capital base at 12 percent will provide an additional $5,286 income, but we need $24,964. With an indexed approach, you are $19,678 short of your goal. Your plan must bridge that gap.

Since the time to achieve your goal is fixed at five years, and for now the maximum amount of capital you have to invest is $25,000, the only way to bridge the gap is with a higher rate of return (reference Figure 22). Using a 28 percent rate of return, our $25,000 nest egg will grow to $85,900 in five years and provide an additional $24,052 in returns thereafter. Add that to your fixed pension of $5,400 and your inflation adjusted Social Security income of $11,171, and you have an annual income of $40,623. Can you make 28 percent from the start, and are you willing to bet our entire nest egg?

If the answer is no, you have two choices. Lower your goal to make it SMARTer, or increase your capital base by converting non-productive assets into productive assets. You can achieve this by converting items that you no longer need or use into cash, items such as second cars and homes, boats, and motorcycles. Doubling your nest egg in this manner will cut the return needed to achieve your goal to 20 percent. However, for the purpose of this illustration, you decide to stay with the 28 percent rate of return and make the $25,000 bet.

Strategy

STRATEGY: Invest your entire nest egg into a portfolio of conservative-growth stocks that offer a minimum annual return of 28 percent.

You must now determine how you will use those resources to achieve your goal. Strategy answers the question, "How?" A dividend approach is unlikely to achieve the returns needed. While a value strategy is capable of achieving 28 percent returns, it is much more intellectually demanding and market-dependent. A conservative-growth investment strategy is more suited to your skill level and plan horizon. Conservative means a company that has demonstrated a history of growth and has a reasonable expectation the growth will continue for the next few years. We are not looking for ten-baggers, penny stocks, or corporate turnarounds.

Assumptions

At present, there are no leading indicators suggesting an economic downturn is expected in the next few years (by the time this book is published that assumption may change). If you anticipated a downturn, you would focus your stock search on defensive stocks (discussed in Chapter 11). Don't let your political biases or the bias of others influence this assumption. When it comes to economics and business cycles, be objective.

Also, there are no health issues that would require the use of your nest egg for extraordinary medical expenses. There are no government regulations anticipated that could interfere with your investment plan. Therefore, the plan will not contain any contingencies to offset a potential negative development. It is also assumed the $25,000 is in a tax-free retirement account. You won't incur any taxes until the money is withdrawn as income at the end of the five-year plan.

Action Plans

In order to implement your strategy and achieve your goal, you will generate several action plans with specific, measurable objectives. Appendix C presents a format for developing an action plan. Chapter 7 contains an outline of a completed action plan. Use the form in Appendix C to build action plans for the following objectives:

1. To acquire access to an Internet stock trading site.
2. To identify a group of stocks with the potential to grow 28 percent per year for the next five years.
3. To create a stock portfolio from the group of potential 28 percent-per-year-growth stocks.
4. To develop and implement a portfolio monitoring and management system.

Results

The cumulative effect of your action plan objectives will equal your overall goal. This can be projected as a simple five-year financial statement. Each year's result becomes a milestone. You can use these milestones to measure your success and take corrective action to keep your plan on track. A copy of a completed strategic plan based on the analysis above is presented in Figure 50.

Goal: To achieve a retirement income equal to $40,000 per year in the year following the completion of the plan.

Timeframe: 5 years

Strategy: Invest my entire nest egg ($25,000) in a portfolio of growth stocks.

Assumptions: There are no negative personal, economic, or governmental obstacles anticipated.

Resources:

Available: $25,000 in capital, $16,571 in cash flow, computer and Internet access.
Needed: Stock trading site, access to reference materials.

Key Action Plans:

● Access an Internet site   ● Select potential growth stocks
● Create a growth stock portfolio   ● Manage the stock portfolio

Financial Results:

	Initial	2007	2008	2009	2010	2011	2012
Capital	$25,000	32,000	40,960	52,429	67,109	85,899	85,899
Cash Flow							
Soc. Sec.		9,636	9,925	10,223	10,530	10,845	11,171
Pension		5,400	5,400	5,400	5,400	5,400	5,400
Investment		-- 0 --	-- 0 --	-- 0 --	-- 0 --	-- 0 --	24,052
Total							$40,623

FIGURE 50: Five-Year Strategic Plan for Retirement Investing Program.

Identifying Potential Stock Purchases (Action Plan #2)

In order to identify stocks to purchase, you will need to develop some selection criteria. Since you have chosen a conservative-growth investment strategy, the criteria will seek to identify low-risk companies in the developmental and growth stages of their life cycle. Using the analysis guideline present in Chapter 9, the initial selection criteria are presented below.

Business

Industry: Eliminate low growth or industries you do not understand.

Size: Choose smaller companies with greater growth potential (under $1 billion in sales).

S/A: There is no fixed standard. However, a value below 2.00 implies there could be room to grow without a major capital outlay for new plants and equipment.

P/S: Below 1.00 would suggest the stock is currently underpriced.

Earnings

GM: This should exceed 35 percent, especially if the S/A is at or above 3.00.

OP: Low operating margins, especially in companies with high GM, implies excessive management, technical, or marketing costs.

Net Income: The average is 3–5 percent; however, it really needs to be compared to similar companies.

Leverage

ROA: Looking for 15 percent or more.

ROE: Depending on the debt, this number should be significantly higher than the ROA.

P/E: At or below the market average of 15–20 is good, but it depends heavily on the projected growth rate and the industry.

Growth

Sales: Prefer double-digit growth for the past three years with acceleration occurring in the past year or quarter.

EPS: Again, look for double-digit growth accelerating to 20+ percent in the past year and quarter.

EG/SG: The EPS growth should exceed the sales growth. This value should be greater than 1.00.

PE/G: Prefer a value below 1.00 or as close to it as possible.

Risk

Debt/Equity: Debt should not exceed the equity. This value should be less than 1.00.

Current Ratio: This should be 2.00 or better.

Interest Coverage: This should be large enough to absorb a 10 percent loss in sales at a 50 incremental margin. This means the income before taxes must be greater than 5 percent of sales.

Cash Flow: Sufficient to finance a 28 percent growth rate. The cash should be generated from operations.

Potential

Industry Position

> **P/E:** Compare the company's P/E to the industry's P/E. Is there room to grow, or is it already fully valued by the market?
>
> **P/S:** The same comparison as P/E.

Shares Outstanding: The fewer shares outstanding the greater impact an increase in net income will have on the EPS and the stock's price.

Markets: Is the company operating in a growing market?

Products: Do the company's products appear to meet customer requirements?

Market Share: What share of the market does the company command? Is there room to grow?

Competitive Edge: Does the company have an edge over competitors? Patents? Brand recognition? Distribution network?

Institutional Ownership: Less than 50 percent.

The Screen

A database is a listing of companies with some of their key performance or descriptive measures (metrics). When you screen the database, you are searching it and selecting those companies that meet your specific criteria. The database you will be using for your screen is at *www.moneycentral.msn.com.* (The analysis in this plan used the *www.reuters.com* database, but that database is no longer available.)

There are two reasons to screen. The first is to develop a descriptive profile, and the second is to develop a selective profile. You will be doing both. Use a descriptive profile if you want to know the sales growth of all the companies in the database, by constructing the screening criteria to include all the candidates regardless of sales growth. If you only want to select companies with sales growth greater than 28 percent, you construct the criteria to retrieve only those companies with sales growth greater than 28 percent. This would select those companies and present them to you as a new database.

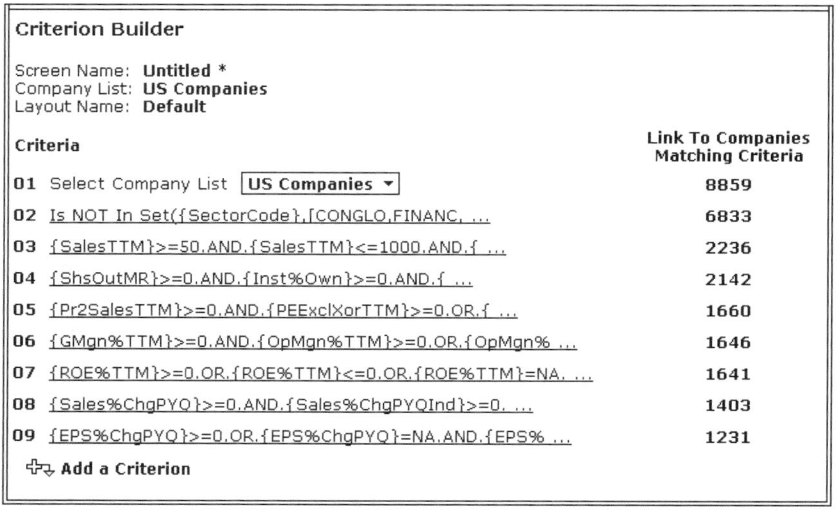

Criterion Builder

Screen Name: **Untitled ***
Company List: **US Companies**
Layout Name: **Default**

Criteria	Link To Companies Matching Criteria
01 Select Company List US Companies ▾	8859
02 Is NOT In Set({SectorCode},[CONGLO,FINANC, ...	6833
03 {SalesTTM}>=50.AND.{SalesTTM}<=1000.AND.{ ...	2236
04 {ShsOutMR}>=0.AND.{Inst%Own}>=0.AND.{ ...	2142
05 {Pr2SalesTTM}>=0.AND.{PEExclXorTTM}>=0.OR.{ ...	1660
06 {GMgn%TTM}>=0.AND.{OpMgn%TTM}>=0.OR.{OpMgn% ...	1646
07 {ROE%TTM}>=0.OR.{ROE%TTM}<=0.OR.{ROE%TTM}=NA. ...	1641
08 {Sales%ChgPYQ}>=0.AND.{Sales%ChgPYQInd}>=0. ...	1403
09 {EPS%ChgPYQ}>=0.OR.{EPS%ChgPYQ}=NA.AND.{EPS% ...	1231
⟱ Add a Criterion	

FIGURE 51: Overview of a Company Screen of the Database at *www.reuters.com*. The progressive nature of the screening process is illustrated. As each new criterion is added to the screen, the number of stocks matching those criteria declines.

You can string together several different screening characteristics to create a focused database meeting all your criteria. Figure 51 provides an overview of the screening results from the database at the Reuters website. Your initial screen selected 1,231 companies. Download this new database from the website to a Microsoft Excel spreadsheet for further analysis.

Analyzing Past Performance

With the spreadsheet, you can sort the downloaded data by growth rate, then sales level, then profitability, or any of the other criteria you placed in your original screen. This allows you to systematically analyze the 1,231 companies identified in your initial screen without eliminating the lower-ranked companies from your database. In that way, you can go back and tweak your sorting system if the initial series of sorts fails to deliver a suitable investment candidate. Figure 52 is a screen capture from a series of sorts that included sales growth, EPS growth, P/S ratio, P/E ratio, and operating leverage. This has narrowed your 1,231 companies to just twenty-five potential candidates. Let's see what the market thinks about these twenty-five companies.

The Chart

The market's attitude toward these companies can be found in their stock charts. The chart you will use to monitor attitude is the five-year monthly with a six-month moving average. To that chart, you will add volume, P/E, and rolling EPS. Figure 53 presents the stock chart for one of the companies—NEGI.

Over the past five years, NEGI has had a significant price run-up. It was a ten-bagger, increasing from approximately $0.40 in May 2003 to $6 in May 2006. However, unlike most ten-baggers, NEGI's P/E is still well below the industry minimum, and at 2.00, is low by any standard. In addition, it appears to be establishing a new trend line (C–D), which would place it on track for a 42 percent price gain next year, well above our 28 percent goal. Clearly, this is a good candidate for investment, but the very low P/E is a red flag. Before you buy, further analysis is required to determine why the stock is valued so low.

Ticker	Industry	Sales $	TotAset	CurAsets	CurLia	ShrsOut	InstHold	GM%	TTMSls%	3YrSls%	5yr Sls%	QteEPS%	EPS%/1yr
LXU	Chemical Manufacturing	463.22	214.4	130.87	72.15	14.53	14.77	18.17	20.27	11.89	7.79	71.95	1398.79
NGA	Misc. Fabricated Products	66.89	45.6	20.8	12.27	7.85	23.9	27.46	54.31	7.83	4.25	481.34	1449.6
PXG	Footwear	144.83	141.57	69.63	21.39	8.38	29.67	37.57	49.73	44.54	26.9	-64.32	714.33
NUHC	Electronic Instr. & Controls	692.89	271.08	260.88	55.87	17.94	71.49	15.3	44.31	22.94	-2.41	295.6	388.89
AWRCF	Electronic Instr. & Controls	274.44	262.35	176.19	92.24	13.83	0	14.62	23.4	3.23	14.33	-93.87	175.19
LMS	Electronic Instr. & Controls	589.29	265.24	150.97	72.89	15.76	95	24.19	31.56	16.52	7.22	109.79	229.72
DTLK	Software & Programming	143.19	67.18	59.13	43.1	11.22	46.94	25.93	33.57	10.63	-3.2	293.42	236.7
BESI	Semiconductors	245.9	409.82	247.18	72.46	32.74	14.45	40.13	28.27	25.44	-3.66	73.64	171.92
INTT	Electronic Instr. & Controls	63.26	37.44	30.54	10.4	9.3	41.6	42.72	23.39	4.23	-9.45	24.33	139
DTRX	Chemical Manufacturing	96.32	49.38	22.97	23.1	1.58	40.49	24.46	25.67	10.29	3.59	221.74	141.2
NEGI	Oil & Gas Operations	72.76	168.48	5.42	7.83	11.19	2.99	84.44	32.13	13.29	2.94	219.24	115.45
NSYS	Electronic Instr. & Controls	101.14	45.05	35.72	23.54	2.67	1.68	11.92	24.93	11.56	8.98	15.11	82.56
SYNL	Constr. - Supplies & Fixtures	147.27	79.16	56.11	22.39	6.13	24.41	11.86	22.94	14.69	2.5	353.11	75.65
DXPE	Misc. Capital Goods	255.2	96.01	73.21	36.38	5.12	16.02	27.92	51.56	7.77	0.3	188.1	165.94
PRZ	Healthcare Facilities	86.75	206.75	35.48	35.29	66.93	10.5	76.2	38.88	109.21	262.96	-123.68	121.36
MAD	Misc. Fabricated Products	940.74	782.6	433.48	148.78	55.41	4.91	15.29	39.82	12.19	3.83	249.28	90.03
CFK	Oil Well Services & Equipment	479.14	182.8	168.36	99.94	18.23	21.36	18.81	26.16	23.66	6.06	9.21	48.96
APNI	Misc. Fabricated Products	170.02	75.08	57.95	21.68	11.19	11.36	14.31	95.36	-31.01	-26.23	170.27	159.09
JADE	Jewelry & Silverware	114.89	129.55	119.81	72.01	18.92	3.15	26.1	30.46	NA	NA	13.7	48.38
GWTR	Construction Services	93.89	64.24	61.63	59.07	6.68	NA	6.95	77.69	35.1	38.97	917.5	117.46
MEA	Iron & Steel	201.45	108.61	46.83	23.1	9.96	2.05	18.68	28.77	40.48	NA	41.4	39.42
STRL	Construction Services	246.87	171.29	112.31	53.94	10.83	57.21	11.9	26.52	17.78	NA	7.13	33.35
XRTX	Computer Storage Devices	946.1	403.68	302.7	177.58	28.74	60.28	21.08	59.61	39.1	NA	123.34	67.68
INTX	Computer Services	189.54	182.49	68.13	43.72	16.83	32.26	63.39	20.05	19	NA	-26.22	21.11
VSEC	Business Services	326.71	87.95	75.47	50.23	2.37	13.88	3.54	19.96	29.69	18.04	18.83	20.01

FIGURE 52: Preliminary Stock Analysis – Microsoft Excel Spreadsheet. The results of your stock screen can be exported to an Excel spreadsheet, where you can sort the stocks by your selected criteria. This allows you to rank them by sales, total assets, shares outstanding, etc.

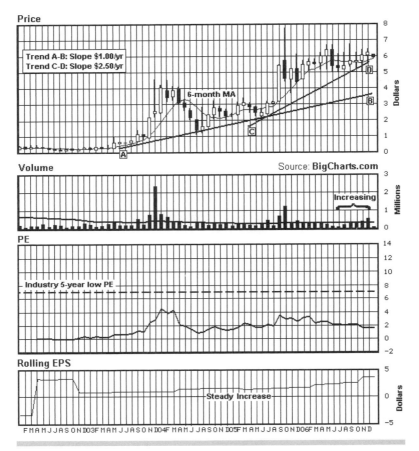

FIGURE 53: Stock Chart for NEGI — Five-year Monthly. This is a five-year monthly chart for NEGI. Added to it is the five-year history of the company's EPS and P/E. Two trend lines have been added to the chart as well as a six-month MA.

Before we continue with NEGI, let's take a quick look at the charts for the other twenty-four companies we identified in your preliminary analysis. They are summarized in Table XVI.

This quick look at the chart further narrows your field of candidates. You now have sixteen companies worth a closer look. Let's return to the Reuter's website to confirm and expand the information you uncovered during the screening process and the chart perusal. (While Reuters.com no longer offers a screen, it is still a good source for company profiles and financial histories.)

TABLE XVI

Summary of Key Observations of Selected Stock Charts (Five-year Monthly)

Company	Shares	Volume	Comments	Rank
LXU	14.53	2	Good market response. Possible.	12
NGA	7.85	4–6	Settling back. Potential.	13
PXG	8.38	0.5	Two strong moves then long-term fallback. No sustained EPS growth.	NR
NUHC	17.94	5–6	Recovering. Volume is up.	NR
AWRCF	13.83	0.5–1	EPS drop.	NR
LMS	15.76	5–10	Very good. Check out.	3
DTLK	11.22	5	Strong chart of TA stock (turnaround).	NR
BESI	32.74	?	No data available.	NR
INTT	9.3	1–2	Could move but need to check EPS vs. price.	14
DTRX	1.58	0.05	Ten-bag. EPS drop to (–). P/E stable at 10.	NR
NEGI	11.19	0.5	Ten-bag. Very low P/E. EPS up. OTC BB stock. Shows volume support on price moves. Check out.	2
NSYS	2.67	0.05	Not exciting.	NR
SYNL	6.13	0.2	Steady increase in EPS. P/E flat.	15
DXPE	5.12	5–20	Ten-bag. EPS is up. P/E is up. Check out.	10
PRZ	66.93	10	Ten-bag to $5. Fell back to $1. Volume is up. P/E is 6.25. Check out.	11
MAD	55.41	0.2	Price collapse from 25 to 5. Slow rise back to 11. EPS drop 60 to 5. Volume is up. P/E 1.5. Could double. Foreign.	5
CFX	18.23	2–4	Made big move then dropped back. P/E down. EPS is up. Possible turnaround. Check out.	4
APNI	11.19	1.5	Good. Check out.	7
JADE	18.92	3–5	No interest. Early warning signs.	NR
GWTR	6.68	40	Price collapse in '02. Low P/E (0.1). Very high volume. Watch for reverse split. Check out.	6
MEA	9.96	1–2	Lots of price volatility. More for trade than invest.	16
STRL	10.83	4	Made move off the construction boom.	NR
XRTX	28.74	10–15	Looks good. NASDAQ. Check out.	8
INTX	16.83	0.5	Potential. Check out.	9
VSEC	2.37	0.25	Good. Good EPS. Check out.	1

A Closer Look

You'll confirm the data in the database by looking at the financial statements of the companies you have chosen for further study. For that, you can return to *www.reuters.com,* where you will find the financial statements of these companies going back five years. While more complex and detailed, these financial statements are fundamentally the same as those presented in Tables VII and VIII for XYZ Company. With practice, you will become very comfortable reading and understanding these statements.[1]

By taking this second look, you achieve two objectives. You clarify your view of the company, and the review provides additional information not readily gleaned from the screened database. For example, the annual sales growth rates presented in the database for NEGI for one, three, and five years was 32, 13, and 3 percent, respectively. This would imply a very favorable and steady growth pattern. However, the reality is very different. Their income statements revealed the actual annual sales growth for the past five years was -11, -11, -6, 21, and 28. By confirming the database, you have discovered that NEGI is more a turnaround story than a steady grower.

The closer analysis allows you to fill in the gaps in your growth story and obtain more detailed descriptions of the company—its products and markets. In the case of NEGI, you discover it is a tangle of oil- and gas-well partnerships and management agreements not easily deciphered by the average small investor. In addition, further investigation into their Securities and Exchange Commission filings[2] indicates they are negotiating the sale of the company. In such situations, the small investor is at considerable risk. For that reason and others, you decide not to buy NEGI.

However, based on your closer look, there are several other highly ranked candidates in Table XVI that you can explore. They include LMS (#3), VSEC (#1), DXPE (#10), SYNL (#15), CFX (#4), APNI (#7), and XRTX (#8). Let's construct a comparative table for these candidates—Table XVII.

Of the seven companies listed in Table XVII, XRTX, LMS, and VSEC appear to be the most promising. Their sales growth is the most

TABLE XVII

Sales Profiles for Select Companies
with Promising Stock Charts

Company	XRTX	LMS	VSEC	DXPE	SYNL	CFX	APNI
TTM Sales	984	599	326	255	147	The Income Statements on CFX end with fiscal year 1997.	170
Sales 2005	680	494	280	185	129		448
Sales 2004	459	387	216	160	100		316
Sales 2003	334	340	133	150	80		302
Sales 2002	253	312	128	148	85		1,364
Sales 2001	Not listed	352	112	174	92		1,747
Current GM%	21.08	24.19	3.54	27.92	11.86	Can't confirm	14.31
Shares out (millions)	28.74	15.76	2.37	5.12	6.13	Can't confirm	11.19

consistent; while the GM percentage is below our original criteria of 25 percent, the consistency of their growth compensates. In the case of VSEC, the very low GM is offset by its small quantity of shares outstanding, which has a magnifying effect on EPS. LMS demonstrated some weakness in 2002, but it has been a steady grower since then. It also has the largest GM percentage of the three. XRTX has demonstrated exceptional growth since its listing, although its EPS growth faltered in 2003 and 2004 because of nonrecurring labor costs. DXPE looks interesting, but it is just beginning to increase its growth rate. It could be a stock to watch. SYNL does not provide sufficient growth or profitability to warrant further study at this time. CFX and APNI are dead ends. On closer examination, their data has not been updated in years (CFX) or they are in the throes of a restructuring (APNI). You decide to continue your analysis on LMS, VSEC, and XRTX, which are charted in Figure 54, Figure 55, and Figure 56.

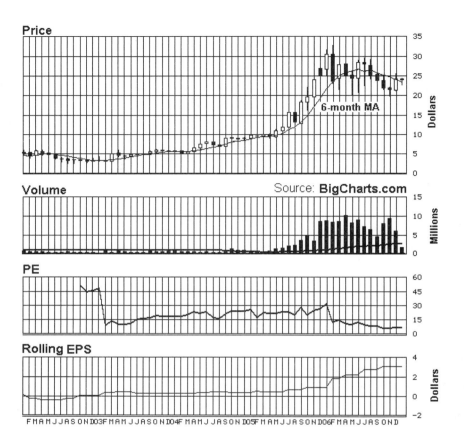

FIGURE 54: Stock Chart for LMS Five-year Monthly. This is a five-year monthly chart for LMS. Added to it is the five-year history of the company's EPS and P/E. The price, volume, and EPS have shown tremendous growth. The recent decline in price has depressed the P/E, which could indicate that the stock is ready for a resumption of its price rise.

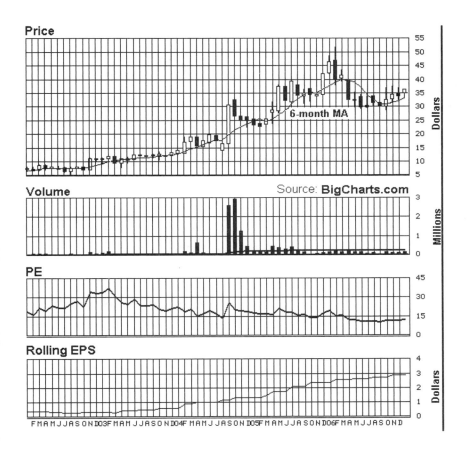

FIGURE 55: Stock Chart for VSEC, Five-year Monthly. This is a five-year monthly chart for VSEC. Added to it is the five-year history of the company's EPS and P/E. The price and EPS has risen steadily over the past five years. The recent price pullback has depressed the P/E, but that appears to be correcting as the stock has moved above its six-month MA in the past few months.

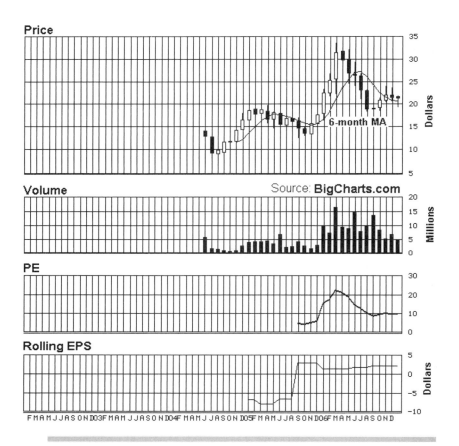

FIGURE 56: Stock Chart for XRTX, Five-year Monthly. This is a five-year monthly chart for XRTX. Added to it is the five-year history of the company's EPS and P/E. This stock has just come on the market in the past 2½ years. Its price and EPS performance do not provide a clear picture where it is heading.

Assessing Potential

Up to this point, you have been assessing the past. To determine what these companies can do in the future, you can look at what other companies in their industry are doing. You can compare your final choices to their competitors. In that way, you can see if they are leaders or laggards. Are they at the top of their game, or do they have room to grow? Table XVIII compares your companies to their industries.

All three of the companies have excellent potential. They command a very low share of their respective markets. Yet, in terms of sales, they are well above the median sales level as well as the median growth rate. Yet, the market has not rewarded this exceptional performance with exorbitant valuations. Both the P/E and P/S ratios are below their industry norms. While net incomes are not consistently higher than their industry average, the ROE for VSEC is close to the industry average, and the ROEs for XRTX and LMS are well above their industry's average. Equally important, all three companies have demonstrated the ability to convert their sales growth into EPS growth. In the case of LMS, the EG/SG was an impressive 45.5. Each of these companies remains a strong buy candidate.

TABLE XVIII
Company Performance Versus Industry Performance

Metric	XTRX	Industry	LMS	Industry	VSEC	Industry
Number listed	—	29	—	235	—	304
TTM Sales	983 (#7)	192 (median)	599 (#53)	78 (med)	326 (#87)	57 (med)
TTM Growth %	45 (#4)	10 (med)	31 (#39)	11 (med)	20 (#79)	6.9 (med)
Market Share %	2.43	—	0.29	—	0.12	—
P/E	9.8	10.7 (low)	7.54	16.9 (low)	12.3	17.4 (low)
P/S	0.62	2.45	0.64	2.00	0.25	2.88
GM%	20.1	37.7	24	30.5	3.5	43.1
Net Income%	5.9	9.4	8.4	6.4	2.1	11.2
ROE	29.4	12.3	49.7	19.3	21.5	21.8
EPS Grw/ Sales Grw	3.7	Negative	45.5	2.2	2.4	3.3

The Story

The story is a very subjective analysis. It includes a description of the company, a resume of its management, and a sense of its prospects. Most of the story can be found in newspapers, magazines, annual reports, SEC filings, on the Internet, and on television. Let's look at the stories behind our three potential investments.

Xyratex Ltd. (XRTX) is listed on the NASDAQ, and is based in Havant, England. The company designs, develops, and manufactures products that support storage and data-communications networks. It was incorporated in April 2002, and operates in two business segments. The first is storage and network systems, and the second is storage infrastructure. The storage systems are primarily sold to OEMs (original equipment manufacturers). The infrastructure devices are sold to computer-disk manufacturers and their component suppliers. They have more than 130 customers and operations throughout the United States, Asia, and Europe. Their listed competitors are Adaptec, Dot Hill Systems, and Engenio Information Technology.

In the past year, they have grown faster than their industry in sales and EPS. However, much of that growth has come from acquisitions. In May 2005, they acquired Oliver Design. In September 2005, they acquire nStor Technologies. In September 2006, they established a headquarters in Japan. And, in January 2007, they acquired ARIO Data Networks and announced Autodesk as one of their newest customers. The architects of this expansion have been Andrew Sukawaty, Chairman of the Board, and Steve Barber, CEO. However, in a recent announcement, XRTX warned against lower sales and profits because of reduced capital expenditures by their customer base. Their reliance on acquisitions and their capital-investment-related product line (as opposed to a consumption-related product) could make them sensitive to business downturns. They also reported a quarterly decline in GM percent (21.7 to 17.4) because of an unfavorable product mix. Profitability at both the GM and NI level has been a persistent problem for XRTX (reference Table XVIII).

At present, institutions own 62.67 percent of XRTX stock. While the analyst's attitude toward the stock remains bullish, the trend has been moving away from a buy recommendation. Institutional activity on the stock confirms the trend with a net sale of 126,542 stocks in the most recent three months. Apparently, the low profit margins and reliance on acquisitions as a means of growth has depressed interest in the stock. However, the large price swings in the chart suggest the market has not yet decided a fair price for XRTX. Based on its growth rate and low P/E relative to its industry, this stock could break up to gains far in excess of your 28 percent annual objective.

Lamson & Sessions Co. (LMS) is listed on the New York Stock Exchange, and is assigned to the Electronic Instruments & Controls industry. However, based on its product line, it may more accurately be classified in Miscellaneous Fabricated Products. It manufactures and distributes a line of thermoplastic electrical, consumer, telecommunications, and engineered sewer products for domestic markets. Its listed competitors are Home Depot, Thomas & Betts Corp., and Georgia Gulf Corporation. However, LMS does include consumer electrical-wiring devices, home-security devices, wireless electrical, and other wireless devices, which may account for its classification.

LMS divides itself into three business segments. The Carlon segment produces raceway systems, electrical boxes, and fittings, which are sold to OEMs, power utilities, cable, and telecommunication companies. These products are used in multicell duct systems and conduit in telecommunication and fiber-optic networks. Carlon accounts for 45–48 percent of LMS's sales. The Lamson Home Products segment provides electrical outlet boxes, liquid tight conduit, electrical fittings, door chimes, and light controls to end-use consumers through home and DIY centers. This segment accounts for 21–24 percent of LMS's sales. Their PVC pipe segment provides PVC pipes and conduits to the electrical, telecommunications, consumer, utility, and sewer markets. The conduit protects wire and fiber-optic cables. PVC pipe generates 30–34 percent of its sales and is considered a commodity product, which means it is a low-profit and price-sensitive product line.

The current COB is John Schulze, who has just announced that he will retire in 2007. Moving up in the organization is Michael Merriman, who is currently president and CEO. They have recently solicited and received approval from the stockholders to increase the number of common shares authorized from 20 to 40 million. The primary purpose of this increase is to facilitate future but yet-to-be-identified acquisitions. This announcement has precipitated a response by Ramius Capital Group. Ramius is a registered investment advisor that manages $7.4 billion in a variety of alternative investment strategies. Ramius owns 5.9 percent of LMS's stock and seeks to alter the management's acquisition plan.[3]

The basic grounds of the disagreement lie in timing and positioning. While Ramius agrees with the LMS strategy to diversify away from the PVC pipe business through acquisition, it believes the first step is to strengthen LMS current stock valuations by selling the PVC pipe business and using the proceeds to reduce debt and repurchase stock. This would increase the price of the stock, which would make any future acquisitions based on a stock exchange less costly for LMS. The LMS management seeks to hold what they have, which they state is in the best long-term interest of the company. Theirs is strictly a long-term approach, while Ramius offers a short- and long-term strategy.

Who is right? Before you invest, you will want to answer that question. Other than your own business expertise, one clue to the answer lies in the institutions and analysts that advise them. Reportedly, fourteen institutions hold 110 percent of LMS stock. This seemingly impossible percentage is caused by the fact that these institutions report holding 17.4MM shares, but LMS reports 15.8MM shares outstanding; there is no explanation for this discrepancy in the references. The two analysts that reported on LMS give it a buy rating, and in the past three months, institutions have added 2.9MM shares to their holdings. Apparently, other buyers are not as concerned about LMS's strategy as Ramius.

VSE Corporation (VSEC) is a NASDAQ-listed company in the Business Services industry. It provides diversified engineering, logistic, management, and technical services performed on a contract basis. They are consultants and contractors located in Alexandria, Virginia. Virtually all their contracts are with the U.S. government. The primary customer is the U.S. Navy (70 percent of sales). The Army accounts for another 20 percent of sales, with the Department of Energy generating 3.5 percent. Most of the key developments for the company are announcements of the latest contracts awarded.

VSEC was incorporated in 1959, and is made up of several divisions that focus on particular areas of expertise such as fleet management, engineering and logistics, management science, and systems engineering. Donald Ervine is the COB, president, CEO, and COO. James Reed is the president of their only incorporated division, Energetics. Mr. Ervine's annual salary and benefits are $648,000 with an additional 49,000 shares of stock options (35 percent of the total options awarded). He joined the company in 1993 as a program manager.

While seventeen institutions hold 13.94 percent of the stock, there are no analyst reports or recommendations. However, in the past three months, institutional holding fell by 50,510 shares. Contrary to that bearish signal, several corporate directors have recently purchased stock at the $25–$35 price range, which is a very bullish signal.

Timing the Buy

You can spend days analyzing a company, only to discover a performance quirk or a forecasted obstacle that raises an insurmountable objection to buying the stock. When that happens, you will have to go back and rethink your goals, strategies, criteria, or assumptions. This is looping, and it is illustrated in Figure 57. Looping, while time consuming, is a good thing; it will prevent you from making costly mistakes. It is better to take the time to loop back and repeat the analysis than it is to buy a doubtful stock and lose both time and money on the transaction.

However, all three of the companies we have isolated in our example have promising stock charts (Figures 54, 55, and 56) and appear buyable. XRTX is in a growth market (technology), and they have aggressively sought out growth opportunities through acquisition. LMS has grown internally over the past five years, and they have announced plans to acquire new companies in order to fuel continued growth in sales and profits over the next few years. VSEC is tied to a very stable market (government contracting), and they have managed to grow both sales and profits within that market (ref. Figure 58). All of these companies have shown promise. However, given your strategy of conservative growth and your 32–55 percent price growth projection for VSEC in Figure 58, you decide to buy VSEC.

Not only is VSEC a good buy, it is also a good time to buy. Figure 59 illustrates the recent run-up of VSEC's stock price with respect to its sales (24 percent) and EPS (39 percent) growth. However, in recent months the price has pulled back below the 39 percent line and found support at $30 per share. This was expected, given the recent slowing of EPS growth (Figure 58). After testing that support several times over a four-month period, the stock has begun to climb to its present price of $37. However, you are projecting VSEC will, on average, maintain its 24 percent sales growth and 39 percent EPS growth

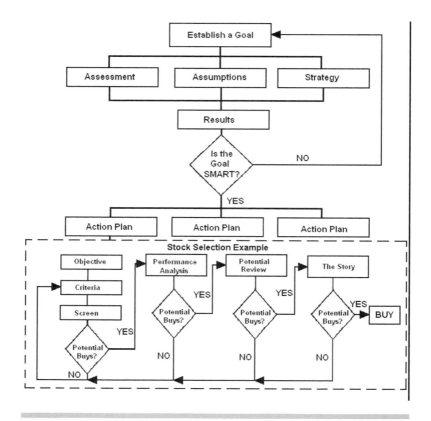

FIGURE 57: Decision Loops. Flow chart illustrating the critical decision points within your plan.

(Figure 58). Thus, with the pullback behind you, it is a good time to buy. You buy 675 shares at $37 each for a total price of $24,975. Adding $25 for transaction costs, you have fully invested your $25,000. This was done the week of January 8, 2007.

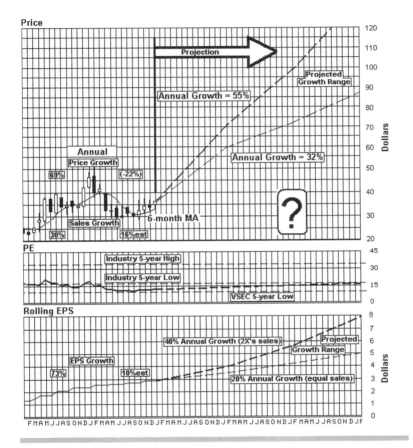

FIGURE 58: Price Projection for VSEC Stock. In order to project the stock price into the future, you will need to consider several factors. First is the growth of the stock's price in relation to the growth in its sales and EPS. Except for the recent price pullback, these compare well. Second, its historical P/E compared to itself and its industry. VSEC's P/E is in the lower range on both counts, which leaves plenty of room for an upward valuation. Finally, the EPS growth is projected based on the potential of the company and its ability to leverage its future operations. Again, a 30 percent sales growth yielded a 73 percent EPS growth. This is all translated into a stock-price projection 32–55 percent, above your plan goal of 28 percent.

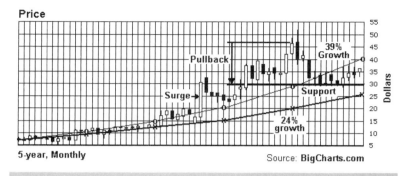

Price

5-year, Monthly   Source: **BigCharts.com**

FIGURE 59: Timing a Stock Buy — VSEC. The recent pullback in VSEC's stock price has dropped the price into its historical growth range. Thus, a buy at this point would reduce the risk that the buyer will experience another short-term price decline before the stock resumes its upward trend.

Monitor and Control

The final step in the process is to establish a selling point. You decide to establish a two-part sell rule. The first part will be chart based. If the stock's price closes below its six-month moving average, you will consider selling the stock. Why will you only consider selling the stock? Because the stock has closed below its six-month MA seventeen out of the last sixty months, and has fully recovered from each of those declines (ref. Figure 55). If you had sold during one of those declines, you may have missed one of the many surges that appear on VSEC's chart (Figure 59). Before you actually sell, the price decline must be confirmed.

Since you are an investor and not a trader, you will take that confirmation from the quarterly income statement or the current news releases of VSEC. In looking at the stock price over the past five years, any price declines were quickly reversed in the absence of a causal sales or profit decline. Thus, without a preceding or subsequent decrease in sales or profits, the price decline will simply be an alert signal rather than a sell signal. Likewise, a decline in sales and profits, which does not correspond to a price decline, will alert us to the need to watch the chart more closely and sell as soon as the price closes below the six-month MA. Thus, the entire sell rule is a chart decline confirmed by a performance decline, or vice versa.

Now you are in business. A quarterly check on VSEC's sales and earnings coupled with a daily check of current news and price fluctuations will give you the information necessary to make a timely liquidation of your position if the company and its stock begin to falter. At the same time, you will want to revisit your other buy candidates to see how they are faring with respect to your forecast for them. If you decide to liquidate VSEC, you may be able to buy one of your backup candidates in order to keep your money working toward that 28 percent per-year objective.

Learn and Grow

Not every stock you buy will make you richer, but every stock you buy should make you wiser. What you have done in this chapter is buy your first stock. It was bought in January 2008 for $37. By the time this book is published, you will know if it was a financial winner. Your objective for the year is 28 percent, which means the stock must be at least $47.44 in January 2009. (If the stock splits, the new chart will be adjusted for the split. Keep that in mind when checking on our choice.) If it is there, you have won your first bet. If it is not there, why isn't it there?

That simple question will lead you to greater understanding and future success. You must learn from your mistakes and your successes. Remember, there is a solution to every problem or glitch in your stock buying and selling system. Your objective in looking back is to spot those problems and solve them; it is not to mourn a dwindling nest egg or lament a missed opportunity. It is to do better the next time, so you can do better than the game, because as a retiree with a tiny nest egg, you must do better than the game.

Now it's up to you to do it on your own. It's time to:

Open your business
Make your plan
Develop your criteria
Run your screen
Select your stocks
Make your buys
Watch and react
Learn and succeed
Use luck—reasoned luck!

What You Have Learned

You have purchased your first stock using the concepts and skills learned in previous chapters. This was an investment decision. If you are a trader, you can trade VSEC stock using whatever system you prefer. Based on the analysis above, a speculator would be interested in further exploring NEGI and GWTR. Both appear to be speculative opportunities. No matter your stock market approach, you have learned to apply several very useful concepts in your new stock buying and selling business.

- First, develop your plan. A well-reasoned and financed plan is the foundation on which you will build your business.
- Looping is good. It allows you to pick the stock with the best chance of meeting your objectives. It will save you time and money.
- Look back to learn. Each trade may not make you richer, but it should make you wiser.
- Be prepared to sell. Don't become emotionally attached to a stock. Establish a reasonable sell point, and stick with it.
- Maintain an inventory of buy candidates. If your initial pick falters, you will be immediately ready to buy one of your backup stocks. This will keep you working toward your objective.

Cautionary Tales

We have taken a journey from fear to understanding. You now know the games people play and the games you are good at. The next step is to develop your confidence. That takes practice, time, and thoughtful analysis. You become good by doing, and it's time for you to start doing. Before you begin amassing your first million, a word of caution.

Economics is the only science created by humans. The other sciences are created by God, or, if you prefer, Nature. They are absolute. They have laws. Mix sodium and chlorine, and you'll get salt. Throw a rock into the air, and it falls to earth. You don't get salt sometimes; you get it all the time. The rock doesn't float because you want it to; it falls in spite of your wishes. It abides by the laws of science.

Economics doesn't have laws; it is governed by human behavior. It is defined by propensities, tendencies, and observations. And because the stock market is a product of the economy, it also doesn't have laws. It, like economics, is filtered through the prism of human behavior. Thus, when we say the stock market is a winning game, this is not etched in stone. It is simply a historical fact; the stock market is a winning game because it has been a winning game for the past 300 years—a fact caused by an increasing world economy, which is driven by the prosperity of individual businesses. If those businesses fail, the economy will falter, and the stock market will cease to be a winner.

Time Is More Valuable than Money

What does *falter* mean? It would take a depression greater than the Great Depression to turn the stock market into a long-term loser. Look at Figure 60, which tracks the Dow Jones Industrial Average from 1920 to 1990, which encompasses the Great Depression. It doesn't matter when you bought your stock—before the run-up of the Roaring Twenties (point A), at the peak of the boom just before the crash (point B), at the depths of the market's plunge (point C), or at the depths of the

Great Depression (point D). If you hold your stock long enough, you will be a winner. With dividends, even if you purchased your stock just before the 1929 crash, your average annual return by 1990 exceeded what you would get with a government bond or a bank account.

The key point illustrated in Figure 60 is the real risk in the stock market is you will run out of time, not money. Your risk tolerance is

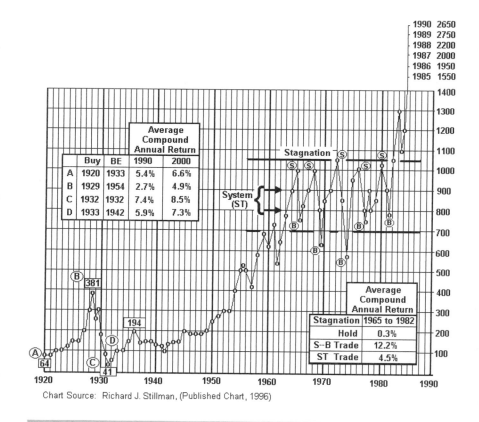

Chart Source: Richard J. Stillman, (Published Chart, 1996)

FIGURE 60: Volatility and Growth of the Dow Jones Industrial Average, 1920 to 1990. At various times over the life of the stock market, different investment strategies are more productive than others. In the 1970s, when the DJIA was essentially flat (0.3 percent annual growth), a trading strategy could yield annual returns 4.5–12.2 percent. The long-term, buy-and-hold investor unfortunate enough to buy an index fund just before the 1929 crash (point B), would still have a 2.7 percent annual return by 1990 and a 4.9 percent return by 2000. If you play long enough, the stock market is a winning game.

not how much money you can afford to lose; it's how long you can afford to leave your money invested. If you have the courage and discipline to stay the course, it will lead you to ultimate success.

Figure 60 illustrates another critical point. While your personality will define the game that's best for you, the game that's best for you isn't always the game the market is playing. During the stagflation years of the 1970s, the market was essentially flat. An investor who bought and held over that period barely broke even. Yet, there were several significant oscillations that provided excellent trading opportunities. It was a trader's market. An astute trader could have earned an average annual return of 12.2 percent. The buy-and-hold investor spent seventeen years watching his nest egg shrink and recover several times until the market finally broke out of its doldrums in 1982. For investors, the stock market of the 1970s was both psychologically and financially depressing.

If you were a retired investor in the 1970s, what would you do? It is easy to say trade after the fact. The problem is no one knows where the stock market is going until it gets there. It's true there are clues, opinions, indicators, and expert advice, but these are often conflicting. Like weather forecasters, they hedge their bets with probabilities and color their views with political agendas. In the end, you are responsible. You must understand the dynamics, make the bet, and suffer the consequences or reap the rewards.

Even the dearth of opportunities in the 1970s applies to only one aspect of investing—the index mutual fund. While the market as a whole was flat, individual stocks were increasing in price. Technologies were being developed. Companies were being born. Investors were making money. For investors, it was a stock-pickers game, which is also the retiree's game, especially a retiree with a small nest egg.

An important defense against the uncertainties of the stock market is liquidity. When the market crashed in 1929, investors didn't have to ride it down to 41. There was plenty of time to liquidate at 300 or 200 or 100. If they bought their stock in 1922 or 1925 or even as late as 1927, they could have sold after the initial crash and still made a very good return.

It is not a loss to sell a loser; it is a strategic withdrawal. You are preserving your capital so that you can play another day, but you must play if you are to be a winner. The people who played the market in 1929 and ran screaming from the game after the crash injured themselves for life. The people who played, withdrew their money a month after the crash, and then reinvested in 1932, tripled that reinvestment by 1936. They liquidated to get out of a losing position; they did not liquidate to abandon a winning game.

Uncertainty—Yes; Controversy—No

The stock market is an uncertain place, but it shouldn't be a controversial place, at least not for you. At the first whiff of controversy, consider moving your money to more settled opportunities. You simply don't have the time to wait for the insiders to sort out their difficulties. Whether it's a restructuring, bankruptcy, or management scandal, you would be wise to move on to other opportunities.

The Lure of Riches

Sooner or later, you will be lured from the relative safety of the New York and American Stock exchanges to the Over-The-Counter exchange. Before you buy any stock on the OTC, you will need to answer one very important question: Why is it listed? Are the owners, or the venture capitalists that backed them, looking to cash out, leaving you with a company that has a glowing past but a dismal future? Or is it a company seeking growth that needs to access equity capital to fund that growth without incurring debt? Determining why a company is listed is no easy task. However, if the owner owns 70–90 percent of the shares outstanding, it suggests the stocks were not issued to fund company growth. Before you buy, determine how widely the stock is distributed and to whom. This information can be found on various websites and in SEC filings.

Caution Is Not Fear

What's proposed in this chapter is caution, not fear. The purpose of the warning is not to drive you away from the market; it is to get you to approach it with a reasoned strategy, based on the fundamental principles underlying a growing and opportunistic stock market. Go slow. Be cautious. Learn, grow, and improve. That is your path to success.

Matching the Player to the Game

Personal Traits Needed to Succeed	✓	Investing	Trading	Speculating
Intelligence		High	Low	Moderate
Knowledge		High	Moderate	Moderate
Discipline		Very High	Moderate	Low
Math Skills		Moderate	Low	Low
Self-Starter		Low	High	Low
Ambitions		Low	High	Low
Patience		Moderate	Low	High
Decisiveness		Moderate	Very High	Low
Visionary		Moderate	Low	Very High
Risk-Taker		Low	Very High	High
Business Acumen		Very High	Low	Moderate
Intuitiveness		Moderate	Low	High
Analytical		Very High	Low	High
Systematic		Very High	Low	Moderate
Curious		Moderate	Low	Very High
Attentiveness		Moderate	Very High	Low
Agility		Moderate	High	Low
Insightfulness		Moderate	Low	Very High
Self-Confident		Moderate	Low	High
add: _____				
add: _____				
add: _____				
add: _____				

Partial Listing of Stock Market Entries

Sector	Industry Examples	Product Example	Company Examples
Basic Materials	Chemical Mfg.	Adhesives	H.B. Fuller
	Gold & Silver	Gold Ore	Golden Cycle Gold
	Metal Mining	Copper Ores	Phelps Dodge
Capital Goods	Aerospace & Defense	Aircraft	Boeing
	Construction & Agriculture Machinery	Construction Machinery	Caterpillar
			Pulte Homes
	Construction Services	Single-Family House	
Conglomerates	Conglomerates	Abrasives	3M Company
Consumer Cyclical	Auto & Truck Mfg.	Automobiles	Ford Motor
	Recreational	Small Arms	Sturm, Ruger & Co.
	Tires	Tires	Goodyear Tire
Consumer Noncyclical	Office Supplies	Pens	A.T. Cross
	Food Processing	Roasted Coffees	Nu Star Holdings
	Alcoholic Beverage	Malt Beverages	Genesee
Energy	Oil & Gas Integrated	Crude Oil & Natural Gas	ConocoPhillips
	Oil Services & Equipment	Oil Field Machinery	Baker Hughes
	Coal	Bituminous—Mines	Peabody Energy
Financial	Regional Banks	State Commercial Bank	The Bancorp
	Consumer Financial	Loan Brokers	E-Loan
	Insurance (A&H)	Accident & Health	AFLAC
Health Care	Biotechnology & Drugs	Diagnostic Substances	Biosite
	Healthcare Facilities	Nursing Care	Sun Healthcare
	Major Drug	Pharmaceuticals	Pfizer
Services	Advertising	Agencies	Monster Worldwide
	Business Services	Accounting	Paychex
	Hotel & Motel	Hotel & Motel	Hilton Hotels
Technology	Communication Equipment	Radio/TV	Motorola
	Computer Hardware	Electronic Computers	Dell
	Storage Devices	Storage Devices	San Disk
Transportation	Airline	Schedule Air Travel	Southwest Airlines
	Railroads	Railroad Equipment	Trinity Industries
	Trucking	Trucking, ex. Local	Yellow Roadway
Utilities	Electric	Electric Services	Duke Energies
	Natural Gas	Natural Gas Transmission	El Paso
	Water	Water Supply	Aqua America

Source: *www.reuters.com* (Powerlite Screener)

Action Plan

Action	Who	When
Objective:		
Strategy:		
Start Date:　　　Completion Date:　　　Responsibility:		

Endnotes

Preface
[1] "Money Advice, by the Book," *The Wall Street Journal*, 24 June 2006, B1.
[2] Burton G. Malkiel, *A Random Walk Down Wall Street* (New York: W. W. Norton & Company, 1990), 215–263.

Introduction
[1] The Social Security benefits calculations were made with the help of the Social Security website at *http://www.SSA.gov/SSA_Home.html*.

Chapter 1
[1] I will often refer to "the market" even though I don't believe in it. So why do it? It is a convenient way to discuss the rational and often irrational stock price movements.
[2] Peter Lynch is a well-known mutual fund manager who has written many instructive books on the stock market.
[3] *Signal* is a term used in trading to mark a buy or sell point on a stock chart.
[4] MACD (Moving Average Convergence/Divergence), DMI (Directional Movement Index), RSI (Relative Strength Index), and OBV (On Balance Volume) are commonly used technical indicators.
[5] An IPO is an Initial Public Offering. It is the first time a company sells stock to the public.
[6] Pump-and-dump schemes are schemes where a manipulator buys a stock and then promotes it heavily in order to attract buyers and raise the price. They then dump their shares at a profit. Since the price rise was not based on a general market rise or an improvement in the company, the stock price usually collapses after they sell.
[7] A bubble is a rapid and irrational rise in stock prices. Bubbles always burst.

Chapter 2
[1] A bull market is one where stock prices are rising. When stock prices are falling, it is a bear market. To earn the title *bull* or *bear*, the rise or fall must be greater than 20 percent. Anything less than that is simply a correction.
[2] I am not including the impact of the crash of 1929 or the Great Depression that followed—that was an exception to the rule. If we have another one of those, you will be burning this book for heat, not reading it for wealth.

[3] Of course, if you have $1 million dollars in your nest egg, a 10 percent return will provide $100,000 a year income. That will place you in an income bracket with the top 5 percent of American wage earners. If that's your situation, take this book to Cancun and read it on the beach. For the rest of us, 10 percent of $25,000 is not going to pay many bills.

[4] The term *ten-bagger* can be found in Peter Lynch's book, *One Up on Wall Street* (New York: Penguin Books, 1989).

Chapter 3

[1] Beta can be loosely compared to the standard deviation of a normal distribution. In that regard, the movement of SP500 would be considered the mean or average and beta would be how far an individual stock deviated from the movement of the mean.

[2] Beta is basically a market-driven metric. It is not a very useful metric to investors, but it can be useful to traders.

[3] The often-touted long-term return rate is presented in many stock market references.

[4] Over the last 100 years, the average stock market downturn was 30 percent. Thus, my contention that 30 percent represents the maximum volatility can be misleading. It is the maximum volatility for this example. In reality, downturns in the stock market can exceed the 30 percent number, but for the purposes of the point being illustrated, that simply means the trend must run longer to compensate for the deeper decline. It is still an issue of timing.

[5] Malkiel, 215–237.

[6] To better understand the mutual fund game, one must apply the concepts of weighted averages. A weighted average calculates the average of a population based on the likelihood of the outcomes in the population. For example, if we state that 70 percent of mutual funds fail to beat the SP500 while 30 percent triple its performance, a simple average of the two outcomes would be 20 percent ($[10 + 30] \div 2 = 20$). If we weight the average using the probability of their outcomes, the weighted average is 16 percent ($[10 \times 0.7] + [30 \times 0.3] = 16$). Thus, the 20 percent number used in Tables IV and V is statistically inaccurate but essentially illustrative.

[7] Leonard J. Kazmier, *Statistical Analysis for Business and Economics* (New York, New York: McGraw-Hill Book Company, 1967).

[8] Based on the Powerlite screening tool at *www.reuters.com*. This screening tool has recently been discontinued.

[9] One of the characteristics of a normal distribution is that 68 percent of the population of the distribution can be found within plus or minus one standard deviation (SD) from the mean. The percentage increases to 95 for a two-standard-deviation spread and 99.9 for a three-standard-deviation spread. The numbers presented in Figure 5 are not calculated or accurate; they are presented for illustrative purposes.

Chapter 4

[1] James K. Glassman and Kevin A. Hasse, *Dow 36,000* (New York, New York: Three Rivers Press, 1999).

[2] The 10–12 percent return is widely reported in the literature. It is reported here as a range because I have seen it stated as 10 percent, 11.8 percent, 12 percent, and various other percentages depending on the historical timeframes used in the calculation.

[3] Notice the 9 percent growth line, while constant in year-over-year percent, is not constant in year-over-year dollar gain. The dollar gain accelerates over time. When I say the price gains are not linear, I am not referring to this acceleration. I am referring to the volatility of the actual price line around the constant growth line.

[4] The number of potential ten-baggers was identified by using Reuter's Powerlite screening tool.

Chapter 5

[1] A bubble is just an extreme version of a fad.

[2] Not only did President Bush cut taxes, the Federal Reserve also cut interest rates. Lower taxes and lower interest rates historically lead to economic recoveries and bull markets.

[3] Not all penny stocks are developmental. Many represent companies in decline or in bankruptcy. Penny stocks tend to reside on either end of the corporate life cycle.

[4] Many brokerage fees are based on a fixed number of shares bought or sold, with 1,000 shares being a common number used to set the fee. Buying more than 1,000 shares will cause a higher fee. Buying fewer shares does not lower the fee.

[5] Lynch, 128.

[6] Powerlite stock screen.

Chapter 6

[1] Answers to the questions:

Did our investor earn a profit at the end of the year?

No. The investor had a net loss of $250.

How much equity did he contribute to his business (Paid In)?

$8,000. Paid in capital is his initial contribution to his business. Any additional money he would add to the business would add to the paid-in account.

How many stocks does he currently own?

None. Any current holdings would be listed in the inventory account.

Was he a successful investor?

Yes. This is indicated by the gross profit he earned on the transactions. This indicates he made $4,350 for the year on an $8,000 investment—a 54 percent return.

Was he a successful entrepreneur?

No. He failed to control his fixed costs, which caused his strong gross profit to be consumed by those fixed costs.

Would it be a good idea for him to add more of his own money to this business; i.e., pay in more equity? Why or why not?

Yes. Since he has demonstrated an ability to generate good returns, more transactions would likely increase the gross profit number. For instance, an additional $5,000 of paid-in capital would allow him additional trades. This could double the gross profits, which would turn his venture from a $250 loss to a $4,100 net profit. At the net-profit level, his new return would be 32 percent.

Name two things he could do to increase his net profit.

As stated above, one is to commit more capital to the venture. Another would be to reduce his fixed costs. For instance, at his level of commitment, the computer and its cable fees are not necessary. By eliminating them, $3,600 can be cut from the fixed cost. This would turn his $250 loss to a $3,350 net profit—a 42 percent return on his paid-in capital.

What would his financial statement look like if he borrowed $5,000 in order to double the number of trades he made? (Assume a 10 percent interest rate on the borrowings.)

ANNUAL INCOME STATEMENT
Revenues:

(6 trades)	$39,000
Dividends	600
Total Revenues	$39,600

BALANCE SHEET
Assets:

Current:	
Cash	$16,600
Inventories	$ -0-
Total Currents	$16,600

ANNUAL INCOME STATEMENT		BALANCE SHEET *(continued)*	
Cost of Goods:			
		Fixed:	
Raw Materials	$30,000	Computer	$ 3,000
Transaction		Depreciation	($3,000)
Fees & Reports	$ 900	Total Fixed	$ -0-
Total Variable	$30,900		
		Total Assets	$16,600
Gross Profit	$ 8,700		
		Liabilities:	
Fixed Costs:			
		Current	$ -0-
Subscriptions	$ 1,000		
Computer	$ 3,000	Debt	$ 5,000
(Depreciation)			
Cable Fees	$ 600		
Interest	$ 500	Equity:	
Total Fixed	$ 5,100	Paid In	$ 8,000
		Retained	$ 3,600
Net Profit	$ 3,600	Total Equity	$11,600
Or (Loss)			
		Total Liabilities	$16,600

Chapter 7

[1] A discussion of SMART can be found on many management websites. One good source is *www.Projectsmart.co.uk/Smartgoals.html*.

[2] Joel Greenblatt, *You Can Be a Stock Market Genius* (New York, New York: Simon & Schuster, 1997).

[3] Leslie Whitaker, *Beardstown Ladies' Common-Sense Investment Guide* (New York, New York: Hyperion, 1994).

Chapter 8

[1] To understand this a little better, let's assume you wanted to receive a 3 percent return on your investment. If the $100,000 is going to equal 3 percent of your investment, how much would you have to invest to make $100,000 a 3 percent return? Or, stated another way, my investment times 0.03 must equal $100,000. The equation looks like this: (My Investment) × 0.03 = $100,000. If you divide both sides of the equation by 0.03, you get [(My Investment) × 0.03)]/0.03 = $100,000/0.03. On the left side of the equation, the 0.03 cancels out, which leaves the following: My Investment = $100,000/0.03. Thus, my investment equals $3,333,333. If my return were 5 percent, my investment would equal $2,000,000. In our example, the requirement was 10 percent and my investment equaled $1,000,000.

[2] By *protected*, I simply mean you are a secured creditor with first rights to the company's assets.

[3] Source: *Wall Street Journal*.

[4] Source: *www.reuters.com* stock screen.

[5] The 12 percent growth rate was observed on a screen of dividend paying stocks. Source: *www.Reuters.com*.

[6] Source: *www.reuters.com* stock screen.

[7] While forecasted growth is the preferred rate to use, quite often the growth rate used is the annual growth rate over the past three years. Using past data makes PE/G a fact-based measure.

[8] Chapman M. Findlay III and Edward E. Williams, *An Integrated Analysis for Managerial Finance* (Englewood Cliffs, NJ: Prentice Hall, 1970), Appendix C.

[9] At a 0 percent growth rate, the P/E would be divided by zero, which is not possible. If we substitute an extremely small growth rate, the resultant PE/G is an infinitely large value.

[10] Making zero growth the reference point establishes that P/E as the growth free measure, which means that any increases in P/E in the table must be related to the growth rate. This allows us to test the ability of the PE/G calculation to equalize the value of the various growth scenarios. If PE/G were effective in that regard, we would expect all of them to be equal, which they are not.

[11] Benjamin Graham, *The Intelligent Investor* (New York, New York: Harper & Row, 1973).

[12] Warren Buffet is the head of the Berkshire Hathaway investment company, which is traded on the New York Stock Exchange.

Chapter 9

[1] The median essentially means there are as many companies with S/As above 2.1 as there are with S/As below 2.1. The average is a more complex calculation. It can be influenced by extreme values. In a database with a high degree of variation, median is often the more instructive measure. In a normal distribution, the median and the average are equal. All the data presented in the chapter with respect to medians, means, and other company statistics were developed using the database that was offered by *www.reuters.com*.

[2] Michael E. Porter, *Competitive Strategy* (New York, NY: The Free Press, 1980).

Chapter 10

[1] John Magee, John Edwards, and Robert Davis, *Technical Analysis of Stock Trends* (Stock Trend Service, 1954).

[2] Bollinger Bands are the equivalent of a series of standard deviations for a moving average line based on the stock price. Thus, Bollinger Bands can be interpreted in the same way we interpret standard deviations on a normal curve. When stock prices reach the upper band, they will tend to move back toward the average,

which means it's time to sell. When the price reaches the lower band, it will also tend to go back to the average, a buy sign. For a more comprehensive discussion on the predictive power of Bollinger Bands, read my article in *Technical Analysis of Stocks and Commodities*, June 2006.

[3] The MACD is a technical indicator comparing two moving averages. One is based on a few readings and measures of the short-term price movement of the stock. The other encompasses more readings and represents the long-term activity of the stock. These are plotted as two separate lines. When the short-term line crosses the long-term line, it signals a change in trend and provides either a buy or sell signal.

[4] The market manager's book contains nonmarket buy and sell orders. Most stock orders are executed at the market, meaning they are to be transacted at the market's current price. However, other orders are sent that are executed at some future price. These future orders are recorded in the market manager's book. This gives the market manager a window into the future and allows her to manipulate prices to her advantage. The SEC would frown on such manipulations, but their facial expressions won't do you any good if you act on a market manager's false signal.

Chapter 11

[1] Everett M. Rogers, *Diffusion of Innovations* (New York, NY: The Free Press of Glencoe, Inc., 1962), 162.

[2] Greenblatt, 1997.

Chapter 12

[1] A helpful guide to understanding more complex financial statements is John N. Myer, *Understanding Financial Statements* (New York, NY: Mentor Books, 1964).

[2] Many of the Securities and Exchange Commission filings can be accessed from the Reuters website.

[3] In this instance, the opinions and actions of Ramius could have either a positive or negative effect on the short-term movement of the stock's price. If they disagree with the management to the point of selling, this will depress the price of the stock as they divest their shares. It may not be a precipitous drop, as they would feed their shares slowly into the market in order to maximize their returns; however, time is important to us, so any action that slows down the stock's price increase is a negative. On the positive side, if they succeed in influencing management or management succeeds in convincing them of the value of their plan, they will hold their stock. This will accomplish two positives. First, it will remove them as a source of stock, which will provide an upward bias on the price movement. Second, it will provide confirmation that the management's plan is achievable. This bodes well for future price increases.

Further Reading

Business and Economics

Findlay III, M. Chapman and Edward E. Williams. *An Integrated Analysis for Managerial Finance*. Englewood Cliffs, NJ: Prentice-Hall Inc., 1970.
An excellent source of present-value and compound-interest tables.

Kazmier, Leonard J. *Statistical Analysis for Business and Economics*. New York, NY: McGraw-Hill Book Company, 1967.
This is an excellent introductory text formatted for program learning.

Lehmann, Michael B. *The Business One Irwin Guide to Using* The Wall Street Journal. Homewood, IL: Business One Irwin, 1990.

Myer, John M. *Understanding Financial Statements*. New York, NY: Mentor, 1964.

Pinson, Linda and Jerry Jinnett. *Anatomy of a Business Plan*. Chicago, IL: Dearborn Financial Publishing, 1999.

Porter, Michael E. *Competitive Strategy—Techniques for Analyzing Industries and Competitors*. New York, NY: The Free Press, 1980.
An excellent exploration of strategic and marketing issues in a modern marketplace.

Stabler, C. Norman. *How to Read the Financial News*. New York, NY: Barnes & Noble, 1951.

Stanton, William J. *Fundamentals of Marketing*. New York, NY: McGraw-Hill Book Company, 1971.

Cautionary Tales

Anonymous and Timothy Harper. *License to Steal*. New York, NY: Harper Collins Publishers, 1999.

Chase, C. David. *Mugged on Wall Street*. New York, NY: Simon and Schuster, 1987.

General Stock Market Guides

The following books provide a general overview of the stock market and the investing process.

Finnegan, Carolyn M. and Staff. *Successful Investing*. New York, NY: Simon and Schuster, 1983.

Fosback, Norman G. *Stock Market Logic*. Chicago, IL: Dearborn Financial Publishing, Inc., 1993.
A good place to start. It is easy to read and filled with insights.

Glassman, James K. and Kevin A. Hasset. *Dow 36,000*. New York, NY: Three Rivers Press, 2000.
A fun read, but not very useful.

Krefetz, Gerald. *The Basics of Investing*. Chicago, IL: Dearborn Financial Publishing, 1992.

Malkiel, Burton G. *A Random Walk Down Wall Street*. New York, NY: W. W. Norton, 1990.
This is a classic, but it is a little too academic for most beginning investors.

Rosenberg Jr., Claude N. *Stock Market Primer*. New York, NY: Warner Books, 1974.

Investment Gurus

These are books written about or by the experts. They are filled with strategies, insights, experiences, philosophies, and techniques.

Brimelow, Peter. *The Wall Street Gurus*. New York, NY: Random House, 1986.

Gardner, David and Tom Gardener. *The Motley Fool Investment Guide*. New York, NY: Fireside, 1996.
They add a lighter touch to a very serious subject.

Graham, Benjamin. *The Intelligent Investor*. New York, NY: Harper & Row, 1973.
This is an investment classic. Or, to quote Warren Buffet, "By far the best book on investing ever written." Of course, Mr. Buffet hasn't read mine yet. So, the quote is a little dated.

Lynch, Peter and John Rothchild. *Learn to Earn*. New York, NY: Fireside, 1995.
Peter Lynch's entire series is an excellent and informative read. They are not too technical for the beginning investor, yet they have plenty of useful insights for the more experienced investor.

Lynch, Peter with John Rothchild. *Beating the Street*. New York, NY: Fireside, 1994.

Lynch, Peter with John Rothchild. *One Up On Wall Street*. (New York, NY: Penguin, 1989).

Mamis, Justin. *How to Buy*. New York, NY: Farrar, Straus & Giroux, 1982.
This is subtitled *An Insider's Guide to Making Money in the Stock Market*. It does a good job of explaining some of the inner workings of the stock market, especially the role of the market managers.

Seto, Matt with Steven Levingston. *The Whiz Kid of Wall Street's Investment Guide*. New York, NY: William Morrow, 1996.
Very basic advice.

Sivy, Michael. *Michael Sivy's Rules of Investing*. New York, NY: Warner, 1996.
Michael Sivy is *Money* magazine's Wall Street editor. He has included several chapters on dividend and value investing.

Tanous, Peter J. *Investment Gurus*. Englewood Cliffs, NJ: New York Institute of Finance, 1997.
Mr. Tanous interviews an impressive list of the stock market's well-known names.

Zweig, Martin. *Winning on Wall Street*. New York, NY: Warner, 1994.
This is a good context book in that it illustrates the effects of economic policy and direction on the stock market.

Investment Strategies

These offer specific investing guidelines and strategies. Some even provide a step-by-step system designed to outperform the market average.

Band, Richard E. *Contrary Investing*. New York, NY: McGraw-Hill, 1985.
Contrarians are people who buy stocks out of favor and beaten down by the market. The approach is much like that of the value investor, only more so. It is either an act of faith or a shrewd speculation. I'll let you decide.

Ellis, Charles D. *Winning the Loser's Game*. New York, NY: McGraw-Hill, 1998.
A lousy title, but a useful overview.

Leeb, Stephen. *Getting In on the Ground Floor*. New York, NY: G. P. Putman's Sons, 1986.

Leeb, Stephen with Roger S. Conrad. *Market Timing for the Nineties*. New York, NY: Harper Collins,1993.
A followup to his book *Getting In on the Ground Floor.*

Mahoney, John E. *Buy Low Sell High*. Toronto, Canada: Pagurian Press, 1978.
The subtitle says it all: *Anyone Can Make Money in the Market, THE FORMULA WAY.*

O'Higgins, Michael with John Downes. *Beating the Dow*. New York, NY: Harper Collins, 1992.
If beating the Dow is your only goal, this book will show you one way to do it.

O'Neil, William J. *How to Make Money in Stocks*. New York, NY: McGraw-Hill Book Company, 1988.
This is written by the founder of *Investor's Daily* and presents his C-A-N S-L-I-M system for investing.

O'Shaughnessy, James P. *Invest Like the Best*. New York, NY: McGraw-Hill, 1994.
This one will show you how to use "your computer to unlock the secrets of the top money managers."

Staton, Bill. *The America's Finest Companies Investment Plan*. New York, NY: Hyperion, 1995.
This one purports to "Double Your Money Every Five Years." Sounds better than it is. The average of the SP500 is 10–12 percent; doubling in five years is 14–15 percent. Yet, it does provide a conservative approach for those with larger nest eggs.

Whitaker, Leslie. *The Beardstown Ladies' Common-Sense Investment Guide*. New York, NY: Hyperion, 1994.
This is a great inspirational guide for older investors. A national bestseller and an insight into how you can pool your limited resources using an investment club.

Zacks, Mitch. *Ahead of the Market*. New York, NY: Harper Collins Publishers, 2003.
Zacks is a well-respected stock-advisory service, and this would be a good introduction to that service to see if it can improve the effectiveness and efficiency of your stock business.

Mutual Funds

Laderman, Jeffrey M. *Business Week Guide to Mutual Funds*. New York, NY: McGraw-Hill, Inc., 1999.
The most recent editions.

Online Investing

Brown, David L. and Kassandra Bentley. *Getting Started in Online Investing*. New York, NY: John Wiley & Sons, 1999.

Jubak, Jim. *The Worth Guide to Electronic Investing*. New York, NY: Harper Collins, 1996.

Pettit, Dave and Rich Jaroslovsky. *Guide to Online Investing*. New York, NY: Crown Business, 2000.
This was written by the people at the *Wall Street Journal's* online division, WSJ.com.

Speculation

Acampora, Ralph with Michael D'Antonio. *The Fourth Mega-Market Now Through 2011*. New York, NY: Hyperion, 2000.

Davidson, James Dale and Sir William Rees-Mogg. *Blood in the Streets*. New York, NY: Summit Books, 1987.

Greenblatt, Joel. *You Can Be a Stock Market Genius.* New York, NY: Simon & Schuster, 1997.
Covers a variety of speculative opportunities like acquisitions and bankruptcies.

Hoover's Handbook of Emerging Companies. Austin, TX: Hoover's Business Press, 1997.
Provides a listing of developing companies, with important financial and strategic descriptors.

Jones, Constance. *The 220 Best Franchises to Buy.* New York, NY: Bantam Books, 1993.
While designed primarily for the Main Street entrepreneur, it can still point you toward some potentially good growth investments.

Trading

Murphy, John J. *Charting Made Easy.* Ellicott City, MD: Marketplace Books, 2000.

Pistolese, Clifford. *Using Technical Analysis.* New York, NY: McGraw-Hill, 1994.
A good place to begin your technical-analysis studies. It is simple, useful, and filled with examples.

Turner, Toni. *A Beginner's Guide to Short-Term Trading.* Avon, MA: Adams Media Corporation, 2002.
Another good starting place, with copious background information and illustrations.

Websites, Periodicals, and Newspapers

Websites

www.TDAmeritrade.com: Stock-trading site where you open an account to trade stocks.

www.etrade.com: Stock-trading site where you open an account to trade stocks.

www.BigCharts.com: Provides free access to stock charts with various performance and technical indicators. Free.

www.Reuters.com: Provides information on companies and their stocks. Free.

www.moneycentral.msn.com: Provides information on companies and their stocks. Free.

Periodicals

Business 2.0: Subscription information: 800-317-9704.
Magazine provides articles on general business, commercial technology, and trends.

Entrepreneur: Subscription information: 800-274-6229.
Magazine provides articles of interest to small business owners and franchisers.

Forbes: Subscription information is online at *www.forbes.com/customerservice*.
The magazine contains articles for businesspeople and investors. Their Makers & Shakers feature provides brief stock profiles and recommendations.

Money: Subscription information: 800-633-9970.
This magazine offers a full range of investment advice and coverage.

Technical Analysis of Stocks and Commodities: Subscription information: 800-832-4642.
This magazine is dedicated to traders and trading techniques.

Newspapers

Investor's Business Daily: Subscription information: 800-831-2525.
Daily newspaper focusing on emerging companies, technologies, and stocks. A useful reference for both investors and traders.

The Wall Street Journal: Subscription information: 800-JOURNAL.
Articles and breaking news about the American and world business communities. A must-read for any serious investor.